Reluctant Aid
or Aiding the Reluctant?

RELUCTANT AID OR AIDING THE RELUCTANT?

U.S. Food Aid Policy and Ethiopian Famine Relief

Steven L. Varnis

Transaction Publishers
New Brunswick (U.S.A.) and London (U.K.)

Copyright © 1990 by Transaction Publishers
New Brunswick, New Jersey 08903

All rights reserved under International and Pan-American Copyright Conventions. No part of this book may be reproduced or transmitted in any form or by any means, electronic or mechanical, including photocopy, recording, or any information storage and retrieval system, without prior permission in writing from the publisher. All inquiries should be addressed to Transaction Publishers, Rutgers—The State University, New Brunswick, New Jersey 08903.

Library of Congress Catalog Number: 89-20575
ISBN: 0-88738-348-3
Printed in the United States of America

Library of Congress Cataloging-in-Publication Data

Varnis, Steven.
    Reluctant aid or aiding the reluctant?: U.S. food aid policy and Ethiopian famine relief / Steven Varnis.
    p. cm.
    Includes bibliographical references.
    ISBN 0-88738-348-3
    1. Food relief. American—Ethiopia. 2. Famines—Ethiopia.
    I. Title.
HV696.F6V37 1990
363.8'83'0963—dc20   89-20575
                                                                                            CIP

Contents

Tables and Figures	vii
Acronyms	ix
Preface	xi

Part I: Conceptual and Analytical Issues
1. Introduction: Power, Responsibilities, and Achievements in Famine and Famine Relief — 3

Part II: Producing Famine and Food Needs
2. Heightening Ethiopian Famine Risk: Inducing Food Shortages and Donor Alienation (1976-1983) — 21
3. Working at Cross Purposes: Production and Concealment of Famine and Confusion of Food Aid Needs (1983-1984) — 47

Part III: Famine Relief Operations
4. Moderating Extreme Strategies During the Emergency Phase: Radicalism, Humanitarianism, and U.S. Prohibitions on Aid for Resettlement and Development (1984-1985) — 79
5. Merging Donor and Recipient Policies for Emergency Food Distribution — 111
6. Stabilization of Relief: Consolidation of Ethiopian Control and Collaboration of Donors in Food Distribution and Development (1985-1986) — 139

Part IV: Developmental and Sociological Conclusions
7. The People's Democratic Republic of Ethiopia, U.S. Food Aid Policy, and the Future of Food Aid in Ethiopia — 169

References	193
Index	215

Tables and Figures

Table 2.1:	Ethiopia's Food Product, Consumption Requirements, and Food Deficit, 1979-84	22
Table 2.2:	Declining Regional Food Production in Ethiopia, 1979-84	23
Table 2.3:	Estimates of Persons Affected by Serious Food Shortages, 1981-84	24
Table 2.4:	Measures of Militarism in Ethiopia as a Soviet Arms Client	36
Table 2.5:	U.S. PL-480 Aid to Ethiopia, 1979-83	42
Table 3.1:	Deterioration of Regional Food Production, 1981/83-1983/85	49
Table 3.2:	Regional Contributions to the Ethiopian Food Deficit, 1984	50
Table 3.3:	Regional Procurement Targets of AMC, 1981/82	54
Table 3.4:	Persons Affected by Serious Food Shortages, 1982-84	56
Table 4.1:	Persons Affected by Serious Food Shortages, and Changes from Previous Years, 1984-86	81
Table 4.2:	Monthly Food Distributions during the Emergency Phase	82
Table 4.3:	Resettled Populations by Regions of Origin and Resettlement as of January 1986	88
Table 5.1:	Contributions of Donors to Food Distribution Systems, 1985-86	112
Table 5.2:	RRC Distribution Sites and Shelters, 1983	116
Table 5.3:	Major Food Aid Donors and Donor Groups, 1985-86	118
Table 5.4:	U.S. Aid to Ethiopia, FYs1984-86	119
Table 5.5:	Allocation of PL-480 Commodities and Nonfood Aid to Distributing Organizations, FYs1984-86	123
Table 5.6:	Planned RRC Distributions of PL-480 Commodities under the Bilateral Agreement	130
Table 5.7	Estimated Amounts of U.S. Food Distributed in Northern and Non-Northern Regions by Phase of Relief	133
Table 6.1:	Persons Affected by Serious Food Shortages, 1985-86 and Changes from Previous Years	140

viii **Reluctant Aid or Aiding the Reluctant?**

Table 6.2: Monthly Food Distributions during the Stability Phase,
           1986   141
Table 6.3: Shares of U.S. Food Aid and Nonfood Aid to Ethiopia,
           FYs1985 and 1986   142
Table 6.4: Arrival of U.S.-Donated Food in Ethiopia, 1985-86   145
Table 6.5: Port of Arrival of U.S.-Based PVOs' Food Commodities
           and Estimates of Regional Distribution   147
Table 6.6: Indicators of Expansion of PVOs' Food Distribution   150
Table 6.7: Registered Shelter Populations, 1985   152
Table 6.8: Growth in Number of PVO-Operated Food
           Distribution Centers   155

Acronyms

CARE	formerly, Cooperatives for American Relief Everywhere
CDAA/JRP	Church Drought Action Africa/Joint Relief Partners
CRDA	Christian Relief and Development Association
CRS	Catholic Relief Services
EECMY	Ethiopian Evangelical Church Makane Yesus
EOC	Ethiopian Orthodox Church
EPLF	Eritrean People's Liberation Front
ERCS	Ethiopian Red Cross Society
FAO	Food and Agriculture Organization of the United Nations
ICRC	International Committee of the Red Cross
LICROSS	League of Red Cross Societies
LWF	Lutheran World Federation
NRDC & CSPC	National Revolutionary Development Council & Central Planning Supreme Council
OFDA	Office of Foreign Disaster Assistance
OLF	Oromo Liberation Front
PDRE	People's Democratic Republic of Ethiopia
PMAC	Provisional Military Administrative Council
PMGSE	Provisional Military Government of Socialist Ethiopia
PVO	Private Voluntary Organization
RRC	Relief and Rehabilitation Commission
SCF	Save the Children Fund
TPLF	Tigrayan People's Liberation Front
UNDRO	United Nations Disaster Relief Organization
UNICEF	United Nations International Children's Fund
UNOEOA/E	United Nations Office for Emergency Operations in Africa in Ethiopia
UNWTOE	UN WFP Transport Operation in Ethiopia
USAID/E	U.S. Agency for International Development in Ethiopia
USAID/W	U.S. Agency for International Development in Washington
WFP	World Food Program of the United Nations
WVRO	World Vision Relief Organization

Preface

This book is the product of research begun in 1983, and is based on two visits to Ethiopia, discussions with many individuals involved in the formation and implementation of U.S. policy, and the review of a wide range of documents.

Reporting this research presents a number of difficulties. Activities of the U.S. government are divided into fiscal year periods, referred to by the year in which the fiscal year ended (for example, FY1985 refers to the fiscal year beginning October 1, 1984 and ending September 30, 1985); Ethiopian government activities and reporting periods are generally referred to with the beginning and ending year separated by slashes (e.g., 1983/84) to avoid confusion. Second, dollar amounts generally refer to U.S. dollars, unless otherwise indicated (for example, E$ refers to the Ethiopian *birr*); these amounts are not adjusted. Third, measurements of food aid quantities are consistently reported in metric tons (1 MT equals 1.1 U.S. ton) except in a few instances; there may have been faulty conversions in some cases. Finally, references to the work of Ethiopian scholars and policymakers have used the individuals' fathers' names as equivalents of surnames for convenience, with regret for any misunderstanding that may result.

Too many people generously made time available to me for expression of gratitude to be made on an individual basis. While each informant contributed to the views expressed in this book, errors of fact and interpretation are my responsibility alone. I would, however, add a special note of appreciation and remembrance for Thomas Worrick.

I

Conceptual and Analytical Issues

1

Introduction
Power, Responsibilities, and Achievements in Famine and Famine Relief

Among the most perplexing issues in the sociology of international development is the persistence of famine in the fourth world despite abundant food surpluses elsewhere, and Ethiopia is a prime example. Famine in Ethiopia during the period 1983-86 also raises controversy between rival sociological formulations of the course of national development in the modern world and the contributions of external factors.

Three viable explanations of the relationship between Ethiopian development and the famine have been advanced, with direct implications for conceptualizing the relief effort: first, that indigenous social factors and traditional food scarcity resulting from population increases and precipitation deprivation leading to drought adequately explain the famine; second, that a "conspiracy" among Western governments to deprive Ethiopia of the resources necessary for food system development caused the famine and retarded relief efforts; and third, that the radicalism of the Ethiopian government's development policy, inspired by a long line of Marxist regimes and Soviet aid, exacerbated the effects of drought and resource scarcity, thereby inducing the famine.

Whether the famine is a measure of the inhumanity of the Western world or the decadence of communist world influence has become the key ideological issue. In explaining the famine, critics of capitalism have come to

4   Reluctant Aid or Aiding the Reluctant?

loggerheads with outlooks critical of the Communist approach to economic and political development. Conflict has arisen over central issues of fourth-world food policy, such as whether state control or market determinism should be dominant, and also over the toleration of political dissent and treatment of military insurgencies. In broad terms of development strategy, the Ethiopian famine and relief operation stand as a valuable case study for examining several of the core elements of these vital sociological issues. Conceptualizing Ethiopian "dependency"—whether in terms of entitlements to foreign food aid and external roles in famine inducement and relief, or in the less precise terms of social underdevelopment—is a highly significant element of this controversy. Post-relief developments in Ethiopia, including the developmental activities of Western and multilateral agencies, and changes in the structure, policies, and programs of the Ethiopian government itself, are important considerations in evaluating the relief effort from a broader perspective. In order to clarify the issues involved, the following sections of this chapter will review the key controversies, first in general terms and then in the sociological context of the analysis provided.

Controversies over Ethiopian Famine and Relief

In contrast to the often ideologically driven analysis of national development, studies of famine and famine relief typically adopt a stance somewhere between hard-headed objectivity and tender-hearted sympathy for victims. No exception is provided by the views that have emerged on the famine in Ethiopia and other parts of Africa during 1983-86. The sentimental and financial costs involved may be measured by the fact that the famine claimed an inestimable number of lives while drawing several billion U.S. dollars in famine relief from a large number of donors. In Ethiopia alone, nearly $2 billion of aid was donated during the period, including $488 million by the U.S. government, despite which a million or more Ethiopians were lost.

Deeply conflicting interpretations of the Ethiopian famine of 1983-86 and the role of the United States in providing relief have been put forth. The memoirs of insiders and participants have been informative, but often contradict one another and clearly reflect the concerns of their authors to demonstrate particular principles or justify certain decisions (e.g., Korn 1986a; Jansson 1987; Wolde Giorgis 1989). The differences that have arisen from these accounts at the cognitive and emotional levels of experience are not easily resolved at the sociological level of explanation.

This book pursues three interrelated theses in describing and attempting to explain the Ethiopian famine and its relief. First, the use of power by the Ethiopian government in producing and exacerbating the famine was the most

Introduction 5

important factor throughout the famine and relief period. However, descriptions of the programs and institutional processes responsible have not been common. When force or power are invoked to explain the origins of famine, they are usually only ambiguously tied to Soviet or Ethiopian policy objectives. Explanations have been sought in the revolutionary policies of the government, and occasionally in assessments of inevitability that viewed the government's hands as being tied without having any options other than those exercised.

Secondly, the assertions of some observers—including members of the Ethiopian government and its sympathizers—that the United States deprived Ethiopia of development assistance and was dilatory in providing emergency aid with the objective of undermining the Ethiopian government's rule, are argued to be untenable in light of the facts. Because of their affluence and visibility, the West and the United States were seen as having primary responsibility for the miseries of Africa, providing the context for sharp attacks on donor governments. Failure to provide larger amounts of developmental assistance was posited as a prime causal factor in inducing famine in the first place. According to this outlook—which operationalizes many of the premises of the dependency paradigm in the sociology of development—in the context of food self-sufficiency and foreign food aid, the donor-recipient relationship is driven primarily by power principles and processes. In rebuttal of this assessment, two rationales for the Western position have been given: First, when policies responsible for producing famine are supported by technical and manpower assistance from the Soviet Union, Western aid is unlikely to satisfy Western desires for equitable distribution of responsibilities for providing relief much less resolve the very distinctive development dilemmas such countries face. Second, denials of Ethiopian government responsibility for the famine have flowed easily from positing the primacy of naturalistic factors and the long tradition of famine in Ethiopia, in which case pointing fingers at the West is likewise misguided.

According to the third thesis of this book, to attribute the dynamics of the Ethiopian famine relief operations solely to the status of Ethiopia in the Communist world would be a mistake. While the U.S. response may be assumed to have been influenced by the developmental orientation and foreign relations of Ethiopia, the donor-recipient relationship displayed many characteristics also evident in other relief operations involving the United States, in which the recipient government's foreign relations were not a key factor; some uniformity if not normative order in the resolution of technical and logistical difficulties rather than geopolitical determinism may be responsible for the final outcome of relief operations. It is not surprising that presumptions about the omnipotence of geopolitical alignments flare in the Ethiopian case, with the aid recipient so closely allied with the Soviet Union.

6 Reluctant Aid or Aiding the Reluctant?

More important in this regard is the assumption of responsibility—in which the Soviets were widely believed to have shirked their duty to a client state—and the likely achievements of aid—that appeared to be limited given the minimal commitment of the Ethiopian government to relief.

This is not to say that a system of normative order or a sense of propriety is presumed in the relief effort; what donor and recipient governments *should* have done without a clear recognition of how governments were *obligated* to act does not resolve the issue. On the contrary, also in this normative vein, but on strictly humanitarian grounds, while some have argued that the United States had no business contemplating any factors in Ethiopia other than need in formulating its response, others have asserted that the United States was perfectly justified in requiring certain conditions for aid and for taking the precautions it did in light of the policies of the Ethiopian authorities. Indeed, some have asserted that the United States should have gone much further in attempting to use food aid to extract major policy reforms from the Ethiopian government.

In attempting to resolve some of these conflicting interpretations, this book aspires to provide a balanced account of the famine and its relief, assessing a range of interpretations of Ethiopian policies and perceptions of U.S. food aid policy. It is the argument of this book that a viewpoint faithful to the facts must explicitly weigh the power factors involved, fairly address the judgments of responsibility that have been made, and measure the positive and negative achievements of the famine and relief operations. A notable byproduct of these efforts may be some advancement of sociological conceptions of Ethiopian national development beyond the confines of dependency theory.

Origins and Dynamics of Power in Famine

Famine[1] in the postcolonial world is increasingly acknowledged to be the outcome of the exercise of power, and few have completely denied the role of state power in inducing famine in Ethiopia during the period 1983-86. As a consequence, analyzing the Ethiopian famine may involve assessments of the very nature of the fourth world and the dynamics of national development in the modern international setting.

Assuring adequate food consumption among their populace has been beyond the competence of national food policies in the subsistence societies of the fourth world[2]. It has been observed that "these areas produce insufficient energy and inadequate food, and hence are basically recipient rather than donor nations in every fundamental respect" (Horowitz 1982:xxiv). Environmental factors in agricultural stagnation and collapse are real in Ethiopia as well as in many other African countries (Harrison 1987), but it is largely through governmental response to crisis conditions—with relatively benign neglect or callous disregard—that the resulting chronic hunger and malnutrition symptomatic of food system underdevelopment in the fourth world escalate into starvation and famine. How state power is exercised to induce famine is the key question.

Equality of international status does not imply uniformity in social structure or policies for food system development. In Ethiopia as elsewhere, famine and patterns of food system development are likely to be embedded in the structure and processes of nation building and social development, as segments and classes of a society struggle for food security. Government options to induce famine range from exploiting traditional social factors and institutions to increasing levels of state power in famine inducement.

To identify the principles and processes of power inducing the Ethiopian famine, the heightening of famine-risk as a structural characteristic in Ethiopia prior to 1983 is analyzed in chapter two. Internal points of responsibility are found to far overshadow the external. An overview of options available for famine inducement will make the actual policy choices of the Ethiopian government and the contributions of external sponsors clearer in their implications.

In some parts of the fourth world, there remain regions where normative famines may occur, resembling those that afflicted ancient and primitive societies that lacked modernizing economies or state structures. These famines are built into the normative order, and the vulnerability of rural areas to famine is an inevitable result of the undeveloped condition of the region or society. Declines in food availability and population pressures operate in a Malthusian manner. Given the strength of state power, it is unlikely that such conditions contributed substantially to the famine in Ethiopia during 1983-86, unless primarily normative or historical patterns of Ethiopian development were engaged.

Just as food production revolutions are prerequisites to development generally (Lewis 1984), political and technological evolution in these undeveloped areas also depends upon conquering food scarcity (Boserup 1981). Nations and peoples may gradually develop famine resistance through evolving a balanced relationship between food production and social development (de Castro 1977). Food systems at the national and regional levels—incorporating as well as intersecting the urban and rural systems— may reflect conflicting institutional arrangements at the heart of national development (UNRISD 1976:9). These systems regulate the allocation of scarce food production resources and the conflicting demands of groups and classes for food. Conflict between urban and rural groups is the most familiar theme, as agents of urban-based sectors attempt to extend control into the countryside through a variety of means. In some societies, including Ethiopia

8 Reluctant Aid or Aiding the Reluctant?

under the Imperial regime of Haile Selassie I (who was coronated in 1930 after 13 years of being Regent and Heir Apparent), laissez faire policy for economic development allowed agricultural entrepreneurs to obtain title to land and squeeze out peasants, further exploiting their plight and exposing them to famine-risk by imposing excessive obligations directly or through taxes levied by the state. Prior to achieving a famine resistant food system for rural populations in developing societies, economic famines have frequently resulted, less from the unavailability of food within the nation or affected regions than from a lack of entitlements to food. In the capitalist world, famine occasionally occurred during the transition to industrialism and large-scale agricultural production. But as rural development proceeds, a mix of modern and traditional food systems in the national society often occurs. Conflict between ethnic groups and regionally-based interests may incorporate or supersede the urban-rural divide. In developing national and regional food systems, government policy may attempt to regulate or to acquire control over the dynamics of conflict.

More commonly, famine in the modern world is induced by food policies, partly the result of attempting to hasten food security in the process of achieving abrupt social change. Normative and strictly economic inducement of famine are now rare because of the growth of state power throughout the modern world. Political famines induced by the exercise of state power have therefore become the model. The vulnerability to famine characteristic of normative famines may be exploited by the state as well as by private interests. Processes similar to those inducing famine under early industrializing economies may also be actively directed by the state. In addition, new and more forceful policies may be adopted, often with much more profound consequences. Militarism and communist economic and political policies are the two classic developmental orientations for state-sponsored famines.

Determining how the Ethiopian famine may have drawn upon different patterns of social development and strategies of food policy requires focusing on Ethiopian social structure, its military setting, and the sequence of external relationships leading toward the Soviet alliance. It is clear that the options open to the fourth world are much broader than the choices available to countries that had attempted earlier to accomplish food production revolutions. Adaptation of developmental options, including implementation of socialist ideology and development strategy and formulating military responses to internal and external threats, becomes more plausible.

Even though the Soviets were heavily involved in Ethiopia prior to and during the famine, external contributions to famine inducement have been attributed to the West and the United States. How democratic politics in donor states may lead to famine inducement in other countries is an intriguing

Introduction 9

question, especially for the United States, which had terminated its relations with Ethiopia during the late 1970s. Such attributions of responsibility were posited on the basis of the failure of these potential donor nations to provide adequate levels of developmental aid. Dependency theory's burden in accounting for external dynamics of famine has heretofore been occupied with patterns of underdevelopment tied to the economic aspirations and policies of the capitalist world. Famines in colonial societies such as Ireland had important external dynamics, while others such as those in colonial India were more internalistic in origin. Theories expressed in neocolonial viewpoints are legion (e.g., Meillassoux 1974). Dependency theory characterizes recipient nations as powerless as a result of a long history of exploitation in which foreign capital and markets transformed social structure into a dependent entity. Foreign development strategies are viewed as being imposed—usually by the West—on developing nations, thereby inducing famine. German inducement of famine in Tanganyika (Kjekshus 1977), and other colonial famines induced through policies sponsored by external governments, took more of a militaristic than a communist form. More recently, external relationships have been stressed in a number of studies (see, e.g., George 1977), often asserting that food surplus countries use this status to exploit fourth-world nations, creating the conditions under which famine occurs. The "world food crisis" in the early 1970s made grain much more expensive to fourth-world importers in Africa; but these countries were also suffering from production shortfalls, which confounds the contribution of external and internal factors.

Despite the increased role of the communist bloc in third-world affairs, the dependency paradigm has been unwilling to extend the scope of dependency to include Soviet-connected external dynamics underlying famines of a political nature. Dependencies on political resources for exercising control over political institutions and military arsenals in order to quell potential revolt—resources that the Communist world has acquired expertise in—are more relevant to Ethiopian famine and other recent famines than are dependencies on Western economic resources. While there is little data on foreign-imposed strategies implemented by high state power regimes, the adoption of communist ideology in Ethiopia and the implementation of revolutionary food policies is an important instance. Inducement of famine by foreign powers during warfare situations is historically a very important factor, but not directly relevant in the Ethiopian case outside of the arms-supplying policy of the Soviet Union.

The early dynamics of the Ethiopian famine, the government's interference with relief, and the initial mobilization of U.S. aid are explored in chapter three. Agricultural development policy was one of the most critical factors in the Ethiopian famine, determining the amount of food that was available for

10 Reluctant Aid or Aiding the Reluctant?

domestic consumption. Declining per capita food production throughout much of Africa (see, e.g., U.S. Department of Agriculture 1985:5) creates an absolute increase in the claims to already scarce food. Food policies in Africa generally have been pointed to as sources of food shortage (Bates 1981). In the Communist world, the state typically aspires to total control of food policy and agricultural development. Policy tools include state ownership and control of food system resources and food production, bureaucracies for food production and procurement, and marketing boards for setting prices and engaging in sales. The use of pricing and taxation policies to achieve agricultural and food policy objectives has been a failure, exacerbated by increasing population pressures and diminishing food production (Eicher 1982). Destroying the incentive structure of the agricultural sector has been a frequent result, leading to stagnating rural economies (Bienen 1987) and then to famine in many countries.

Under the communist development strategy, the Soviet and Chinese orientations provide two basic models for analyzing the Ethiopian famine. Classical communism in the Soviet Union was closely connected with militarism during the war communism policy of the civil war period. Perhaps the most critical factor is the food procurement policies of the government, by which rulers obtain the economic wherewithal to support their commands and further militarize their rule if necessary. The Ukrainian famine in the Soviet Union during the 1930s was induced by the Soviet state's procurement policies for acquiring food surpluses to support industrialization and militarization (Dalrymple 1964) and to eliminate sources of internal opposition to Soviet economic policies (Conquest 1986). In postrevolutionary China, famine flowed directly from Communist development policy independent of militarism; during the Great Leap Forward, policies of the government produced famine in the countryside through excessive procurements (cf. Bernstein 1984). Agricultural development is based on collectivization of production and state control of surpluses. Famine-inducing food procurement policies are often facilitated by collectivization of food production by the state, rationalizing production to make procurements more sizable in theory and more easily extracted in practice. The difficulty or impossibility of collectivizing agriculture in Africa (Bienen 1987) suggests that when it is attempted massive amounts of state power will be involved. While procurements by Ethiopia's food procurement agency increased prior to the onset of famine, any direct connection between such procurements (for military or any other purpose) and famine inducement at the regional level has not heretofore been demonstrated.

Of perhaps greater importance in inducing the Ethiopian famine were the dynamics of military dictatorship and the unresolved military and political conflicts throughout the country. Militarism may go hand in hand with

Introduction 11

Communist development strategies, or military development and action may be independent of such policies for economic and political transformation. Militaristic strategies have been evident in the recent famines in southern Sudan in the mid-1980s and in Biafra during the secessionist war, although creating food shortages has been a long-standing military strategy in internal civil wars no less than in international wars (Mudge 1970). Military actions, political controls and economic policy may converge to produce food shortages and famine conditions.

State control of food system development and sponsorship of famine may guarantee weak famine relief institutions because of the social contradiction between inducement and relief, but also because it is likely that private intervention will be regarded as a challenge and strictly controlled, if not prohibited. Even so, in recent years, recipient governments have begun establishing government agencies involved in famine relief (UNITAR 1982). They include agencies with administrative and technological competence (Kent 1983) as well as ideological ones with primarily theoretical and rhetorical jurisdiction. The ideological functions of relief and rehabilitation bureaucracies have been understudied but are being remedied in studies of the Soviet case (cf. Conquest 1986). Revelations about the Ethiopian relief agency are certain to advance the debate.

Even if they are responsible for the crisis itself, fourth-world governments may be dependent on the relief policies of donors during such periods, being limited by their ability to attract and their effectiveness in implementing food aid donations because of lack of internal resources and commitment. The promptness and regularity of appeals to solicit outside aid are important determinants of the effectiveness and scale of the relief effort in relation to need. The degree of openness of recipient governments to Western food aid and operations for famine relief is critical. Relatively open societies are likely to permit outsiders untrammeled access to the famine districts, while closed societies tend to limit access to "prepared" regions made ready for foreigners. Those societies that are largely closed to outside aid are also more likely to use any food aid to consolidate power rather than to provide relief. There was, for example, a shift in the Soviet regime from being relatively open during the 1921-22 famine to being closed during the 1930-33 famine (Conquest 1986). Ethiopian regulation of foreign aid efforts is thus an important variable.

In a world where food surpluses and deficits are national attributes, the responsibilities of donor and recipient governments in response to food shortages are best viewed in terms of interdependence. With respect to emergency food distribution, recipient government responsibilities for making aid viable[3] clearly arise first, and the responsibilities of donors arise only upon the satisfaction of this obligation of the recipient. The main option

12 Reluctant Aid or Aiding the Reluctant?

open to donors is to withhold aid (assuming it is needed) or to spearhead relief efforts from their position outside the recipient nation (provided that aid is viable). For the United States, aid to Ethiopia was far more a political than a financial controversy. The value of the lives of Ethiopians was never at issue, nor were economic costs or benefits to the United States ever calculated. Estimates of the magnitude of donor costs during the famine varied widely, but usually were greatly underestimated (see, e.g., Insel 1985). During the 1983-86 period in Ethiopia, viability of aid clearly conflicted with need for aid. The kinds of calculations performed were of a political but not necessarily non-humanitarian nature. Cost effectiveness was contested only insofar as there was little assurance that aiding people under the control of an authoritarian regime would satisfy *individual* entitlements to food (see Phillips and Fisher 1984:11) rather than subsidize the Ethiopian government's avoidance of responsibilities to its own people. Being able to effectively distribute aid was an important factor in the decision to donate aid in the first place.

Given the ascendancy of politics over economics in mobilizing U.S. aid, ideological bases and structural contexts of U.S. food aid become equally important in measuring the fulfillment of responsibilities in responding to Ethiopian famine and providing relief. Both foreign aid doctrines and democratic constraints of foreign food aid policy formation influenced the balance obtained between duties of the United States to rescue the starving and its neutrality in relief. Ideologically, the Reagan Doctrine, humanitarianism and sentiments underlying sanctions against Ethiopia all figured in Ethiopian famine relief policy. Despite legal restrictions on U.S. developmental assistance to Ethiopia, the technical doctrines of relief and rehabilitation permitted U.S. aid that had a developmental impact.

Priorities and Performances in Relief Operations

Responsibilities of donor and recipient nations in relief operations are defined partly by their governments' orientation to normative principles, partly by geopolitical context, and partly by humanitarian impulse. Contributions of the United States to the Ethiopian relief effort were substantial. Describing the actual division of labor for famine relief between donor and recipient governments in the Ethiopian situation may expose shortcomings in the effort but may also reveal the division of responsibility that is most appropriate. Moreover, the central role of nongovernmental organizations in performing relief operations places responsibility in a multilateral context. One level of concern that arises in such large-scale relief operations revolves around effectiveness, accountability, and assessing violations of normative relief principles. Generalizing achievements is

Introduction 13

difficult because the nature of constraints is so variable in different relief settings. Corruption and nonneutrality in distribution may be prevalent in any relief operation (Green 1977), but opportunities may be greatly heightened in a setting like Ethiopia.

Normative operations in providing relief developed only slowly in the Ethiopian camp as the dual systems of the recipient government and international donors gradually merged to broadly comply with relief principles. Basic principles of relief include the duty to rescue famine victims, the obligation of recipients to be open to outside aid, and the commitment of donors and recipient to neutrality in providing relief. The principle of rescue creates obligations for one government to assist another, as well as for the recipient government to assist the persons under its sovereignty (Samuels 1979:248).

The conflicts between donor and recipient governments over the need for food aid and for population redistribution through resettlement during the emergency phase of the famine are discussed in chapter four. Openness to outside aid requires that a government accept aid from without if internal resources are insufficient. Fulfilling this obligation may conflict with obligations from the principle of neutrality, which include providing aid in accordance with need rather than on the basis of the loyalty, ethnic attachments, or economic background of individual recipients (cf. Green 1977). Such principles may conflict with donor and recipient objectives, as donors are required to provide aid regardless of political alliance of a recipient government. Ostensible forfeitures of state sovereignty and embarrassment have long been rationales for closing borders to foreign relief operations and food aid. Whether bilateral arrangements suffice in these circumstances may depend upon geopolitical alignments as much as upon whether multilateral and nongovernmental organizations are poised to act.

In some cases, power-seeking donors may exploit opportunities for providing food aid in order to assert their interests. In the Ethiopian case, the range of options was made clear by the assumption of responsibilities. Groups of donor nations quickly formed to divide responsibility. Soviet responsibilities were largely disavowed, and the aid that it actually provided was limited and rarely used for famine relief. For the United States, aid to Ethiopia and the responsibilities of donor status conflicted with its disinterest in Ethiopia's pursuing a communist path of development and with the recipient country's relationships with the Soviet Union and other communist nations. Both roles—as donor nation and international power holder—converged in the Ethiopian famine relief effort. In Ethiopia, until the Ethiopian government took some kind of action, U.S. intervention and other donor involvement could have been construed as a violation of Ethiopian sovereignty (it was labelled counterrevolutionary by the Ethiopian government), unless a

14 Reluctant Aid or Aiding the Reluctant?

sufficiently compelling justification could be identified (e.g., human rights violations justifying nonmilitary humanitarian intervention [cf. Bazyler 1987]). Resettlement programs have been prominent tools for agricultural development and nation-building in Asia and Africa, but in Ethiopia resettlement and villagization programs were implemented during the famine. The Ethiopian program during the height of the famine was one of the most brutal, notwithstanding the fact that it was promulgated as a "famine relief" policy. In its harshest form, such policies and famine inducement may constitute genocide in advancing a "coherent policy of group destruction" (cf. Gurr and Harff 1988:363). Whether the Ethiopian program had developmental objectives or more closely resembled deportation programs aimed at the extermination of participants is one of the central dilemmas of the day. Deportation and resettlement of persons such as Ukrainians and "kulaks" in the Soviet Union, urban residents in Kampuchea, and other victim groups elsewhere, have often promoted genocidal objectives. Such policies may be promulgated by the government with the goal of controlling support for revolutionary or counterrevolutionary forces; penalizing aspirations to comfort, preventing the formation of alternative elites and repressing political opposition is more straightforward in such circumstances. In Kampuchea, Khmer Rouge policies served to cleanse the nation of potential counterrevolutionaries (Shawcross 1984). Creating and controlling involuntary migration (see Hansen and Oliver-Smith 1982), including the *ujamaa* (or "family-head" socialism) schemes of Tanzania's President Nyerere and other villagization approaches, may or may not lead to collectivization.

The Ethiopian government infrequently asserted a sovereignty right to control foreign food aid donations or to force rebels into submission by blockades, a stark contrast to the Nigerian government's actions only 15 years earlier. In-country distributions typically arouse some suspicion, and recipient governments may impose restrictions on the numbers, activities, and movement of expatriates engaged in relief activities. After some delay, Kampuchean authorities eventually permitted donors to maintain some personnel in the country, and allowed evaluations to be performed (Scoville 1985). Cross-border famine relief operations, as opposed to in-country food distribution, highlight more clearly the sovereignty and diplomatic relationships involved, as Sudanese assistance was required. The negotiated character of cross-border operations in other recent famine relief efforts, including Biafra (Jacobs 1987) and Kampuchea (Shawcross 1984), have likewise required cooperation of neighboring governments.

Private voluntary organizations (PVOs) with headquarters based in the United States and a humanitarian mandate played a key role in distributing food for relief and supporting the U.S. Agency for International Development's (USAID) programs during the emergency phase of the famine.

Perhaps the greatest limitation of recent assessments of U.S. humanitarianism in Ethiopia (Nichols and Loescher 1989) is their neglect of the social dynamics of U.S. responses to the famine. Democratic constraints and institutionalized conflict over aid objectives were embedded in congressional and administration relationships, and realist and idealist outlooks fueled the tensions arising over diverging assessments of food aid viability and needs in Ethiopia. Funding decisions and program choices of the United States were largely reactions to Ethiopian policy, seeking primarily to mediate the extremist strategies of the recipient government. Supporting the Ethiopian government with food aid dispels notions of a uniform or power-seeking foreign policy based solely on the Reagan Doctrine.

In this context, chapter five discusses the merging of donor and recipient food distribution systems in Ethiopian relief operations. The administrative patterns in food aid distribution are described, including the division of labor and responsibility between donor and recipient governments and international agencies. Food distributions of the Ethiopian Relief and Rehabilitation Commission (RRC) system and the U.S.-supported PVO system were coordinated by UN organizations and gradually merged in many respects. Responsibilities for in-country operations voluntarily assumed by private and nongovernmental organizations may have deflected the conflicts between donor governments and the recipient government. Such organizations are widely presumed to be able to act more quickly and in a neutral manner relatively independent of governmental interests. In the case of Ethiopian famine relief, they played a key role but raised new questions about responsibility and accountability. How their conduct is to be assessed and their performance evaluated in terms of the overall achievements of famine relief is uncertain. Understandings and practices resembling a normative order did develop, even if less technical than those prescribed by the United Nations Institute for Training and Research's (UNITAR) (1982) Model Rules.

Stabilization of relief operations is discussed in chapter six. Reliable mechanisms for delivering and transporting food commodities were gradually developed. While normative in procedure, Ethiopian government control was consolidated through beneficiary selection and primary distribution. As PVOs expanded their food distributions, institution building, and the villagization program in particular displaced need-based operations throughout the country. Bringing scattered producers together in controlled villages, as was done in Ethiopia's villagization program, and transforming pastoralists into agriculturalists usually requires particularly strong force. Somalian schemes for settling already displaced nomads demonstrate the difficulties of settlement even when migrations have already been accomplished (cf. Schraeder 1986).

Facilitating recovery to prefamine conditions is a common goal of foreign relief efforts, and the infusion of such massive amounts of aid resources inevitably leads to questions about reforming the pattern of development responsible for famine in the first place. Assessing the impact of relief activities in rehabilitation and developmental terms in Ethiopia is relatively straightforward. Strengthening traditional infrastructure for development and creating new institutions may be the explicit goals, or may be contrary to the interests, of the recipient government. Rural institutions may support policies for genuine agricultural and social development leading toward food security. Alternatively, relief activities may create dependent populations and, in a case like Ethiopia, strengthen the socialist institutions responsible for the famine in the first place. While unlikely to induce further famines, largely because of the presence of Western relief agencies, food deficits in Ethiopia are likely to require substantial food aid in the future.

Western Aid and Socialist Development

The fundamental measure of the achievements of famine relief must be the number of lives saved from the onslaught, and there can be little doubt that the relief effort in Ethiopia substantially achieved this in the short term. Despite calculations of up to 2 million Ethiopians dying during the period, it has been estimated that without U.S. aid alone, a further 7 million might have perished. Achievement of long-range goals of donor and recipient governments in terms of developmental orientation is much more difficult to assess. Chapter seven evaluates the famine and relief effort in the broader terms of Ethiopian national development, U.S. food aid policy, and the future of famine and food aid in Ethiopia. Among states of socialist orientation, the Ethiopian case may be an exception to the general understanding of the dependency paradigm. In the case of a nation with as strong a history of autonomy as Ethiopia, disavowing independent action in famine and famine relief in favor of foreign dependency is shortsighted. This is concluded with respect to Ethiopia's resistance to foreign intervention, operation of political institutions, management of foreign aid, and economic development.

If underdeveloped countries undergoing a socialist revolution are generally attempting to normalize relations with the capitalist world (Chase-Dunn 1982:47), Ethiopia has continued to distance itself from the West and rejected several modest overtures of the United States. The limp diplomatic and military aid efforts of the United States during the famine period are explained by the scale of humanitarian action at the time. This was due in part to USAID's autonomy from the foreign policy establishment in conducting relief operations, the democratic constraints on U.S. foreign policy, and the norms of developmentalism in food aid policy.

Despite the norm of developmentalism, humanitarian activities contributed

Introduction 17

to the almost certain prospect of food deficits in Ethiopia's future. International organizations, PVOs, and donor nations of the West and East share responsibility with Ethiopian authorities for guaranteeing a fourth-world position for Ethiopia well into the future.

Notes

1. Defining famine is a difficult matter, and a combination of definitions of the United Nations Research Institute for Social Development (UNRISD 1976:3) has been adopted here. The important language in brackets is omitted in the 1976 UNRISD definition. Requiring individual calamities to progress to death is not a universal criterion. For example, for Torry (1984:234), "famine signifies some complex of extreme, large-scale suffering instigated by extraordinary constraints on food accessibility," but does not require mortality. In general, famine may be characterized by the widespread lack of food resources "on a scale sufficient to [take as well as] threaten the lives of a significant number of people;" it entails massive deaths and is "a crisis of mortality caused by starvation and starvation-related disease, a crisis measured by the increase in the numbers of deaths" (Appleby 1978:1).

2. Some would restrict the scope of the fourth world to the famine-prone countries in Africa (e.g., Ostefeld 1986), a sensible determination in light of the fact that two-thirds of fourth-world nations are in sub-Saharan Africa (Wood and Mmuya 1986). But there can be no doubt that Ethiopia has fallen into the quagmire of the fourth world. It ranks among the worst of low-income economies on the World Bank's indicators for life expectancy, infant mortality, per capita daily caloric supply, and per capita food production during the 1980s (World Bank 1984).

3. Viability should be defined not only in terms of the friendliness of the recipient to the donor, but in terms of the likelihood that the aid will fulfill the needs of famine victims.

II

Producing Famine and Food Needs

2

Heightening Ethiopian Famine-Risk: Inducing Food Shortages and Donor Alienation (1976-83)

The inducement of food shortages and heightened famine-risk in Ethiopia that resulted in widespread famine during 1983-86 was the consequence of internal policy decisions and external reactions thereto. These primary sources of action and reaction run contrary to the expectations of dependency theory. The Ethiopian government sponsored the famine by implementing revolutionary food policies, reinforced by a restructuring of external relationships from West to East. The response of the United States, as well as other donor nations, was shaped and limited by the Ethiopian alliance with the Soviets as well as by domestic policy factors. Accounting for internal and external sources of heightened famine-risk prior to the famine period is important in attempting to assess the factors responsible for the outbreak of the famine itself. The main Western contribution lies in the misuse of foreign resources donated from abroad rather than insufficient levels of aid aligned more closely with Ethiopian policy than with donor recommendations.

Indicia and Dimensions of Famine-Risk

The famine-risk that exploded into famine in 1983 had been intensifying since shortly after the Ethiopian revolution's consolidation in 1978, and lay barely dormant in the structural food deficit being produced by the military

22 Reluctant Aid or Aiding the Reluctant?

regime's domestic and foreign food policies. Entirely apart from precipitation shortfalls, Ethiopian policy was generating food shortages and long-term obstacles to food security. The emergency deficit produced by the short-term effects of adverse natural conditions heightened a crisis already in the making.

Declining productivity is the pattern evident in the food product prior to the outbreak of famine. Table 2.1 describes the gross food product of Ethiopia during the 1979-84 period. Total food production fluctuated greatly, but the general pattern is a decline after 1979-80, with the exception of the strong harvest of 1982-83. With population increases, productivity declines are clearly evident, as per capita food production fell from 154 kg in 1975-76 to 135 kg in 1983-84, a 12 percent decrease. Nor were productivity declines offset by foreign imports. Food aid from abroad consistently accounted for only 2-4 percent of the gross food product in Ethiopia. Less consistent increases result when commercial food imports are included, but a dramatic reduction between 1977-78 and 1981-82 indicates the declining importance of this factor. Even apart from increasing governmental food procurement, the result of productivity declines was less food available for per capita consumption.

Disaggregating productivity declines in terms of regional and sectoral performance must proceed with caution. Regionally, the declines in production are indicated in table 2.2. Excluding Eritrea and Tigray, 10 out of 14 administrative regions experienced absolute declines in production between 1979/80 and 1983/84, without taking population increases into account. Only

TABLE 2.1
Ethiopia's Food Product, Consumption Requirements, and Food Deficit, 1979-84
('000 MT)

	1979 1980	1980 1981	1981 1982	1982 1983	1983 1984
Grain Equivalent of Local Production	6,712	5,881	5,668	6,940	5,687
Annual Consumption Requirements [a]	6,113	6,292	6,471	6,650	6,846
Population (mil)	37.5	38.6	39.7	40.8	42.0
Locally produced food available for consumption (kg per capita)	179	153	143	170	135
Estimated Food Deficit [a]	+599	-411	-803	+290	-1,159

Source: Faught (1987)

a. Calculated on the basis of 163 kg per capita, which is the mean of FAO (143 kg) and RRC (182.5 kg) standards (FAO 1988).

Arsi and Ilubabor showed (short-lived) production gains. Similarly, sectoral performances showed declines. In the smallholder sector, peasant producers were unable to meet government taxes, procurement quotas, and increased demand resulting from population increases, much less ordinary consumption requirements. Declines were experienced in the war zones and unstable regions of Eritrea and Tigray, but also in the marginal regions, the typically deficit regions, and even the typically surplus-producing regions. This was the case for the grain-producing Amhara as well as the sedentary highland Oromo peoples; among the nomadic, pastoral food producers (mainly Somalis and 'Afars in the peripheral lowland areas of the east

TABLE 2.2
Declining Regional Food Production in Ethiopia, 1979-84
(Cereals and Pulses) (in '000 MT)

	1979 1980	1980 1981	1981 1982	1982 1983	1983 1984	Average 1979-84
Arsi	437	504	561	602	469	515
Bale	143	81	156	198	130	142
Eritrea [a]	217	222	201	225	226	218
Gamo Gofa	116	123	93	148	99	116
Gojam	794	727	748	898	775	788
Gonder	600	485	529	773	515	580
Hararghe	653	334	364	481	353	437
Ilubabor	206	106	132	218	247	182
Kaffa	386	312	223	352	362	327
Shoa	2035	1731	1475	1989	1633	1773
Sidamo	207	192	153	212	193	191
Tigray [a]	200	204	186	207	207	201
Welega	651	432	521	585	527	543
Wollo	762	1000	866	788	503	784
CSO Total [a]	6990	6027	5821	7244	5806	--
Difference [a]	417	426	387	432	433	--
TOTAL [a]	7407	6453	6208	7676	6239	6797

Sources: Based on Ethiopian Government Central Statistical Office and FAO data in USAID/E (1987:41), except for total production, which is from Faught (1987).

[a] Production figures for Eritrea and Tigray are estimated by allocating the per capita share (52 percent and 48 percent respectively) of the difference between the Faught (1987) total production and the CSO total (which did not include Eritrea and Tigray). These estimates are probably far too high, given 1984/85 production estimates (94,000 MT for Eritrea and 80,000 MT for Tigray).

24 Reluctant Aid or Aiding the Reluctant?

and northeast), livestock holdings were less influenced by government policy during the period. Not only has the state farm sector been unable to make up the difference, its productivity has been a drain on costs and inputs (FAO 1982:22).

Consumption shortfalls resulting from declining per capita production have never been evenly borne in Ethiopia. Government controls over food consumption have favored the urban and military sectors over the rural population. Productivity declines and consumption shortfalls were compounded in recent years by the fact that procurement for urban and military consumption requirements have conflicted with rural consumption needs, production incentives, and surplus disposal. The entire cycle has been affected by increasing governmental grain procurements that nearly quadrupled between 1976/77 and 1981/82 according to World Bank estimates (Dejene 1987:91). Procured food has been subsidized for distribution to the urban and military sectors largely through low farm gate prices paid to producers. Moreover, in general, food is only circulated from the rural areas to the military and urban centers; within the regions with the largest food deficits the shortfalls are not spread out because there is typically no transfer of food from surplus to deficit regions (Griffin and Hay 1985).

TABLE 2.3
Estimates of Persons Affected by Serious Food Shortages, 1981-84
(in '000)

	1981	1982	1983	1984
Arsi	185	220	60	21
Bale	275	109	35	53
Eritrea	650	713	800	877
Gamo Gofa	232	-	-	80
Gojam	-	84	20	35
Gonder	67	202	425	325
Hararghe	420	384	285	279
Ilubabor	-	20	-	-
Kaffa	-	-	-	-
Shoa	239	533	195	204
Sidamo	-	303	145	355
Tigray	500	600	1000	1300
Welega	-	-	-	-
Wollo	450	592	1100	1821
TOTAL	3018	3760	4065	5349

Sources: RRC (1985d); USAID/E (1987:1) for Eritrea, 1984.

The social consequences of the structural food deficit and food shortages in the rural areas prior to the onset of famine in late 1983 are evident in the indicators of food system collapse provided in table 2.3. Ethiopian Relief and Rehabilitation Commission (RRC) figures for persons affected by food shortages show an increase from 3 million to 4 million between 1981 and 1983, and then to over 5 million in 1984. The number of people affected by serious food shortage in Wollo and Tigray doubled during the period, exceeding 1 million in each region in 1983. Gonder experienced the greatest increase in the number of people affected, from 67,000 in 1981 to over 400,000 in 1983, while in Eritrea the number remained fairly stable at over 500,000. These four northern regions accounted for 80 percent of the number of people affected in 1983. Other indicators of food system crisis such as shelter populations showed similar increases.

Two factors explain why the Ethiopian government allowed food shortages to escalate into famine. First, the government was not concerned with the threat of famine (as will be made clear in chapter three). Despite the revolutionary government's early promise upon seizing power to abolish famine-risk, and despite early productivity gains and good international prices for export products (i.e., for coffee exports, which increased dramatically), Ethiopia experienced its worst famine in recent history during 1983-86. Even if the government had been open to the problem, regional variations in the types of famine-risk (because of food system differences and government policy tools) would have required a response the government was incapable of mounting, given its military and political activities at the time. Second, in pursuing a military agenda directed toward installing the infrastructure for a "communist" society in Ethiopia, the government continued to alienate the West and spurn the advice of donor (and potential donor) nations. It lost credibility as a government as a result, and by alienating donors and refusing to be open to assessments of the encroaching famine, delayed an effective response from any quarter. The Ethiopian government must therefore bear responsibility for sponsoring the famine through building a food system and implementing food policies that created a structural food deficit.

The Ethiopian Government's State Sponsorship of Famine

A dramatic change in orientation toward food system development and famine inducement followed from the Ethiopian revolution. Under Selassie's government, it had been largely the failure of the government to act that had resulted in famine. In contrast, affirmative policies promulgated by the revolutionary government heightened famine-risk and actually induced famine in many parts of the country.

Many of the sociopolitical sources of famine-risk may be traced to the origins of the revolutionary government. Achievements as well as failures in food policy marked the early days of the revolution: Recovery from the 1972-74 famine and the production gains during the first few years after the land reform were encouraging, but the breakdown in marketing and the shortages of food in the urban sectors cut against these primarily rural achievements. Later developments reversed this pattern, working against the interests of the rural population.

Whether the regime's early problems—that had more to do with resources and infrastructure than with incentives—could have been resolved by strengthening marketing mechanisms while simultaneously undertaking agrarian reform is now a moot question. Ensuring food security was not, and has not become, one of the regime's priorities. Distinguishing its rhetoric for ensuring famine resistance and food security from the reality of the regime's composition and evolution will put its policies in bold perspective. Attaining a position of rule amidst a plethora of groups contending for power had been the initial aim of the junta that eventually came under the grip of Lt. Col. Mengistu Haile Mariam. Thereafter, assuring its survival and the territorial integrity of the nation through state control over every segment of Ethiopian society became its driving force.

In food policy especially, a close association between consolidating military dictatorship and preparing a socialist veneer had been evident at each step of the regime's efforts to transform Ethiopia into a Soviet-styled social structure. A dialectic in food policy was early set in motion between satisfying the need for controlling food production and distribution on the one hand, and following the socialist program for social development on the other. Distinctively Ethiopian devices have also been drawn upon by the revolutionary government.

Overhauling the entire infrastructure of Ethiopian society, including the establishment of a centrally-controlled food system exposing peripheral food systems to famine-risk, has been accomplished by installing throughout the country a variety of socialist development institutions poorly adapted to the Ethiopian setting. By the time famine began in 1983, steady progress had been made in installing such institutions throughout the country; by the end of the famine in 1986, the process had advanced much further. Just as the famine would most likely never have occurred without the strong push for socialist transformation, without the famine—and the rationales for radical action it provided and the external aid it attracted—the transformation would not have progressed to its current stage. In short, state sponsorship of famine was accomplished by six policy factors in the revolutionary government's rule:

1. Administering the rural sectors through military, state, and then party structures has been motivated by the desire to consolidate military-political

control more than to increase food productivity and improve nutritional statuses.
2. Resolving conflict and dissension by military means has been the hallmark of the government. while in the militarized zones and in the unstable zones of potential revolt, it has treated political opponents as military enemies.
3. Economic stagnation in the countryside measured by productivity shortfalls and heightened famine-risk has resulted from both the withdrawal of positive incentives and the escalation of surplus-extracting policies.
4. Central planning of food policy and economic rationalization of production and distribution have become founded solely on state- and party-controlled institutions.
5. Diverting scarce inputs to collective institutions and depriving small-scale farmers of modern agricultural inputs pushed peasants over the line of food shortage into famine-risk.
6. The government took advantage of the suffering of famine-risk to launch further programs for resettlement and villagization to extend its control, meanwhile allowing death tolls to escalate, further reproducing the cycle of misdirected food policy.

By 1983, strengthening these institutions had become more important than responding effectively to the food shortages that were becoming apparent. Some of the programs to advance these policies were partly implemented prior to the onset of famine; others were intensified during the height of famine, while still others were implemented during the stabilization period of relief. Yet the system devised by the Ethiopian government to implement revolutionary food policies has a grand coherence in terms of socialist design.

Implementing Revolutionary Food Policies

Internal restructuring of Ethiopian society along socialist lines and promulgation of revolutionary food policies commenced with the Declaration of Socialism issued by military leaders upon their seizure of power in 1974. The military junta quickly breached its mandate to combat famine, as military administration took priority over food security. Thereafter, food policy, socialist development strategy and military tactics worked hand in hand to induce famine in the countryside.

The major transformation to account for in the revolutionary government's food policy is the shift in the sectoral origin of surplus extraction from the tributary and tax-based system of traditional authorities to the state-based agricultural procurement through socialist agencies. For Ethiopian governments, national food policies have traditionally sprung from attempts to subdue recalcitrant regions and extend the scope of loyalty to central government rule. While this has been a project of the Ethiopian state since its borders were established by Emperor Menelik II (who ruled from 1889 to 1913) in the 1890s and throughout the reign of Emperor Haile Selassie I (1930-74), the current government has utilized much more sophisticated programs and instruments to implement food policy.

Commitment to socialist development strategies was expressed early in the "Declaration of Socialism" promulgated by military leaders in December 1974, shortly after their seizure of state power away from the monarchical rule of Selassie. Following a period of general turmoil sparked by increased food and petrol prices and during which strikes, demonstrations and riots surged through the Ethiopian capital (Erlich 1983a:466-469), the military staged a "creeping coup" in the spring of 1974. Mutinies and arrests of commissioned officers resulted in the formation of the Armed Forces Coordinating Committee (later known as the *Derg*, which is Amharic for Committee). It initially consisted of representatives of all ranks of the military but was dominated by noncommissioned officers. The Imperial regime was gradually dismantled, Emperor Selassie was deposed, and the Provisional Military Administrative Council (PMAC) was established in September. Executing 57 to 60 members of the old regime in late 1974 was perhaps the first sign of the radicalism of the coup leaders. It soon became clear that "the Ethiopian revolution concurrently adopted socialism, predicated on Lenin's and Stalin's interpretations, as both its means and ends" (Schwab 1985:115). Ethiopian nationalism and the norm of *Ytiopia Tikdem* (Ethiopia First) were partly subordinated to the revolutionary strategy of the regime, readily apparent in its inability to resolve the nationalities issue vis-a-vis the Eritreans, Oromos, Tigrayans, 'Afars and Somalis.

Upon the assumption of power, the military regime proceeded to articulate and implement its revolutionary policies for restructuring food production and consumption, simultaneously defining and eliminating its enemies while attempting to coopt potential supporters. The military men obtained the ideological foundations for revolutionary strategy and food policy from returned exiles and others armed with left-wing ideology.[1] A series of proclamations for economic reform of the rural and urban sectors was followed by programs for mobilizing and organizing the social sectors targeted to be overhauled.

In the rural areas, the regime adopted a transitional theory of development, the first stage of which was accomplished by the creation of Peasant Associations (PAs) formed after the land reform proclamation of March 1975. The *Zemecha* (National Development Through Cooperation Campaign) that was launched at the time to achieve the first level of rural reorganization into Peasant Associations (PAs) was implemented largely by urban elites (some 50,000 students and teachers from secondary schools and the national university). Class transformation in the countryside was limited to eliminating landlords and organizing farmers, but students were reported in some regions to have been more zealous in engaging in revolutionary violence. However, it was not until after the 1976-83 period that food policy itself was directed toward the transformation of the peasantry. The government took over the larger estates and transformed them into state farms. Later, the formation of service cooperatives and producer cooperatives was encouraged as intermediate rural institutions in the transformation of smallholder production into state farming.

Food policy was almost immediately redirected after the stabilization of the coup in order to service urban and military consumption requirements. The recruitment of students and faculty to participate in the Zemecha drew upon revolutionary and reform-conscious zeal, but also served to dilute urban opposition to the military council. Urban land reform and the creation of *kebeles* (neighborhood units) destroyed the rentier class and provided the government with additional revenues based on rent. Nationalization of foreign capital also diluted the class of wealthier landowners and entrepreneurs. Kebeles served as militia units during the later Red Terror-White Terror period, but also established the basis for urban political control and subsequent rationing and distribution of food.

Conflicting prescriptions for the direction of the revolution did not immediately cleave along military and civilian lines. At every step, provoked by reforms of food policy no less than eagerness for absolutism, the military regime defined its enemies. The process of centralizing power into the hands of smaller and smaller groups entailed eliminating competitors, both civilian and military. The Program of the National Democratic Revolution (20 April 1976) was largely an attempt of the military government to legitimate MEISON's ideological and political position. Even so, by the end of 1976, resources were diverted away from meaningful food policy reforms by the civil war that broke out primarily in the major urban centers, and by efforts to control the revolution and the nationalist revolts throughout the country. These outbreaks also delayed the implementation of socialist policies for a period of time.

By 1977, the new regime had established control. It then proceeded to destroy its civilian and military opposition. In many ways, Mengistu was able to ride out the storm by brutalizing his opponents. A split between military and civilian groups, exploited by the military to further confuse and divide the civilians (Sauldie 1982), was a major factor responsible for the rise of military control in the revolutionary order (Abate 1984). Experience with insurrection in the 1960 coup attempt had instilled in the military a sense of a need for strong central control to prevent a countercoup (cf. Marcus 1983). Originally "a parliament rather than a junta" (Clapham 1985:260), with representatives from all of the major units of the armed forces, the Derg

30 Reluctant Aid or Aiding the Reluctant?

presumably contained some diversity in ideological outlook. But shortly after the relatively junior officers had mutinied, command from above became the moving force. The execution of internal competitors for power paralleled the elimination of opponents outside the Derg during the Red Terror.

Efforts to create a civilian organization for controlling the masses—responsive and perhaps advisory to the military leaders—are most evident in the progression of political organizations formed by military leaders. Starting from the POPO (People's Organizing Provisional Office) to POMOA (Provisional Office of Mass Organization Affairs—a civilian politburo of Marxists dominated by MEISON), party-building proper in the communist sense began with COPWE (Committee to Organize the Workers' Party of Ethiopia), which became the WPE (Workers' Party of Ethiopia) during the famine period. Whether this maneuvering toward COPWE is best viewed as preventing the emergence of a viable civilian opposition or as a "process of party building from above" (Clapham 1988:70), is subject to some debate, but the end result and the process of centralizing authority into a single political organization is clear.

Supporting civilian organizations sympathetic to the revolutionary process took a different turn after 1976 and the return of the Zemecha participants. Civil war was being waged by MEISON, the Ethiopian People's Revolutionary Party (EPRP), and other organizations. Rival organizations and civilian groupings were eventually extinguished through three waves of Red Terror launched by the Derg against counterrevolutionaries, the EPRP and finally MEISON itself (Lefort 1983).

Unwillingness to engage in the frictional activity of political accommodation was even more obvious in the military government's handling of ethnic and regional struggles. The revolutionary government resurrected intense hostility in Eritrea under the leadership of the Eritrean People's Liberation Front (EPLF), which had wavered under several rebel groups since the federation was dissolved by Selassie's formal incorporation of Eritrea as an administrative region in 1962. Mengistu's ascent to the head of state followed from the February 1977 mortal resolution of the conflict with Teferi Banti over Eritrea, partly aroused by the Soviet promise to provide military aid on the condition that American military assistance be discontinued (Henze 1983:169-170). In Tigray, another "nationalist" movement emerged in early 1975 with the formation of the Tigrayan People's Liberation Front (TPLF), largely the result of dissatisfaction with the Derg's rule, but also drawing upon nationalist sentiments aroused by the Imperial regime in the early 1940s. Two branches of the Oromo Liberation Front (OLF) emerged: one in 1976 in the southeast (in Harar) that was militarized largely in response to the Ethiopian government's land reform policy and the military expulsion of the Somalis, and the other in 1982, in the West, having military and political strongholds in Welega (OLF 1986). Several other liberation fronts were also formed, including the 'Afar Liberation Front in the Awash Valley that emerged from conflicts between the Derg and the Sultan Ali Mirah (Shehim 1985:343).

Experience in using food supplies as a weapon of war and the command of a war economy was gained from engagements in the north. Plans for a peasant march in May 1976 to subdue Eritrean rebels were cancelled after many of the recruits were attacked and the plan received adverse reactions from abroad (Erlich 1983b:75-76). After two more years of battle in the north, military resources were redirected toward the eastern border with Somalia.

Mounting a defense against the Somali invasion (the strongest threat to the Mengistu regime's survival) further depleted military food reserves and manpower. The weakness of the revolutionary regime was clearly perceived in the Somalian capital of Mogadishu by the Soviet-supported military units of Said Barre, which seized the moment to support and mobilize ethnic Somalis in the Ogaden. Rekindling the long-standing tension between Ethiopians and Somalis allowed Somalia to make a deep thrust into Ethiopia, taking Jijiga, attacking Dire Dawa, and laying siege to Harar until February 1978 (Zartman 1985:13). (The massive military buildup to expel the Somali forces, sponsored by the Soviets in a dramatic change of proxies, will be described below, including its drain on every sector of the Ethiopian economy.)

Finally resolving the Somali border threat, the Derg returned its attention back to internal restructuring and pursuing war in the north and other areas. Such concerns were hardly independent, as imposing controls over civilians for maintaining order converged with mechanisms for extracting the maximum amount of food surpluses. This is perhaps most clearly illustrated by the villagization of Bale (Clay 1988). Not only did it prevent inhabitants from resurrecting loyalties to Somali rebel forces, it also created government-controlled production units. Ethiopian government grain procurements from Bale increased by over 800 percent between 1978/79 and 1981/82—from 12,000 quintals to 97,000 quintals (Lirenso 1984:53).

In other regions of open and potential revolt, prefamine-period military activities resumed with six major Ethiopian offensives launched against the TPLF by the fall of 1981. Military offensives against the OLF occurred in Bale and Sidamo in 1980-81, including air strikes by fighter bombers (Clay 1988:225). The Red Star Campaign in Eritrea in late 1982 and other offensives against the EPLF and TPLF in 1983 regained many of the northern positions lost during the Ogaden War. Promulgation of the National Military Service Proclamation in 1983 served notice that the Derg was serious about continuing military activities and had a conscription system in operation for recruiting combatants.

Having secured military-political control, the regime proceeded with further revolutionizing of food policy. It created and strengthened centrally-controlled economic institutions. Further, destruction of private marketing systems for food was partly motivated by the regime's desire to retain control of Addis Ababa and regional capitals. Urban centers in Ethiopia have traditionally had a key role in both the rationale for and the magnitude of food procurement to support non-farmer consumption. However, the growth of urban-based populations dependent on the market for food grew from 19 percent to 34 percent of the total population between 1970 and 1983, while marketed grain declined by 9.2 percent between 1977 and 1981 alone (Lirenso 1984:13-14). Even though urban growth in Ethiopia has not been as great as in many other African countries, Addis Ababa continues to require food from outside the Shoa region. While food merchants have been tolerated in the capital because the Ethiopian Agricultural Marketing Corporation (AMC) and its distributor (the Ethiopian Domestic Supply Corporation) are unable to meet the demand, they are as tightly controlled as they are strongly discouraged.

Both the operation of economic institutions and agricultural development strategy reflect this dilemma. A new Central Planning Commission, established in 1977, which was replaced by the National Revolutionary Development Campaign and Central Planning Supreme Council in 1978, strengthened central control and developed new tools for economic management. After the National Revolutionary Development Campaign (NRDC), surplus extraction and economic rationalization of agricultural production were facilitated in 1978 by changing the role of the AMC from competing with private traders to procuring agricultural products on a quota system (Clapham 1988:126). Agricultural development theory and policy became based on the commitment to state farms and service and producer cooperatives (the latter cooperatives being collective farms), even though collectivization had been moderate until the 1979 decree on collectivization (Cohen 1984:197). The dual objectives of controlling rural populations and rationalizing agricultural production to maximize state procurements have been only partially served thereby. State farms are the most frustrated tools of the government, and have not worked out in practice. Labor control and conscription problems, poor incentive structures and mismanagement of resources have all contributed to failure (Griffin and Hay 1985). Even though the amount of land under state farm control increased from 67,000 ha in 1976 to 250,000 ha in 1980, by 1983 state farms still accounted for only 4 percent of cultivated land (World Bank 1983:11). Peasants were deprived of needed inputs through diversion of resources to the state farm sector. Between 1977/78 and 1981/82, the share of fertilizers distributed to the private sector declined from 75 percent to 53 percent, while the state farm share increased from 23 percent to 39 percent

(Teferi 1984:28). Taxes on agricultural income also skyrocketed between 1976 and 1981, rising five-fold from E$9.7 million to E$53.6 million (IMF 1987:355). Productivity, measured in terms of crop yields and production costs, has decreased. But the government continues to pump agricultural resources into the state farm sector.

Establishing state control over smallholder producers has been achieved less abruptly through the cooperative sector. Emphasizing Service Cooperatives (SCs) has been suggested to be the most realistic approach for increasing both the autonomy and the productivity of PAs (Dejene 1987). However, SCs may be only a prelude to the organizational form of collective farms represented by Producer Cooperatives (PCs), evident in the patterns of growth in both types of coops.[2] Service cooperatives showed only a slight growth in terms of numbers and participating members between 1980 and 1982, although their capital nearly tripled. In contrast, the number of PCs nearly doubled during the same period and the participating members increased by over 25 percent (World Bank 1983:11). Substantial external support, in ideological as well as economic terms, was obtained from the Eastern block as well as several United Nations agencies.

Along with revolutionizing the domestic fabric of Ethiopian society, the military government's relationships with the external world underwent a similarly deep restructuring. The Ethiopian government seized a model of sociopolitical control that carried with it a development strategy and food policy program. External restructuring and implementing the revolution were mutually reinforcing processes, evident in the evolution of Ethiopia's switch from West to East in external orientation.

Restructuring External Relationships

With its long history of independence, it is difficult to interpret Ethiopia's recent restructuring of external relationships toward the East. Ethiopian nationalism has never been strong in relation to the many ethnic strains in the outlying areas. Militarism, in contrast, has always been a central feature of the Ethiopian state, and a core tradition in Ethiopian culture and social structure. It was perhaps the imperial tradition of Ethiopia that made the Soviet approach attractive, and explains how communism was grafted onto the traditional aspects of Ethiopian society. A switch to the East is accurate in political terms, but economically and socially, ties with the West have been retained while restrained.

Characterizing prerevolutionary Ethiopian development as "dependent" has limited interpretive value. The most vehement yet weakest proposition of dependency theory in Africa is that an impoverished nation like Ethiopia must have been dependent upon the West and especially the United States for its very existence as a nation. Contrary to most other African nations, the origins of the Ethiopian nation-state are found firmly within its borders and institutions (Mazrui and Tidy 1984). Ethiopia's long tradition of independence survived repeated attempts on the part of Middle Eastern, African, and European forces to subordinate the country to outside control (Rubensen 1976). The failure of the Italian colonial occupation (except for Eritrea) remains a source of African pride. Indeed, Ethiopia can find no place in the grand scheme of African dependency on Europe proposed by Amin (1972:504).

Western involvements in Ethiopian affairs since the 1930s provide somewhat stronger evidence of an external role in preserving or maintaining Ethiopia's national existence. The earliest official European foray into Ethiopian territory was a Portuguese intervention in the early sixteenth century, either in response to Ethiopian requests for assistance in quelling threats to Ethiopian survival posed by a Muslim jihad (Hess 1970:44-45), or a European attempt to outbid the Ottoman Empire for control over Ethiopia (Eshete 1982:14). But greatest success in European domination was achieved by the colonization of the Red Sea coast in the north by the Italians, who named the region "Eritrea." It was accompanied by European colonization of the territory around Ethiopia's borders. But Menelik's and then Selassie's empire stood firm until the Italian invasion of the highlands in 1935; indeed, it succeeded in its own colonization program in the south and the east. Subsequently, the Italian military occupation of the heartland was brought to an end, and its colonial aspirations—that had been fulfilled only in Eritrea—were dashed. Restorationist forces from without allied with Patriots within to allow Ethiopians to resume control over the domestic political economy. British assistance in restoring Emperor Haile Selassie I to power was extended to civil and military administration of the periphery until 1951, even though the penetration was shallow rather than deep (Farer 1979).

Ethiopia remained outside the sphere of strict Western control. Although finally becoming a member of the League of Nations after formally outlawing slavery, Ethiopian participation in the lend-lease program as a supplier to the Allied powers marked a watershed in its diplomatic relations with the West and the United States (Marcus 1983:18-21). The replacement of the East African shilling by the Ethiopian dollar in 1945 was an initial step toward basing Ethiopian currency on the U.S. dollar (Spencer 1976:23). The United States later filled the administrative position in Eritrea vacated by the British, as the tradeoff for assisting with the United Nations' resolution of the Eritrean situation in 1950 led to the establishment of the Kagnew communications base in Asmara.

Eventually, the United States replaced the United Kingdom as Ethiopia's major Western patron, which illustrates the flexibility of these ties rather than any kind of dependency. Selassie's government received substantial support from the United States during his reign. All indications are that Ethiopia was never dependent on or handcuffed by the United States in the way dependency theorists have traditionally characterized dependent relationships (see Marcus 1983; Spencer 1984).

During the early years of the Ethiopian revolution, anti-Western rhetoric soon went beyond the milder criticisms of "imperialism" and assertions of self-reliance characteristic of some African socialisms. The Ethiopian government undertook a program to reverse decades of moderate development strategy supported by the United States and other Western nations in favor of the revolutionary strategy of the East. Breaking with the United States and the West followed a not unfamiliar pattern. Expropriating foreign and domestic investments and asserting state control over the economy was an early step, and the PMAC failed to pay its bills for U.S. military equipment. The value of the property of 21 U.S. citizens and firms nationalized was estimated at $15-20 million. On the social front as well, the government showed no mercy, as documentation of human rights violations against Ethiopians appeared (see, e.g., Amnesty International 1978). Antipathy extended to harassing foreigners generally, including missionaries.

Associating with the Soviets was clearly a factor in these domestic actions. Any Soviet influence during the coup and the early stage of the revolution has not yet been documented. But after Mengistu's rule was secured, Moscow wasted no time in rushing in to befriend the radical soldier. Soviet and Cuban military aid to rebuff the Somali invasion provided an opening for furthei entrenchment of Soviet ideology. Soviet military aid to Ethiopia was escalated on the condition that U.S. aid be terminated (Henze 1983), and Soviet developmental ideology became dominant within the state, although Marxism already had a strong appeal to Ethiopian ideologues in MEISON and other groups. A treaty of Friendship and Cooperation was concluded between the two in November 1978, even though a military aid agreement had been signed nearly two years earlier (Henze 1985:20). The Soviet command to dissociate from the United States was followed by Ethiopia's eschewing the advice and recommendations of donors and Western agencies, ranging from the Swedish International Development Agency (SIDA) to the World Bank (Cohen 1984:197-9), and the replacement of Western advisers with their Eastern bloc counterparts.

Militarization undoubtedly had a stronger implication for food policy than did communism prior to 1983. In food policy, the reversal of Western-oriented development strategies by replacing market institutions with state-controlled quotas and procurements was strengthened by a general subordination of traditionally private-sector activity to state-sector control. An analogy with the "war communism" period of Soviet development is

36 Reluctant Aid or Aiding the Reluctant?

appropriate in the Ethiopian case. Under Mengistu's rule and Soviet guidance, militarism reached a new peak. As a consequence of the Derg's rule, which must be distinguished from the advisory roles of committees like the Mengistu clique during other Ethiopian political crises (see, e.g., Marcus 1983:33, 91), the military replaced civilians as the administrative authority. Selassie's military development policies mirrored Menelik's, but after World War II, Selassie consolidated the previously private armies of the major nobles, with the central army professionally trained and equipped by Americans (Cartwright 1983:260, 263). As table 2.4 indicates, Ethiopia experienced a dramatic escalation in all measures of militarism once it associated with the Soviets. The size of its military grew from 50,000 to 250,000 between 1975 and 1979 (see Henze 1984:646; see also Snyder 1986:121), and a similar growth in the size and proportion of its military expenditures is evident. While the Soviets "donated" military hardware to the Provisional Military Government of Socialist Ethiopia (PMGSE), as the Derg was designated after 1977, without expectation of total repayment, no monetary support for the manpower required to operate the equipment was provided, leaving the burden on the Ethiopians to raise money and goods for maintenance. The debt may be as significant as the prospect of repayment. According to one estimate, Ethiopia had a hard currency debt to the Soviets of about $2 billion at the end of 1982 (Luckman and Bekele 1984:17). Feeding the men at arms became a major determinant of food policy, as procurement of peasant produce for hard currency purposes no less than soldier subsistence has been necessary.

Just as the Soviets filled Mengistu's orders for military assistance in the late 1970s, Soviet ideology was called upon to manage the process of state development and food policy implementation. Modelling Soviet state structures was the most obvious sign of influence. In nearly all respects the structure of the Ethiopian government is based on the Soviet model as a state

TABLE 2.4
Measures of Militarism in Ethiopia as a Soviet Arms Client

	1974	1977	1978	1979
Defense as percent of GNP	3.2	5.0	7.4	n.a.
Defense as percent of Government Expenditure	17.9	21.1	21.6	30-40
Size of Armed Forces ('000)	45	225	233	250
Arms Imports as percent of Total Exports	3.7	132.3	358.3	54

Sources: Henze (1984:646, 651); Nelson and Kaplan (1981:318).

of "socialist orientation" in official Soviet third-world policy terms (Legum 1987). The PMGSE consisted of four distinguishable units. Mengistu, referred to in the vernacular as "the chairman" after the formation of the Worker's Party of Ethiopia, sat at the helm of the party system constituted as COPWE until late 1984. He was also head of the state apparatus proper, a number of "auxiliary units," as well as several bureaucratic institutions with food policy responsibilities.

Whether Ethiopia's current relationship with the Soviet Union is a "dependent" one is more difficult to determine, even though the Ethiopian government has relied on the Soviets for arms, has a large military debt, and has transformed itself along the lines of the Soviet model. Soviet involvement was peripheral until at least 1977, which was after the domestic sphere had been radicalized. The fact that direct Soviet involvement followed Ethiopian radicalism is a major barrier to extending this tenet of dependency theory to Ethiopian development. One explanation for the radicalization of the Ethiopian government after 1977 is that its very survival, and that of the Ethiopian nation, was guaranteed only after Soviet and Cuban aid supported the Ethiopians against the Somali invasion of the Ogaden. From the point of view of dependency theory, it is necessary (unless one views the Soviet alliance as a liberation) to identify a "dependency substitution." This is consistent with the prevailing outlook among analysts of the region: Ethiopia is almost routinely described as having switched from the United States to the Soviet Union for support.

The Ethiopian government's military base had been ideologically but not economically problematic for the Soviets until 1989[3]. Military control had conflicted with party formation and leadership, but continued to be a useful source of demand for Soviet military aid and its accessories. Whether control by Moscow extended to extinguishing any Derg policies contrary to Soviet wishes is unclear. At the most, any "balancing" as a civil tactic of Mengistu served to diminish conflicts between pro- and anti-Moscow factions (Keller 1985:13). Early struggles over party formation were resolved in favor of the anti-Moscow position as pro-Soviet intellectuals with some sympathy for the pro-Soviet faction "fell out with Mengistu" (Henze 1983:172). But the formation of COPWE and then WPE revealed a return to Soviet principles. Mengistu had interviewed all cadres "appointed to the central committee," his suggestions during the first COPWE Congress were "endorsed without demur," and all regional appointments were likewise controlled from the center (Gilkes 1982:24-25). As the general secretary of the WPE after 1984, Mengistu had control of the party apparatus, including the executive and central committees. The "Politburo" was formed after the WPE was appointed and simply added four positions to the seven-man Derg (Keller 1985:13). It is presumed to be heavily Amharic and Tigrayan in constitution, while Mengistu maintained an effective dictatorship. As the head of state, Mengistu commanded the Derg as chairman and was also the chairman of the Council of Ministers and commander in chief of the Revolutionary Armed Forces.

Regardless of the inputs and interests of Moscow, the Ethiopian government adopted the communist approach to food policy and its orientation to famine inducement wholeheartedly. The Soviet model of social, political and agricultural development appears to have contributed directly to policies leading to famine inducement. At the very least, Ideological support was provided for policies of collectivization, resettlement, villagization and economic centralization, even though the support appears to have been solicited by pro-Moscow elements in the Ethiopian government rather than compelled from without. The entire bureaucracy responded to Mengistu as head of state and as chairman of the Council of Ministers (and as party chairman after the formation of the Workers' Party of Ethiopia). Because of the state's control over all sectors of Ethiopian society, the bureaucracy had little independence. In food policy, several ministries and associated agencies and staffs had special responsibilities for food system development. Mengistu's power position limited the autonomy and dictated the conformance to political consolidation of the Ministry of Agriculture, the Agricultural Marketing Corporation, and the Relief and Rehabilitation Commission. Party authorities came to supersede administrative rationality, as Party officials were simultaneously bureaucratic agents. The former RRC commissioner was on the central committee; later, a high-ranking Party member was assigned to supervise RRC operations.

In light of the Soviet's near monopoly of external influence over Ethiopia, expecting that the West would seek or be able to fill any gap to prevent famine-risk from escalating as a result of famine-inducing activities is difficult to understand. For the most part, the policies of the West and the United States were reactions to the Ethiopian government's spurning of the "imperialist alliance."

A common explanation for Ethiopia's embrace of the Soviet Union is the abandonment thesis. According to this view, the West—especially the United States—abandoned Ethiopia in its time of need. However, total Western abandonment of Ethiopia after the revolution would have been a very severe reaction and is not supported by the facts. To be sure, changes in the major Western aid donors were registered between 1976 and 1983. But, while U.S. aid declined over the long run, aid from the European Economic Community and its member states increased "from an average of $9.8 million in 1971-73 to $82.4 million in 1979-82, and Ethiopia became the sixth largest recipient of Community aid under the Lome Conventions" after 1975 (Clapham 1988:122). Most posit the U.S. abandonment of Ethiopia at the time of the

Somali invasion, during which the United States refused to supply additional arms. But an earlier abandonment by the United States has been proposed: in August 1974 in favor of the Soviet Union "in the larger hope of preserving world peace" (Spencer 1984:356), or following the increasing political involvement of the Ethiopian military (Marcus 1983:188-9).

Two alternative explanations for the U.S. "abandonment" have surfaced, as well as an insider rejoinder to the abandonment thesis (Peterson 1986). One is that the United States was clumsy and out of control in Ethiopia due to administration crises in Washington stemming from the Watergate scandal, and due to disorganization of the U.S. embassy in Addis Ababa as the result of having no Ambassador in residence during 1974 (Korn 1986a:7-9; see also Henze 1983). Another explanation is that the instability of the revolution, which quickly passed through four different leaderships, made any U.S. commitment to any particular regime dangerous (Agyeman-Duah 1986:297). Perceptions of the consequences of the Soviet military presence were doubtless underestimated at the time. Possible motives and procedures for "abandoning" Ethiopia or withdrawing from the donor-recipient relationship are reviewed below. But it seems unlikely that the United States would have "abandoned" Ethiopia in the absence of serious breaches of what the relationship required. The absence of other instances of U.S. abandonment of aid recipients, and the Ethiopian tradition of switching sponsors, suggest that an Ethiopian variant of Nasserism may be a plausible explanation.

Positing U.S. responsibility for the 1983-86 famine on its withdrawal of developmental assistance, in particular, is based on a mistaken view of the strength—and reasons for the termination—of the donor-recipient relationship between the United States and Ethiopia. The strength of U.S. interest in Ethiopia prior to the revolution suggests a deep relationship that the United States would not have simply abandoned without a rational calculation of the value of the relationship and what stood to be lost (cf. Farer 1980). Western reactions to the Ethiopian revolution must therefore be viewed in terms of Ethiopia's relative independence of Western influence as well as its spurning of it in favor of the East. It is possible that neither the United States nor the Ethiopian government unilaterally renounced its donor-recipient relationship. Rather, there may have been a gradual divergence between the two during the 1974-77 period, when each came to denounce its respective status.

Evolution of the U.S. Position

The response of the United States to the Ethiopian revolution was a gradual one—not at all what would have been expected if Ethiopia had been a "dependency" about to be lost. Even prior to the revolution, U.S. policy toward Ethiopia was characterized by a kind of "development diplomacy," as U.S. funds for education, health and agriculture projects gradually outstripped military aid (Selassie 1984:262, 261). Even though the United States was the third largest importer of Ethiopian goods as early as 1889-1900 (Pankhurst 1968:403), substantial U.S. involvement in Ethiopian development did not begin until after Ethiopia was liberated from the Italian occupation in 1941. An American was named the Governor of the Bank of Ethiopia in 1943 (Perham 1969:207). The United States's Point-Four Program began operations in Ethiopia in 1952. While the U.S. administration and State Department had earlier contacts and personnel in Ethiopia, the official relationship was formally defined by the Mutual Defense and Assistance Agreement (MDAA) entered into in 1953. Subsequently, many other treaties for technical cooperation in diverse areas were also agreed to.

Many have argued that the obsolescence of the communications base at Kagnew, which had been obtained after the incorporation of Eritrea into Ethiopia, led to a loss of U.S. interest in Ethiopia. Certainly, Kagnew and having friends in the region (as testified to by Ethiopian troops in Korea and the Congo), were important to the United States, which provided large amounts of military aid for the maintenance of Ethiopian boundaries and for internal security purposes. But military assistance was far from being the "linchpin" of the relationship around which all other aspects revolved (Agyeman-Duah 1986:288). The Peace Corps was a key ingredient of the U.S. development program in Ethiopia (and the largest Peace Corps program in Africa), which included aid for education and agricultural development, even though diverging interpretations of the position of the Peace Corps in Ethiopia have been offered, ranging from a comfortable one (Vestal 1986) to an eventually hostile assessment on the part of Ethiopian students (Balsvik 1985:243). In addition, both Alameya Agricultural College in Hararghe (established in 1951) and Gonder Public Health College (established in 1954) were greatly assisted by USAID (cf. Vestal 1986:20-22). The Ford Foundation sponsored a massive legal development program at Haile Selassie I University, a form of "political" development assistance with long-term consequences for revolutionary leadership.

Withdrawal of aid rather than abandonment is the more accurate assessment of the U.S. response to the Ethiopian revolution. Events unfolding in Ethiopia during 1974 led to U.S. suspicion, but no decisive action. As one long-time observer of Ethiopian affairs describes it, the "hackles" of the United States were raised by the Marxist-Leninist vocabulary of the military officers who deposed Selassie. The U.S. government became "decidedly upset" in November when a large group of Selassie's former officials were executed, and "anxious" when "socialism and land nationalization were proclaimed" (Marcus 1985:192-193).

U.S. withdrawal was based on broader principles than perceptions of the revolution and Ethiopian development alone. The United States had become disenchanted with Selassie's rule, and its support had waned as his regime became more repressive and less democratic (Spencer 1976). These principles, including notions of responsibility and self-interest, are evident in the relationship that developed between the United States and the revolutionary government in Ethiopia. According to the charge d'affaires of the U.S. Embassy in Ethiopia during the early 1980s, the United States was willing to tolerate an Ethiopian version of "African socialism" as late as mid-1975 (Korn 1986a:13). U.S. military deliveries in 1976 were the largest ever—Ethiopia received in aid "$6.6 million in grant military assistance, $5.3 million in grant economic aid, $6.6 million in Public Law 480 food sales and grants, and $.5 million in Peace Corps assistance" from the United States in 1976 (Agyeman-Duah 1986:298).

This period of U.S. suspicion was followed by a period of monitoring Ethiopian development after Mengistu seized control of the state. The response of the United States to developments in Ethiopia was certainly limited by regional considerations—especially the Somali aggression and Soviet incursions in the Horn. But adjustments in U.S. policy required by congressional decisions and administrative changes also had implications for official assistance. Ethiopia was gradually put outside of the developmental aid program and acquired a different status within the food aid program, although food and other humanitarian aid continued (see below). This change of status occurred just as dramatic shifts in Ethiopian development policy resulted in adverse consequences for U.S. interests. Both factors were apparent in the refusal of the United States to approve Ethiopia's request for additional arms. U.S. interests were aired in House and Senate hearings of 1975 and 1976. Hearings in the House (U.S. House 1975) addressed a full slate of Ethiopian development issues in order to determine whether a "turning point" had been reached in relations with that country. Deciding whether military aid should be continued was the top item on the agenda. Similar questions were raised in Senate hearings a year and a half later (U.S. Senate 1976). After the refusal, the PMAC denounced the MDAA (Korn 1986a:132), and U.S. operations were administratively quashed by the restrictions on U.S. embassy personnel and the eviction of USAID staff and Peace Corps volunteers.

A reduction in aid to Ethiopia on the basis of human rights abuses of the Ethiopian PMAC was announced by Secretary of State Vance in February 1977 (*New York Times* 1 May 1977). Brooke Amendment sanctions followed from the failure of the PMGSE to pay for military equipment, although the Ethiopian government claimed the United States had failed to deliver hardware already paid for. Ethiopia was estimated to be $4-6 million in arrears on loan repayments to the United States for military equipment (U.S. Senate 1985b:7). But Brooke Amendment sanctions were suspended in 1980, to be reimposed in 1981 (Nelson and Kaplan 1981:222). The U.S. response to property expropriations pursuant to the Hickenlooper Amendment to the Foreign Assistance Act, which required termination of developmental assistance to countries having nationalized U.S. property, was somewhat slower to unfold. Although Ethiopia had declared that compensation would be provided for the expropriations of 1975 and 1976, "no meaningful progress toward resolution of the claims had occurred by 1979" (Finney 1983:232). Even so, it was not until July 1980 that the U.S. embassy in Addis Ababa was informed that all aid except for humanitarian purposes had been suspended (Peterson 1986:641).

In addition to terminating bilateral aid as required by the Hickenlooper Amendment, the United States also took action in multilateral institutions, opposing proposed World Bank loans to Ethiopia under the authority of the Gonzalez Amendment (*New York Times* 26 November 1984) It also "abstained" on votes for loans to Ethiopia by the International Development Association, and opposed African Development Fund loans.

Two important observations must be made in assessing the U.S. response to the Ethiopian revolution. First, the United States did not try to subvert the revolution or take a directory role in rebel activity. The proposal during the Senate hearings on the Ethiopian regime's request for military aid in 1976 to use a reduction in food aid as a weapon against the Derg does not merit the serious attention given it by some (e.g., Medhanie 1986). The perception that a food power option existed makes the fact that the United States did not even come close to using it much more significant. More importantly, the United States continued to show respect for the territorial integrity of Ethiopia as

TABLE 2.5
U.S. PL-480 Aid to Ethiopia, 1979-83

Fiscal Year	Amount (MT)	Value ($)
1979	42,634	9,081,000
1980	43,532	10,880,000
1981	24,370	8,103,000
1982	6,224	2,201,000
1983	14,285	9,300,000

Sources: U.S. House (1983b:79); U.S. G.A.O. (1985a:10).

officially constituted, and provided only token support of a less than viable group of dissidents based outside the country.

Second, U.S. withdrawal was selective rather than absolute. This was partly due to the limitations on cutting off aid, especially for emergency purposes. For example, termination of U.S. developmental assistance had a necessary but unclear impact on PL-480 food aid policy. The U.S. commitment to Ethiopian food system development survived, as evidenced by the 1975 Drought Recovery Program Agreement and USAID's participation in the construction of an Early Warning System. The United States also continued to operate a PL-480 program—largely through Catholic Relief Services, but also through the World Food Programme and a government-to-government program—albeit at reduced levels. Figures for the period 1979-83 are reflected in table 2.5. The United States had also provided a grant to Ethiopia in late 1978, and continued to engage in diplomatic jockeying with the government through the end of 1980 (Korn 1986a:55).

In addition to what remained of U.S. aid programs, aid from other countries and agencies came to fill the gaps. Not only did many other Western nations increase their bilateral aid (as noted above), but further aid was channeled through multilateral institutions so that Western aid to Ethiopia, including large increases from Italy, the World Food Programme and the International Development Association, actually increased after the revolution (Clapham 1988:121, 123). Direct substitutions in the area of food policy included the replacement of USAID assistance by UNICEF support in the further development of Ethiopia's Early Warning System. Many U.S.-based PVOs continued their work in the areas of relief and development.

Because there was no depletion of new external resources for Ethiopian development, it is certainly not clear that the position of the United States vis-a-vis Ethiopia was responsible for the deterioration in the development of the Ethiopian food system or the heightened famine-risk that exploded into famine in 1983.

Assessing Responsibilities for Famine-Risk

Accounting for the origins of heightened famine-risk is ordinarily no easy matter. However, the depth of Ethiopia's plunge into food deficiency makes the assessment of responsibilities for the outbreak of famine in 1983 somewhat more straightforward: By mid-1983, the food deficit had reached crisis dimensions, as 4 million people were at risk of famine. Responsibility may fall in various proportions on natural factors, the programs and policies of the ruling government, and the policies of donors such as the United States. In the case of the Ethiopian famine of 1983-86, the configuration of factors is fairly clear.

44 Reluctant Aid or Aiding the Reluctant?

Natural factors such as precipitation shortfalls and pest and locust invasions should not be discounted in terms of production costs, but they should not be treated as independent variables in the inducement of famine, as is often done (e.g., Bush 1985; Hancock 1985). Adverse rainfall patterns and unreliable precipitation are longstanding features of Ethiopian agricultural production (Degefu 1987:33-35). Smallholder producers have traditionally been able to adjust consumption to the climatic constraints on their seasonal cycles of sowing and harvesting.

Normative factors in famine inducement, inherent in the long legacy of famine in Ethiopia that "has always been in the Ethiopian socioeconomic setup" (Zewde 1976:57), should likewise not be disregarded. After the Great Famine of 1888-92 claimed up to two-thirds of the population (Pankhurst 1968:217), a cyclical pattern in famine began, including: the 1916-20 famine, the 1927-28 famine, the 1934-35 famine, the 1947-50 famine, the 1957-58 famine, and the 1964-65 famine. In the past two decades, the ravages of famine have been particularly severe, particularly during the 1972-74 famine, which caused an estimated 200,000 deaths. Initially concentrated in Wollo, Eritrea and the lowlands of Hararghe, the 1972-74 famine gradually spread to other areas (Hussein 1976), although its impact in Wollo was most severe. It was followed by another famine in 1977-78 (Bondestam 1981).

That the Ethiopian government failed to support peasant farmers and denied them assistance by neither responding to adverse natural conditions nor overcoming the historical defects in Ethiopian food policy is more than clear (cf. Mengisteab 1989:21). Instead it exploited their vulnerability to famine through its military, political and economic policies and programs. To the extent that vulnerability to famine has traditional origins, it is hard to hold the PMGSE accountable, but harder to hold the United States and West responsible. Even if normative or natural factors had a primary role in heightening Ethiopian famine-risk, U.S. responsibility for such developments must be held to be close to none. Neither the United States nor the West had any control or influence over Ethiopian food policy. Nor is there any evidence that increased aid would have been used to contain the growing famine-risk and to reform food policy in the direction of food security. The relative responsibilities for heightened famine-risk are made clearer in the actual inducement of famine, which followed directly from the radicalism of Ethiopian authorities in the areas of military strategy, economic and agricultural development, and exercising political controls.

Notes

1. The French Communist Party's influence is notable in Ethiopia as elsewhere. Just as many Khmer Rouge officials committed to "restructuring people" to the extent of massacre had associated with the French Communist Party (Shawcross 1984:51, 43), the principal drafter (Haile Fida) of the Ethiopian Program of the National Development Revolution (PNDR) and many of his associates within MEISON (All-Ethiopia Socialist Movement) were French Communist Party fellow travellers (Lefort 1983:166, 169).
2. The importance of the fact that there was no necessary connection, "in Marxian logic or otherwise," between SCs and PCs is diminished by the Ethiopian government's policy of conditioning the benefits derived from formation of a SC upon the PA's having a "firm" plan for the formation of a PC (Rahman 1979:13).
3. It was the Soviet complaint about and threat to discontinue military aid that prompted Mengistu to request arms in East Germany prior to the coup attempt in May 1989.

3

Working at Cross Purposes: Production and Concealment of Famine and Confusion of Food Aid Needs (1983-84)

By 1983, food shortages in Gonder, Tigray, Wollo and Eritrea had reached crisis levels, reflected both in the large increases in the number of people seriously affected by food shortage and in the number of people registered at shelters. At this critical point for mounting a relief effort to prevent widespread famine, the Ethiopian government was exacerbating the need for food. The government's responsibility for the impending famine was largely the result of its pursuing military objectives and implementing collectivistic programs for advancing the regime's revolutionary development strategy instead of pursuing food security. The structural food deficit was heightened by the drain of resources from the rural regions and by the accelerating process of class transformation in the countryside. For several months, the government also successfully concealed famine conditions by sealing off regions and restricting access to the affected areas.

On the other hand, the United States was struggling to assess food needs in Ethiopia while proposing policies to satisfy the myriad objectives and constituencies involved in its own policy formation process. If the 1977-78 period in Ethiopia is properly called the Dark Year (Lefort 1983:181-218; Clapham 1988:59), then 1983-84 in Ethiopia may be called the Secret Year for the West, in that the United States and the West had a poor sense of current developments in Ethiopia. During this period, U.S. foreign policy for the Horn of Africa region was also somewhat disoriented, there being some

48 Reluctant Aid or Aiding the Reluctant?

uncertainty as to which foreign policy doctrines were most applicable to Ethiopia. The Reagan Doctrine's policy of supporting rebellions against communism in the third world conflicted with the perceived milder diplomatic opportunities for regaining Ethiopia to the West. Despite both kinds of confusion, a U.S. response to famine conditions was being formulated and implemented as early as May 1984, and by early 1985 the United States was delivering large quantities of food aid.

Sufficient evidence of PMGSE activities and U.S policy has now surfaced to permit assessment of the Ethiopian government's revolutionary programs and U.S. reactions during this early stage of the famine. These programs not only induced famine in many regions of the country, but also had an adverse affect on the humanitarian response. The constraints on the U.S. response to the famine may also be assessed in the process of reviewing these activities.

Building the Structural Food Deficit: Militarism, Collectivism, and Revolutionary Strategy

At the time the U.S. embassy in Addis Ababa declared a state of emergency on 5 May 1983 (U.S. G.A.O. 1985a:15), the Ethiopian government was holding its course on food policy despite the fact that its effects were becoming increasingly clear to inside observers. Food deficits were being transformed into consumption shortfalls and famine.

Some measure of the magnitude and distribution of the structural food deficit, and the further extent of the productivity decline just prior to the onset of widespread famine, may be gleaned from observing the deterioration of national and regional food production during the 1983-85 period in comparison to the 1981-83 period. Table 3.1 contains estimates of the annual domestic food production by administrative region. Every region showed a decline in production except for Ilubabor and Kaffa (which showed only minor increases). By the latter part of 1983, with an estimated population of 41 million, the food deficit had reached approximately 319,000 MT, the largest shortfalls being evident in the highland regions in the north.

Estimating the Emergency Food Deficit

Finding a connection between Ethiopia's food deficit and the programs and policy decisions of the Ethiopian government requires disaggregating the deficit into its structural and emergency portions. Deriving plausible estimates of the emergency deficit is important because of the recognition that not all production outcomes are policy driven, but problematic because of the unreliability of the available data and the enormous analytic consequences of such a disaggregation. The total food deficit in Ethiopia during the period

1979-85 most likely ranged from 500,000 to 2,000,000 MT per year (see Faught 1987:1; Worrick 1986:1,3; Atwood 1987). The annual emergency deficit is equivalent to the annual consumption requirements less the shortfalls attributable to the structural deficit produced by poor food policy decisions. The structural portion of the deficit has been estimated to be from one-fourth to over one-half of the total.

Several hypotheses may be advanced to explain the relationship between these two sources of the deficit. Some portion of the emergency deficit may be attributable to unforeseeable precipitation shortfalls and pest invasions against which no policy response could reasonably be expected. A small part of the variance in food production may be taken as an initial estimate of the emergency deficit due to these factors, since they are irregular and arguably unforeseeable in the Ethiopian context. Other parts of the food deficit, such as those attributable to the inability of the Ethiopian food system to keep pace with population increases, levels of Agricultural Marketing Corporation (AMC) procurements, military diversions, and diminishing productivity, must be included in the structural deficit.

TABLE 3.1
Deterioration of Regional Food Production, 1981/83-1983/85
(Cereals and Pulses) (in '000 MT)

	Two-Year Totals		
	1981/83	1983/85	Percent Change
Arsi	1163	841	-28
Bale	354	189	-47
Eritrea	426	320	-29
Gamo Gofa	241	154	-36
Gojam	1646	1455	-12
Gonder	1302	954	-27
Hararghe	845	551	-35
Ilubabor	350	367	+4
Kaffa	575	596	+4
Shoa	3464	2812	-19
Sidamo	365	332	-9
Tigray	393	287	-27
Welega	1106	843	-24
Wollo	1654	654	-60
TOTAL	13,884	10,355	-25

Sources: Calculated from Ethiopian Central Statistical Office data (USAID/E, 1987:41), except for Eritrea and Tigray, which are estimated as described in Table 2.3.

50   Reluctant Aid or Aiding the Reluctant?

Accounting for the Structural Deficit

Deficits due to population growth are structural in origin because of the predictability of demand and the failure to boost production and/or increase imports to meet increased demand. The burden in accounting for the structural portions of the food deficit above and beyond those resulting from population increases alone is to demonstrate how regionally-specific policies interfered with food production and then with consumption during 1983-84. Interregional movement of food outside of AMC procurement channels is severely restricted, making regional consumption more heavily dependent on regional production. Table 3.2 presents the contributions of regional deficits to Ethiopia's total food deficit for 1984.

TABLE 3.2
Regional Contributions to Ethiopian Food Deficit, 1984

	Population ('000)	Food Requirement (MT)	Food Production (MT)	Food Deficit ('000 MT)
Arsi	1662.2	270.939	420,500	+149
Bale	1006.5	164,059	94,500	-69
Eritrea	2704.0	440,752	160,000	-280
Gamo Gofa	1248.0	203,424	77,000	-126
Gojam	3244.9	528,919	727,500	+198
Gonder	2905.4	473,580	477,000	+3
Hararghe	4151.7	676,727	275,500	-401
Ilubabor	963.3	157,018	183,500	+26
Kaffa	2450.4	399,415	298,000	-101
Shoa	9503.1	1,549,005	1,406,000	-143
Sidamo	3790.6	617,868	166,000	-451
Tigray	2409.7	392,781	143,500	-249
Welega	2369.7	386,261	421,500	+35
Wollo	3609.9	588,414	327,000	-261
TOTAL	42,019.4	6,849,162	5,177,500	-1,671

Sources: Population: Office of the Population and Housing Census Commission, *Ethiopia 1984: Population and Housing Census Preliminary Report*, 1984 (in Wubneh and Abate, 1988:135).

1984 Food Requirements calculated on the basis of 163 kg per person (see table 2.1 for explanation).

1984 Food Production: average of 1983/84 and 1984/85, from table 3.1 and artificially decreases the estimated food deficits in Eritrea and Tigray; does not include non-grain production (e.g., milk) and therefore artificially increases the estimated food deficits of pastoral regions.

Three Ethiopian policy factors interrelated at both the micro and macro levels of explanation account for the structural food deficit. (They also contributed directly to the inducement of famine through shortages of food for rural consumption.) First, militarism had a direct role in producing food shortages in the war zones, especially in the north but also in parts of the southeast and southwest. Second, advancing civilian-side programs for collectivization had clear control targets for preventing revolt. The third factor—the revolutionary economic strategy of the Ethiopian government—converged with rural collectivization programs to spread the adverse impact of regionalized food policies throughout the economy.

Militarism continued to be the defining characteristic of Ethiopian government rule during the 1980s, heightening the adverse effects of food policy at the micro and macro levels. Both types of effects were evident in the war zones of Eritrea and Tigray, but also in parts of Hararghe and other regions where military contingents were based. In Eritrea and Tigray especially, military activity escalated prior to and during the famine period. In 1983, an Ethiopian offensive of the same magnitude as Operation Red Star was waged against the EPLF (Kaplan 1988:67). Also in early 1983, an offensive against the TPLF in Western Tigray was mounted (Kaplan 1988:96). Military actions heightened the structural food deficit at both levels, even though population decreases resulted from war deaths.

At the micro level, several factors of militarization contributing to lower levels of food production may be identified. Despite the nearly country-wide need for more extensive land cultivation, destruction of farm land as a result of military engagements between Ethiopian government troops and rebel units certainly occurred, although its extent cannot be even crudely estimated.

Diminished amounts of food available for local consumption followed directly from these lower levels of food production, reduced further by procurements of food supplies by Ethiopian military and rebel units while in the field. Evidence of grain seizures by the Ethiopian forces has been widely documented (Clay and Holcomb 1985; Dines 1988); it must be assumed that rebel units did the same, despite the claims of many of their patrons and supporters to the contrary. Economically-based food procurements for supplying the military with foodstuffs through the AMC also reduced the supply of food available for consumption by peasants.

Further decreases resulted from disincentives to production created by militarization. Military activity in the government- and rebel-held regions undermined the confidence of farmers that they would be able to successfully plant and harvest their crops and consume and market any food surpluses. Such effects have been amply documented through interviews with Eritrean and Tigrayan refugees in Sudan (Clay and Holcomb 1985). Less intense conflicts produced similar confidence deflation in Hararghe and other regions.

52 Reluctant Aid or Aiding the Reluctant?

Recruitment for military service further drained manpower resources from agricultural production. The National Military Service Proclamation was promulgated in May 1983, and its first batch enlisted in May 1984 (Clapham 1988:140). Government men at arms increased to their highest level of 300,000 and incorporated another generation of men and women into the rebel forces. There were reports of persons "volunteering" for military service in order to provide food for starving family members (Dines 1988:153). Conscription in southern regions—a major source of military personnel—reduced the productivity of those areas, and they experienced production shortfalls, especially during the latter part of the famine period. The swelling of rebel ranks, even though more voluntarily, increased food requirements in rebel-held areas while decreasing the manpower capacity for producing it.

Further depletion of manpower resources for agricultural production resulted from the migration and adoption of refugee status induced by military activities, and also through fear of victimization and conscription. By August 1983, more than 1 million Ethiopians had already adopted refugee status, including 460,000 in Sudan and 700,000 in Somalia (Rogge 1985:13). This was to be only a prelude to the great migrations of 1984-85, and did not include the large number of internally displaced persons whose productivity also declined.

In macro terms, the buildup of the war economy in the wake of the formation of the Soviet alliance has already been discussed, but the drain on agricultural development budgets must be further emphasized as contributing to the structural food deficit. In 1984, 46 percent of the government's expenditures were for armaments (see Kelemen 1985:11). Food bills for feeding 300,000 regular units and supplying the militias took food and production resources away from peasant producers. Government expenditures committed to military activities retarded opportunities for industrialization, lowered levels of public investment, and decreased private investment, thereby reproducing a cycle of economic stagnation (Aboucher 1984; Abegaz 1988).

The Ethiopian government's revolutionary economic strategy converged with militarism at many points in increasing the structural food deficit. Overall productivity declines resulted from the poor decision making exercised over the economy by central planning institutions. Economic stagnation and other adverse effects were compounded by efforts to collectivize agricultural production and control upward mobility through economic channels.

In the smallholder sector, 1983/84 food production fell to only 90 percent of the average production level for fiscal years 1980/81-1983/84 (USAID/E 1987:42). These declines were at least partially due to attempts to control agricultural decision making through central institutions, as well as to the substance of the decisions themselves. Evaluations of the performance of smallholders under the influence of Peasant Associations, PCs and SCs have

Working at Cross Purposes 53

not been uniform, but the general conclusion is that overall they have not resulted in productivity increases. The adverse effects of land reform without meaningful social reforms, including reducing the autonomy of peasants, not taking population increases into account in redistributing land, the insecurity of tenure resulting from not having title, and threats of redistribution, all undermined the farmers' commitment to produce and return surplus value to investments in the land for production.

Disincentives to production—resulting from these uncertainties as well as from input scarcity, unfavorable procurement expectations, and lack of consumption opportunities—reached their high point between 1982/83 and 1984/85, as is evident in the large production declines during the period and the overall trend since the late 1970s. At the regional level, the PMGSE's economic policy for altering production patterns continued to result in declines, but with a much steeper slope. At the individual level, declines resulted from resistance to the restructuring of food entitlements. Adjusting from an individualized system based on the market and traditional exchange values to a state-controlled system requiring initial satisfaction of obligations to pay taxes and fulfill procurement quotas cut against Ethiopian character. Traditionally, in the north, surplus extraction was legitimized by *gult* rights (similar to fief rights), which allowed for some flexibility in the levels of produce delivered by farmers to their lords (Markakis and Ayele 1986:22); in the south, the relationships of landlord and tenant could be dissolved through eviction from the land. Difficulties throughout the country were heightened by the fact that participation in consumption programs was restricted by membership in collective institutions. State ownership of land, and encroachments on individual ownership of agricultural implements, created further uncertainties about the value of efforts to produce.

Politicization of agricultural inputs and extension services clearly reflected the priority of agricultural development policy in favor of collective institutions. Food policy continued to neglect smallholders in favor of collective institutions, including Producer Cooperatives (PCs), Service Cooperatives (SCs), and state farms. Tax policies, procurement quotas, marketing options, and consumer items were similarly skewed against smallholders in order to encourage the formation of collective institutions (Cohen 1984). As a result, the productivity of the smallholder sector could only be expected to decline.

Quotas for excessive AMC procurements during 1983/84 were perhaps set and partly motivated by the deceptively large harvest during the previous year. Table 3.3 sets forth the targeted procurements by region for the 1981/82 period preceding the outbreak of famine. Levels for the 1982/83 period were likely even larger because of the favorable harvests and successful procurement program of the previous year. Food procured by the AMC from

54 Reluctant Aid or Aiding the Reluctant?

smallholders was removed from the sphere of smallholder consumption, being targeted to urban populations and the military. In Ethiopia, as elsewhere, planned procurements over a period of time may be more important than actual procurements in affecting production because of the emergence of the belief that "what is not produced cannot be requisitioned" (Abegaz 1988:71).

Consumption-side incentives to increase production were quashed by procurement of any otherwise disposable surplus as well as by restrictions on access to markets for consumer goods. Dejene (1985:141) has noted the dissatisfaction of the relatively affluent rural populations in Arsi with the consumer goods made available to them through SCs. Except for the free trade zones in Hararghe, that are difficult to access, only poor quality goods are made available through the Ethiopian Domestic Distribution Corporation (EDDC).

An assumption of only a 5 percent decline in 1979-83 average production levels due to these factors would result in over 300,000 MT being reasonably attributed to the structural deficit, which would leave only approximately

TABLE 3.3
Regional Procurement Targets of AMC, FY1981/82

	1981/82 Procurement (MT)	1981/82 Planned	1980/81 Actual	Percent of 1980/81 Planned	1979/80 Actual	1979/80 Planned
Arsi	65,489	151	183	167	377	187
Bale	9,676	231	230	90	105	276
Eritrea	-	-	-	-	-	-
Gamo Gofa	-	-	-	-	-	-
Gojam	101,187	108	103	184	257	202
Gonder	33,284	108	152	124	387	416
Hararghe	-	n.a.	n.a.	n.a.	n.a.	n.a.
Ilubabor	326	14	31	14	37	13
Kaffa	3,640	49	70	51	93	81
Shoa	62,432	70	89	66	69	89
Sidamo	847	91	419	6	314	42
Tigray	-	-	-	-	-	-
Welega	12,293	138	136	114	259	224
Wollo	17,281	99	175	133	185	192
Total	306,455	103	119	112	162	153

Source: Calculated from AMC, Data Book on AMC Operations (March 1983) (in Lirenso 1984:555).

Working at Cross Purposes 55

19,000 MT as the estimated emergency deficit; both figures were doubtless much larger. Regardless of proportion, for individual farmers the structural food deficit translated into famine through a complex set of processes put into motion by the central institutions of the Ethiopian state.

Inducing Famine: Allocating Consumption Shortfalls

Building the structural food deficit was consistent with several plausible interrelated military, political and economic objectives of the Ethiopian government. Military victory over the rebels and prevention of further insurgencies was the primary objective. Class transformation was certainly the result if not the goal of Ethiopian food policy decisions during the 1983-84 period. The food deficit would have to born by someone in the form of consumption shortfalls. While increasing control over the peasantry, what better way to destroy any remnants of their freedom than through restricting their access to food?

Consumption shortfalls throughout the country produced by the mounting food deficit may be measured by RRC estimates of the increasing levels of persons affected by serious food shortages between 1982 and 1984. As table 3.4 indicates, the northern regions experienced the greatest increases, while in other regions increases did not occur until 1985. Some measure of the relationship between production declines and famine is provided by the correspondence between production deficits and persons affected by food shortages presented in the table. These estimates and shelter populations may be the best measures of the encroachment of food shortages into famine.

Mortality rates due to the encroaching famine are impossible to measure in absolute terms. However, increases in estimated mortality rates provide valuable relative figures for estimating fluctuations in severity. (In eastern Tigray, during the six-month period ending May 1983, there were approximately 4,400 famine and famine-related deaths (Clark 1986:6). Former RRC Commissioner Dawit Wolde Giorgis's (1989) mortality estimates are probably the best available even though the regional distribution of deaths is not documented.) Through late 1983 and early 1984, the "death rate in the villages increased steadily. By the end of February, approximately 10,000 a week were dying in the shelters, distribution centers, and villages. After March it rose to 16,000-17,000 a week" (Wolde Giorgis 1989:133). Combining these estimates, it may conservatively be estimated that approximately 500,000 Ethiopians had already died by the middle of 1984.

Allocating consumption shortfalls to induce famine was accomplished through the progression toward collectivism that was a major element of the Ethiopian government's plan for designing a system of central control; utilizing economic, political, and social institutions to achieve this stability

56 Reluctant Aid or Aiding the Reluctant?

TABLE 3.4
Persons Affected by Serious Food Shortages, 1982-84

	1982	1983 (In '000)	1984	1982-84 (% change)	Food Deficit 1984 ('000 MT)
Arsi	220	60	21	-90	+149
Bale	109	35	53	-31	-69
Eritrea	713	800	877	+23	-280
Gamo Gofa	---	---	80	--	-126
Gojam	84	20	35	-58	+198
Gonder	202	425	325	+61	+3
Hararghe	384	285	279	-27	-401
Ilubabor	20	---	---	--	+26
Kaffa	---	---	---	--	-101
Shoa	533	195	204	-62	-143
Sidamo	303	145	355	+17	-451
Tigray	600	1000	1300	+117	-249
Welega	---	---	---	--	+35
Wollo	592	1100	1821	+208	-263
Total	3760	4065	5350	+42	-1671

Source: RRC (1985d); USAID/E (1987:1) for 1986 and Eritrea, 1984 and 1985; and table 3.2 for Food Deficit.

was at the core of the government's development strategy. Transforming state structures and encouraging military and party supervision of bureaucrats and church hierarchies clarified the emerging pattern of power. By 1979, half of the members of the Derg held "powerful provincial and other executive positions" (Selassie 1980:47) while appointments of military personnel were made to take over administrator posts at the *kifle hager* (administrative region), *awraja* (sub-region), and *woreda* (district) levels (Cohen 1984). Party officials and cadres penetrated the administration and rural institutions to supervise peasants and implement commands from above. Political controls and reshuffling ministers prevented officials from developing ties with their clients but also kept them ignorant of conditions existing within their jurisdictions.

Attempts to undermine religious authority followed an analogous pattern. Expropriation of church buildings (including the conversion of the Bible Society of Ethiopia's building into COPWE headquarters), seizure of radio stations, abductions of church leaders such as the general secretary of the Ethiopian Evangelical Church Makane Yesus, infiltration of the Ethiopian

Orthodox Church and replacement of its head by a radical—all were among the government's programs for undermining religion (see, e.g., Doulos 1986).

Processes for controlling the flow of commands from the top down, that also prevented the flow of influence from the bottom up, were consolidated prior to the famine. Such arrangements had a major role in implementing famine-inducing policies and a great impact on the government's inability to respond to the famine. This pattern is especially clear in the one sector where some institutional influence by farmers might have been possible. Mass organizations or "auxiliary structures" (Schwab 1985) built by the regime, such as the All Ethiopia Peasant Association (AEPA), Revolutionary Ethiopia Women's Association (REWA), and the Revolutionary Ethiopia Youth Association (REYA), were ultimately controlled by elites at the center. The reorganization of AEPA in 1982 was designed to increase party control over PAs. One study of the relationship between PAs and Women's Associations in Arsi region found the latter to be subservient to the former (Dejene 1987). In its Tenth Regular Meeting, REYA stressed the "duty of Ethiopian youth to continue to expose and foil counterrevolutionary propaganda" (*Ethiopian Herald* 12 April 1987) indicating that the group had come firmly within the grip of Mengistu. Mass organization building also had the effect of destroying alternative institutions such as religious ones.

Implementation of Ethiopian food policy has been accomplished by the devolution of policy commands down the line of state and party institutions to PAs. In this context, the September 1984 reorganization of the regime, especially the creation of WPE and the Office of the National Committee for Central Planning (ONCCP), brought the PMGSE one step closer to the Soviet model of government (Clapham 1987:155-156). The party-building exercises culminating in the celebration of the Tenth Anniversary of the Revolution and the launching of the Workers' Party of Ethiopia reflected the concentration of authority in an institution guided by principles of ideology rather than practical performance or economic rationality. Rather than being the participatory institutions originally envisioned, PAs have evolved into little more than organizational structures for the implementation of policy formulated by state and party officials (see, e.g., Rahmato 1985:81-84). PAs had been delegated responsibilities for fulfilling agricultural produce quotas, for collecting taxes, and for filling quotas for participation in the resettlement and villagization programs (Clapham 1988:161). They had become little more than disciplinary tools.

A reasonable economic explanation for the PMGSE's food policies during the period is preparation for increased procurements. It seems clear that the motivation for increasing agricultural procurements was to underwrite further military activities and elite development, but not to nourish industrialization, that had grown only minimally (Aboucher 1984; Henze 1985). Moreover,

58 Reluctant Aid or Aiding the Reluctant?

strengthening the infrastructure for procurement consolidated the political grip of central institutions on rural populations. Using food to test the political loyalty of the rural population is therefore a reasonable political explanation for Ethiopian food policy, compatible with the economic objectives of the government.

This analysis of Ethiopian food policy is consistent with the government's failure to respond to the famine in a relief mode. By the time the famine was in full swing, the regime was no longer consolidating its power; it was launching a program for guaranteeing its survival, creating a new class of elites based on connections with the party already being formed by COPWE. When the government finally acknowledged the famine, it did not prepare for policy reform. Instead, it used the famine as an opportunity to extract resources from the West to further advance its food policy. Manipulating foreign nongovernmental organizations proved to be only a slightly easier task than coercing the complicity of donor governments in its programs.

RRC Activities and the PMGSE's Response to Famine

In this context of induced famine, responsive programs on the part of the Ethiopian government would hardly have been expected. Assessments of the RRC's efforts to mount a relief effort and its subsequent activities in the area of relief and development must take into account the Ethiopian government's policy orientation to the famine. Prior to the Ethiopian government's acknowledgement of the famine near the end of 1984, its response had evolved from willful blindness regarding food shortages to vehement denial of the widespread suffering, and then to concerted efforts to conceal the famine for domestic and international political purposes. After the party seized control of the relief operation away from the RRC, it aspired to direct relief resources away from relief and toward the government's programs for collectivization. The RRC's activities are especially important in light of the central government's interference with relief, the misguided resettlement program, and eventually bringing the spoils of famine relief under central control for further consolidation of socialist food production and distribution.

Refusal of the government to acknowledge the encroaching famine is not surprising given the revolutionary fervor underlying Ethiopian food policy. From the beginning of its rule, signals from the PMGSE to domestic groups and the international community regarding food shortages displayed a callousness of outlook. Previously, during the famine of 1977-78, warnings of famine had been made to the PMGSE repeatedly by sympathetic advisors and by relief and development organizations, but without effect (Bondestam 1981). During a three-day budget meeting in the summer of 1983, neither the famine nor the drought were even mentioned (Wolde Giorgis 1989:127),

Working at Cross Purposes 59

making it clear that at the highest levels food shortages were not even viewed as an issue.

After knowledge of the famine had surfaced, the Ethiopian government's first internal response was to prohibit the RRC from making public appeals for aid during May through October of 1984. The government also broadcast propaganda in the domestic sphere, denying the famine and attributing famine claims to counterrevolutionary forces (Korn 1986a:131; *World Affairs Report* 1985:550-2). These actions were related to the efforts of the Ethiopian government to hide the famine while preparing to celebrate the anniversary of the revolution and the establishment of WPE. The government "severely restricted" travel to the affected areas during July and August (Goyder 1988:91). Party-building activities and rhetoric made it organizationally and ideologically impossible to acknowledge the disastrous effects of revolutionary policy at the very time it was to be officially celebrated (cf. Korn 1986a:120). Roadblocks were constructed outside of Addis Ababa to keep the hungry out (Wolde Giorgis 1989:169).

The effects of the PMGSE's failure either to mobilize or to be mobilized by domestic social forces inside or outside of the government in order to respond to the famine can hardly be exaggerated. Between March 1984 (the date of the RRC's initial request for aid) and September 1984 (the month of the anniversary celebrations), "hundreds of thousands had died" (Wolde Giorgis 1987:521). The Ethiopian government's disavowal of the famine affected the way in which the RRC responded: it also blocked foreign efforts to respond by placing sovereignty limitations on their relief efforts. Later, television programming continued the litany of anti-imperialist propaganda, ignoring Western aid while inflating meager levels of Eastern bloc aid (Korn 1986a:131; *World Affairs Report* 1985:550-2).

Lack of central government support was one major structural constraint on the RRC's famine relief operations from within. Indeed, according to the commissioner at the time, the RRC's "most difficult task was convincing [PMGSE] leaders of the very existence of a widespread famine" (Wolde Giorgis 1989:134). Even so, the RRC had been the internal vanguard, making an early presentation to the UN Conference on Least Developed Countries in May 1981 (Hancock 1985:72). It began publicizing the impending famine in the international arena in September 1982, as low-level RRC officials issued warnings. RRC Commissioner Dawit's presentation in March 1984 requested nearly 1 million MT of food (later reduced to 450,000 MT) for the "over 6 million of our people in absolute jeopardy" (Wolde Giorgis 1984:12). Similar requests were made during pledging conferences and visits with Western donors to solicit aid.

Expecting the RRC's vanguard position in sounding the alert on famine to easily mature into a normative role in famine relief would be shortsighted.

60 Reluctant Aid or Aiding the Reluctant?

Throughout the famine, the RRC attempted to administer a complex system for relief, responding to the food power commands of the PMGSE and Party apparatus, attempting to expand its own domain and mandate in the Ethiopian bureaucratic setting, and responding to the normative pressures of the international relief community. The RRC was required to bear the entire official Ethiopian responsibility for relief.

The RRC's dilemma may be gleaned from its own bureaucratic structure and development. Since a detailed study of the RRC's budget, activities, and sources of funding has not yet been performed, the single best source of information remains the RRC's own glossy presentation in *The Challenges of Drought* (RRC 1985a). Typical of fourth-world bureaucracies and famine-relief agencies in particular, the RRC's internal structure and linkages with international systems for famine prevention and relief suffered from numerous bureaucratic and technical flaws. Prior to mid-1983, under the leadership of Commissioner Shimelis Adugna, the RRC was "guilty of minor corruption and widespread maladministration (Shepherd 1985a:6n). The fact that Shimelis was then also the head of Ethiopian prisons must have diluted his relief authority, as he was presumably a trusted member of the security administration. When Dawit Wolde Giorgis—himself a former military officer and an admirer of Shimelis—replaced him as commissioner in the spring of 1983 (in order to remove Dawit from his COPWE work in Eritrea and effectively "get rid of him" [Wolde Giorgis 1989:129]), RRC performance improved. But its flaws as a normative relief agency became most evident in its inability to cure the defects of the resettlement program (Wolde Giorgis 1987).

Limits on the RRC's relief mandate may be clearly assessed by examining its origins in Ethiopia's revolutionary order. It is overly simplistic to attribute the downfall of the Selassie regime and the onset of the revolutionary process to the famine of 1972-74 or its ineffective relief, a thesis more often asserted than substantiated. There is certainly some connection between the famine that claimed 200,000 lives and the ascendance of the military in 1974 that overthrew the Imperial regime. The military rebellion was partly inspired by the breakdown in civilian maintenance of the social order that was "combined with a famine relief operation necessitated by the government's lethargy, and competing with the army's need for transport" (Harbeson 1979:358). One important outcome of the early assault on the Imperial regime, however, was the creation of a bureaucracy for investigating the failure and for overseeing relief efforts (RRC 1985c).[1]

Given the subsequent rise of military administration in Ethiopia, it is not surprising that the RRC was called upon to assist with the implementation of military policies or that the Ethiopian government made use of food for military purposes, a typical rather than exceptional policy in warfare (see,

Working at Cross Purposes 61

e.g., Mudge 1970). From the outset, the RRC's mandate[2] has been infused with the military objectives of the early revolutionary regime. By 1975, the government:

> had a functioning relief agency. And there was food to distribute. But this little impediment to conscripting famine as an ally was overcome by fiat: The agency would not function in rural Eritrea. The Dergue [i.e., Derg] also ordered foreign and international relief agencies to close their feeding stations in the countryside. Food in excess of needs of the garrisons and, barely, the population of the occupied urban areas was barred from the province [of Eritrea] (Farer 1979:44).

An admission made in the presence of the U.S. charge d'affaires in December 1984 by the acting foreign minister that the regime had used food as a "major element" in its military strategy "against the secessionists" in the north (Korn 1986a:137) serves to support other allegations of military cooptation and interference with relief efforts in the famine regions.

In the economic and developmental dimensions of revolutionary food policy, a structural dilemma was long posed for the RRC by its relationship with the central government. The RRC's manifest functions and operations had originally been diverse. They ranged from administering famine relief to taking responsibility for resettlement, with some additional functions in the state farm sector (Holt 1983:190-191; IDI 1983:164). Its mandate and strategy for discharging food allocation and distribution functions, including the disposition of food aid commodities, was structurally compromised from the outset. The PMGSE's central distributive mechanism for food commodities operated to move food from the rural to the urban areas—just the reverse of famine relief needs. This flow also restricted the development of inter-regional mechanisms for transferring food from surplus to deficit regions, as would operate in a market system through price behavior; all food must go through the state and be made subject to its military and revolutionary priorities. Urban food rationing centers were supplied by the Basic Commodities Supply Corporation from AMC procurements.

Even though the RRC's authority to administer famine-affected regions without military or party supervision may be doubted, the RRC was the sole Ethiopian organization with a relief mandate during the early part of the famine and the main institutional system for getting foreign donations into the government's coffers. The RRC's sources of domestic funds were limited. It had been authorized to tax the salaries of workers earning in excess of E$125 per month in an amount equal to one month's salary, payable over a one-year period (RRC 1985b:108). The RRC also received some amount of direct funding from the PMGSE. For 1978/79, for example, it was budgeted E$10 million for drought relief—a minuscule amount equal to about .47 percent of the total PMGSE budget (Bezabih 1981:82). A RRC request for E$95.5 million in July 1983 was rejected; only the usual E$10 million subsidy was approved (Wolde Giorgis 1989:126-7).

Technological resources for predicting famine and estimating needs for relief centered around the development and operation of the Early Warning System (EWS) and the RRC's Pre-Disaster Planning Program that was established in 1975 and originally cosponsored by USAID. Claimed to be the best in Africa (ICIHI 1985:37-38), the EWS nonetheless had many defects, and an urgent need for technical and accounting assistance had been identified. The EWS's principal defects related to its bureaucratic setting and its vulnerability to political commands.

In developing its plan for operational development, for early warning, as for other activities, the RRC was to work closely with military authorities and other agencies (RRC 1975:4). Governmental participation in EWS included the Ministry of Agriculture, the National Meteorological Services Agency, the Ethiopian Nutritional Institute, the Central Statistical Office, and the RRC (RRC 1984b:13-14). But EWS presumably came to be supervised by WPE authorities.

It issued monthly as well as special reports. The monthly reports of the Early Warning and Planning Service contained rainfall and grain price trends (e.g., RRC 1986). Special reports (such as RRC 1985d) documented trends by administrative region, including those of prices and estimates of the number of people affected. Despite the preparedness rationale for these measures (Cutler 1984), there is also evidence that EWS information was used to identify farmers and areas with modest surpluses that might support increased procurements (Clay 1989:248).

A well organized bureaucracy had been made of the RRC by the 1980s. In June 1982, it had a staff of 434 employees, growing to 17,000 employees in 1985 (Wolde Giorgis 1987:523). The departmental organization of the RRC largely followed recommended patterns. The RRC had also developed food distribution operations and established distribution centers by the time of the famine. Its transport apparatus was largely built by foreign donors on the basis of a 1977 UN agreement (see UNDP/ILO 1982:2). In December 1981 the RRC took over the fleet of the National Transport Corporation (NATRACOR), adding it to the RRC's own fleet of 168 trucks and 124 trailers. As of November 1984, the RRC had 400 trucks, although the conditions of the fleet left much to be desired (Wolde Giorgis in USAID/W 1984:4). The RRC also operated central warehouses for food storage in Nazareth, Kombolcha and Asmara (OFDA 1985:26). By the end of 1983, the RRC operated 193 distribution centers throughout the country (ADAB 1984:47).

Like other agencies and organizations in Ethiopia, the RRC was subordinate to the politics of the PMGSE and came to be controlled by the

Working at Cross Purposes 63

WPE after its emergence from COPWE. Early subordination of the RRC to higher Ethiopian authorities may be measured by the fact that although it had reported impending famine in September of 1984, the PMGSE and Mengistu were occupied with other matters, particularly the overhauling of Addis for the celebration of the Tenth Anniversary of the Revolution. And, while it had effectively monitored food system operation and crises, the RRC had only a narrow political base in the PMGSE and was unable to find a listening ear until the famine was raging.

Even so, the RRC had primary, if not exclusive jurisdiction within the PMGSE for regulating the relationship between donors and the recipient state. But the RRC's famine relief operations were largely dependent upon its ability to circumvent PMGSE restrictions and to attract relief from donors. Unlike the majority of undeveloped countries, Ethiopia had no indigenous nongovernmental organizations able to respond to the famine in a vanguard mode, primarily because the PMGSE had effectively banned private organizations not connected with the party or state institutions (although Ethiopian organizations, especially churches, did assist with food distribution in some areas). The RRC also had few relationships with Ethiopian institutions having economic power, and commercial channels for distributing substantial amounts of food did not exist. As foreign donations began to pour in, the RRC was clearly caught between the cross-purposes of the PMGSE's development strategy and the norms of famine relief of its international sponsors.

There is little evidence that the RRC operated as a norm-bearing organization. Its links to international norms were largely based upon food aid donated by Western donors. Bureaucratic reorganizations further subordinated the RRC to higher authorities. The RRC's authority for famine relief was combined with the Settlement Authority (Clay and Holcomb 1985:165), and the resettlement authority was then transferred from RRC to COPWE (Survival International 1986). But the WPE rather than state institutions became the sole body for dealing with famine as the Politburo asserted decision-making authority (Clapham 1988:83), and it was not until after the urging of the Italian Embassy—and presumably the diplomacy of other foreign governments as well—that the WPE recognized the famine and began to assert control over relief operations.

Interference with normative processes of relief operations was also evident, as the former RRC commissioner revealed that for his agency, the "most serious problem was the interference of party officials, who saw the situation entirely from the political point of view" (Wolde Giorgis 1987:523). Initially, the RRC effectively distributed food in the permitted areas but succumbed to revolutionary politics in the process. Directing aid toward the development of a Soviet-style food system—and away from effective famine relief—became a part of its mandate by default if not by Party direction.

Former RRC officials have reported purges within the RRC by WPE, cleaning up the agency to "ensure more efficient control" by WPE over the RRC (Clay and Holcomb 1985:166). The result was further control over RRC operations by the WPE, and the assignment of RRC to the supervisory responsibilities of implementing Party policy. After the Central Committee was appointed, Politburo officials trumped relief officials in implementing Ethiopian policy. The number-three man in the Politburo, Feseha Desta, became chairman of the Transport Committee for Relief, and Berhanu Bayeh was appointed chairman of the Political Bureau's Famine Relief Committee. Local party officials also gained control over relief operations in the field (Jansson 1987).

Prior to the entry of WPE into the field, famine relief was spearheaded by private agencies, foreign embassies, and international organizations that had to operate within the constraints of the Ethiopian government, their sponsors (often Western donor governments), and the space occupied by UN agencies. The development and operation of the RRC continued to be an important consideration for donors in their formation of policy for famine relief. Confidence that aid donated would be distributed effectively was important to donors. While private agencies were certainly in the vanguard during the early stages of relief, Ethiopian authorities eventually pre-empted the field and were able to at least partially coopt many of the agencies. Later, the RRC may have had to compete with ethnic and other famine relief organizations (REST, ERA, and ORS) for funding. But the division of funding labor among different donors generally left the relief wings of the liberation movements with very small amounts of aid. Controlling aid, PVOs, and relations with religious and voluntary organizations (e.g. the regional branches of the ERCS) became the RRC's operational posture. The RRC coordinated foreign aid from nongovernmental organizations from abroad on the basis of their plans of operation, while it deferred to the mechanics of the UN system for aid through FAO and the World Food Programme (WFP) (Novicki 1984:49).

Mobilizing the Donor State

Ethiopian famine in the early 1980s presented special difficulties for the U.S. government. When a former recipient of massive aid has nationalized the private investments of American citizens, expelled U.S. embassy officials, denigrated Western development strategy wholesale, ruthlessly handled its farmers and political opponents, dived deeply into the Soviet orbit, and been unwilling to help its own people to survive a famine largely of its own making, the responsible course of conduct for a donor such as the United States would hardly be clear. Uncertainty surrounding famine conditions would have hampered the response mounted by a commander of foreign policy, but the ambiguity of the Ethiopian situation thoroughly confused the democratic institutions involved in mobilizing U.S. donations. Other preoccupations influenced the initial response, but signals from the U.S. Embassy and PVOs in Ethiopia, as well as congressional missions, triggered a series of aid packages. Only Canada, the European Economic Community (EEC), and Australia responded more quickly to the Ethiopian famine, which is not to say more generously or rationally.

It is apparent that structural characteristics of donor status no less than foreign policy doctrines came into play in the mobilization of U.S. aid. Conflicts involving the Reagan Doctrine in Ethiopia, technical problems in needs assessment, the ambiguity of the situation, humanitarian impulses and capabilities, and assessing the viability of aid to Ethiopia all had a role in mobilizing U.S. aid. Other Western donors faced similar problems in responding to the Ethiopian famine (cf. Gill 1986). Different donors struck different tradeoffs between the need of Ethiopians for aid and the viability of providing aid under the circumstances.

U.S. Preoccupations

The initial mobilization of U.S. aid was defined and delayed by several preoccupations of U.S. foreign policy. These included concerns over the general policy for emergency food aid and U.S. policy with respect to Ethiopia in particular. Domestic politics had a role in providing competing policy interests during the famine period as well as in imposing democratic constraints and concerns for efficiency over the process of policy formation.

Among foreign policy considerations, the greatest issue was the applicability of the Reagan Doctrine to the insurgencies in Ethiopia. Hopes of bringing Ethiopia back to the West were frustrated by the realities of the situation. Legal controls over foreign food aid and development assistance had an independent significance for both foreign policy positions. Even though the Reagan Doctrine for aiding rebellions against Soviet-supported regimes in the third world would have found a nearly perfect ideological fit in the case of Ethiopia, the doctrine had little applicability to U.S. policy in the country, partly because there was no credible noncommunist movement in Ethiopia, and partly because of countervailing policy considerations (including the hope to retrieve the Ethiopian government). The only certain application of the doctrine in Ethiopia was the donation of $500,000 to the Ethiopian People's Democratic Alliance (EPDA) in 1981/82 (although there have been suggestions that the TPLF also received some financial aid from the United States). Of the grants to EPDA, half went to the organization's central committee and the rest to its headquarters in Sudan (*Africa Confidential* 7 May 1986). The support was thus infrastructural in character rather than strictly military. Nevertheless, the EPDA collapsed in late 1983.

Failure to bring the Reagan Doctrine to bear on Ethiopia in a meaningful way did not result from a total lack of effort. (See, e.g., *Wall Street Journal* 4 April 1986.) The White House "carried out several preliminary studies to determine how best to escalate CIA support for Ethiopian rebels," and President Reagan "signed a presidential 'finding' under the National Security Act, authorizing the CIA to contribute to a 'nonlethal' campaign against the Mengistu government" (*Africa Report* July-August 1986:49). Explanations for the failure of these efforts may include the fact that the EPDA had no real domestic support in Ethiopia and that the Iran-Contra deal was casting suspicion on U.S. foreign policy. Preoccupations underlying the Reagan Doctrine had an at least indirect influence on the formation of the humanitarian response. (See *Washington Post* 26 June 1986 et seq.)

There was general reluctance on the part of the U.S. administration to become overly visible in Ethiopia, in either a hostile or a cooperative posture. The State Department's finding of continuing problems with the Mengistu regime, despite some improvements revealed in its Country Report on Human Rights Practices for 1983 (U.S. Department of State 1984), advised against a confrontational strategy. The State Department mistakenly reported that the PMGSE's food system development policies and programs had resulted in "an overall increase in food consumption in rural areas." It also noted the inadequacy of food production and stated that "widespread starvation and food shortages had been prevented by food aid shipments" (U.S. Department of State 1984:128, 130).

Activism in Congress and among a small segment of the administration was characterized by a quite different set of concerns. This activism was also associated with the U.S. Embassy in Addis Ababa, staff in USAID bureaus, and minority elements higher in the State Department who sought to encourage Ethiopia to turn toward the West.

In legal and structural terms, U.S. foreign food aid policy was itself oriented toward diverse policy concerns. On the one hand, PL-480 budgets are routinely approved on an annual basis for each fiscal year, and policy agents are committed to advancing their interests within that time span. On the other hand, longer-term interests in Ethiopian famine relief and food system development, and countering communism and the Soviet influences in the Horn, extended beyond the annual cycle. With the apparent termination of the donor-recipient relationship, and Soviet adoption of the Mengistu government, mobilizing the U.S. food aid program required circumventing an initial obstacle in terms of diplomatic relationships. This foreign policy pivot was sharpened by the famine that surged through much of sub-Saharan Africa and that required decisions to be made about the judicious deployment of

U.S. resources, as U.S. involvement with other African famines also competed with Ethiopia for the resources available for commitment. The entire formation process, from identifying problems for U.S. food aid policy in Ethiopia to fashioning U.S. targets for famine relief, was affected by this dynamic.

Technical concerns over the assessment of actual food needs exacerbated the U.S. government's policy dilemma. The actual situation in Ethiopia was very unclear to outsiders and even to those in Ethiopia, and apprehension over "crying wolf" doubtless arose. In fact, the regularity of proclaimed crisis conditions in East Africa generally, as well as diplomatic chaos with Ethiopia, may have been partly responsible for the circumspection in mounting relief efforts. This knowledge of chronic agricultural problems in Africa was shared by Congress. The House Subcommittee on Africa, for example, had held hearings on Food Needs in East Africa in June 1980, in which there was testimony that "Severe famine exists in parts of [Ethiopia]" (U.S. House 1980:32). While the Catholic Relief Services' (CRS) request to USAID in December 1982 was the first input to the U.S. foreign food aid community about the problem of potential famine in Ethiopia, a CIA report had predicted famine as early as 1983.

International organizations contributed to needs assessment. However, assessments of need resulted in conflict and compromise between USAID, the RRC, and the Food and Agriculture Organization of the United Nations (FAO). RRC assessments were loosely based on its Early Warning System, FAO's were based on a variety of sources culled by FAO and World Food Programme (WFP) field staff (FAO 1983:39), and USAID's were based partly on its own surveys (e.g., in May [U.S. G.A.O. 1985a:4] and September 1984 [Korn 1986a:125]). The Ethiopian office of the UN's Office for Emergency Operations in Africa (UNOEOA/E) issued monthly status reports that were widely relied upon, including by USAID until it established its own system.

To an extent, technical disputes over needs displaced ideological disagreements over the obligation of donors like the United States to provide needed aid. Two levels of dispute were apparent: technical ones over the assessments of the need for food in the countryside, and political ones over the determination of how much of what type of aid was needed and where. These disputes converged in the initial U.S. response. Several policy issues were identified by a General Accounting Office study as having influenced the initial U.S. response. The hesitancy and cautiousness of the U.S. government were attributed to the desire for assurances that an emergency existed, that food would reach the starving instead of being diverted, and that food aid would not support the Ethiopian government.

68 Reluctant Aid or Aiding the Reluctant?

NGOs in the Vanguard?

Despite the revolutionary government's efforts to cleanse Ethiopia of foreign imperialist influences and to promote Ethiopian nationalism, a number of Western private voluntary organizations had continued to operate in the country. Addis Ababa also remained the site of a complex of UN agencies as well as of the Organization for African Unity (OAU). During the famine period, as many as seven international agencies monitored the food situation in Ethiopia (Cuny 1989:278). Their presence was useful to the Ethiopian government even though the agencies and organizations were on the cutting edge of the response to famine. In this sense, the response was in stark contrast to the bungled effort to detect and relieve famine during the 1972-74 crisis (see Shepherd 1975).

Among the vanguard in responding to the famine were two private voluntary organizations (PVOs) based in the United States. The speed of their early response is not surprising in light of the fact that they had been engaged in relief activities in Ethiopia for some time. For the same reason, they evolved into two of the most influential distributors of emergency food aid donated by the United States, even though they had only modest bases of operation in Ethiopia prior to their huge growth during the famine period. Catholic Relief Services (CRS), which made the earliest requests (beginning in December 1982) to the U.S. government for food, had been operating in Ethiopia since 1958. In addition to operating its own assistance program utilizing "the private infrastructure of the local church with the [Ethiopian government's] full cooperation" (CRS 1986:3), it was the only U.S. agency to have operated a U.S. government-sponsored feeding program in Ethiopia since 1975, distributing PL-480 food commodities to children and pregnant and lactating mothers in Addis Ababa and Dire Dawa. Although a relatively small program in comparison with the larger PL-480 program during the 1979-80 period (cf. table 2.5), CRS distributed around 10,000 MT of food in fiscal years 1983 and 1984.

Also having a previous presence in Ethiopia was the World Vision Relief Organization (WVRO), which had been involved "in relief and development activities in Ethiopia since 1971, initially [as] a funding partner in a variety of small projects, then since 1975 as an Ethiopia-based PVO with an all Ethiopia program staff" (WVRO 1985:1). WVRO began its operations in the south in 1971, providing relief to Nuer refugees fleeing the Sudanese civil war, and opened an office in Addis Ababa in 1975 (WVRO nd:14). It operated a $3.6 million relief operation in the south in 1981, expanding to $5.8 million in 1982, and began a $8 million relief operation in Gonder and Wollo regions in 1983.

Among the many missionary operations in Ethiopia, and one to survive the

Working at Cross Purposes 69

revolution, SIM, International (formerly Sudan Interior Mission) had been operating in Ethiopia since 1927, distributing PL-480 food it received from U.S. agencies such as Lutheran World Relief through its 2,700 churches (SIM, International 1986).

The position of these agencies in relatively close proximity to the experience of food shortage and famine doubtless made their prompt response to famine more likely. CRS in particular was quick to request governmental assistance from the United States, beginning with a request for 838 MT of food in December 1982. Subsequently, requests were made by other international agencies and UN organizations. An Ethiopia-based consortium in which several U.S.-based PVOs had membership—the Christian Relief and Development Association (CRDA)—transmitted a telex in September 1984 that was signed by 18 of its member organizations (Gill 1986:89).

In contrast, the UN agencies were generally sluggish in their response. This was true for those housed in the UN complex in Africa Hall as well as those with compounds in the outlying areas of Addis Ababa. The World Food Programme (WFP) was drawn into the relief effort the soonest, partly because of its food distribution infrastructure for food-for-work programs. Similarly, the Food and Agricultural Organization of the UN (FAO) was drawn into the fray, and greatly underestimated the amount of food needed. The UN's Disaster Relief Organization (UNDRO) issued the first UN appeal for famine relief in mid-March 1983, after completing its one-week needs assessment. The UN's International Children's Fund (UNICEF) followed with an appeal in mid-April.

Within the central UN organizations with food aid responsibilities, bureaucratic infighting rather than specialized responses or coordinated action characterized the early response to famine and the initiation of relief actions. Competition between FAO and UNDRO over the leadership role, and delays in coordinating the functions of FAO and WFP, dampened their performances. According to one agency official, the WFP/FAO mission report of March (published in June 1984) was more damaging for the confusion it generated over food needs estimates than for its errors in making estimates (Goyder 1988:91-92). It was not until the UN Office for Emergency Operations in Ethiopia (UNOEOA/E) was established in November 1984 by UN Secretary General de Ceullar that UN operations contributed productively to the relief effort.

Contributions of PVOs and UN agencies to the initial response should not obscure the role of other nongovernmental organizations and Western government embassies in Addis Ababa. Among Non-Governmental Organizations (NGOs), the International Committee of the Red Cross (ICRC) responded in perhaps the most disciplined manner, having extended its mandate from its programs for assisting civilian victims of the Ogaden war to programs for feeding victims of civil war and government policy in association with the Ethiopian Red Cross Society. The U.S. and other embassies in Addis Ababa also had a role in obtaining information and influencing relief policies (Korn 1986a).

As the installation of PVO operations in Ethiopia increased the viability of aid, the factors responsible for the hesitancy of the U.S. response also served to prevent ideological extremes from controlling the dynamics of the policy formation process. Administration authorities were accountable to congressional groups with a broader range of ideological outlooks and political interests. Technological considerations provided a counterbalance to ideological concerns by providing tools for needs assessment and overcoming logistical constraints. Finally, mass influence in terms of private donations, fund-raising efforts, and political pressure took matters out of the exclusive hands of elites to incorporate a wider range of interests and objectives into U.S. policy.

Dynamics of the Initial U.S. Response

By 1983, policy makers in Washington were convinced of the seriousness of the famine in Ethiopia and other African countries, acknowledged the failure of the Ethiopian government to act, and understood what would happen if the United States failed to respond. By the middle of the year, the United States had mobilized its resources to provide relief aid for the Ethiopian famine. However, the speed and depth of the U.S. government's response to changing conditions in Ethiopia as well as in its own country fluctuated greatly. This was due to ideological factors as well as the process of foreign food aid policy making. Ideologically, the administration and Congress were initially polarized but later integrated during the course of policy formation. On one side were those who defined U.S. policy toward Ethiopia exclusively in terms of famine relief; for those on the other side, Ethiopian communism as a cause of famine and future problems loomed equally significant.

Throughout the famine period, problem identification and policy responses of the United States were driven by a dialectic between administration and congressional actions. It is not realistic to attempt to determine whether Congress or the administration took the lead. The dynamics of ideological skirmishing and convergence is an important but incomplete measure of progress in policy formation. But their respective ideological positions and policy decisions provide substantial evidence of the institutional workings of U.S. food aid and the dynamics of the response to the Ethiopian famine.

Sometimes, administration actions set the congressional agenda; sometimes Congress sets the pace. Probably the highest level of administration decision making was vested in the Interagency Group on Ethiopia and Sudan (IGETSU). IGETSU was established in April 1983 by the State Department, USAID, and the National Security Council (NSC) to address problems regarding the rebel-controlled areas and the possible increase in refugee outflows to Sudan (U.S. G.A.O. 1985a:7). An Interagency Task Force on the African Famine, consisting of representatives of the same agencies, was established in late 1985. Reports suggest that the NSC had recommended earlier against providing famine relief to Ethiopia (Clay 1989:233), and had insisted on having veto power in IGETSU. (See, e.g., *Washington Post* 16 January 1985.) Cast in these terms, the problems of Ethiopian famine took on a regional dimension and highlight the political motivations and consequences of U.S. food aid.

The administration's problem assessments were doubtless affected by congressional influence and international pressure.[3] It was on 5 May 1983 that the charge d'affaires of the U.S. Embassy in Addis Ababa declared a state of emergency in Ethiopia (U.S. G.A.O. 1985a:15). By 6 May, the value of U.S. food aid to Ethiopia totalled $602,000, and an additional $1.5 million was provided to an international agency by 17 May (Bread for the World 1983). Congressional influence was perhaps clearest in the decision to reinstate the Title II program in Ethiopia. Prior to proposing legislative solutions to the famine situation in Ethiopia, congressional groupings had engaged in less formal activities to define the nature and scope of the problem and to urge administration action. Congressional activists had accused the administration of shuffling its feet earlier, but had also acknowledged that by May 1983 the United States had begun responding to the crisis in a humanitarian manner (U.S. House 1983a:3). The earlier criticisms were partly in response to USAID's intention to terminate the Title II program in Ethiopia during 1983; the program had already shrunk in FY1983 to a $3.7 million feeding program in Addis Ababa and Dire Dawa administered by Catholic Relief Services (U.S. G.A.O. 1985a:9). On 1 June 1983, a group of 74 members of the House submitted a letter to the administrator of USAID urging that the PL-480 program be continued in Ethiopia. and that it provide aid through UNDRO. In July, substantively similar House and Senate resolutions sent signals to the administration (U.S. G.A.O. 1985a:16, 20) that domestic constituencies perceived a food problem and supported a relief effort in Ethiopia, and that they opposed terminating the U.S. food aid program.

USAID announced in July that the Title II program administered by CRS in Ethiopia would be reinstated. Whether the reinstatement of PL-480 aid was a normative response to food needs in Ethiopia or the result of congressional actions has not been conclusively determined, but a simple congressional pressure model would posit a causal connection between the congressional pressure and the administration's decision. One informed source, however, has concluded that reinstatement was the result of "strong protest" against the proposed cancellation of the Title II program in Ethiopia (*Africa Report* January-February 1985:39).

Regardless of the cause, the reinstatement of the PL-480 aid program triggered an institutional mobilization to rationalize problem assessment and activated a technical process for assessing Ethiopian food needs. Initial investigations of the famine situation were characterized more by an overlap than a division of labor between Congress and the administration. A three-person USAID team arrived in Ethiopia around 1 August 1983 to assess transport and other functions (U.S. House 1983a:159). According to unofficial reports, rain and fighting were the main reasons for transport difficulties, as measured by the fact that the road between Assab (the main port) and Addis was cut. The first of several congressional missions followed shortly thereafter. Seven congressmen visited several African countries, including Ethiopia, during 6-25 August 1983 (U.S. House 1984a). This delegation produced a document that demonstrated congressional fact-finding abilities and expertise, and perhaps constituted a congressional bid for an administrative role in Ethiopian food aid policy.

Agreement rather than difference soon marked the outlook of Congress and the administration on Ethiopian food problems. Both the administration and a major proponent of Ethiopian aid (Congressman Howard Wolpe) agreed in July 1983 that the problem in Ethiopia now was not additional food but rather transporting food already at the ports inland to points of distribution, USAID having made that determination somewhat earlier.

The rate at which Ethiopia's food situation deteriorated and the vacillation of policy makers' assessments thereafter can be marked by evidence of food needs and relief problems submitted during congressional hearings. Some interaction, if not coordination, between the House and Senate was evident even at this early stage. Senator John Danforth's trip to Africa in January 1984 spawned a second set of congressional hearings and, perhaps more importantly, a meeting with President Reagan on African famine. Senate hearings were held on 1 March by the Foreign Relations Committee, Subcommittee on African Affairs (U.S. Senate 1984a). This was the first time that this body had had a hearing on African food problems since August 1982. This March 1984 Senate hearing was largely a response to the House Appropriation Committee's approval just the day before of $150 million for the FY1984 supplemental and $90 million to expand the Commodity Credit Corporation's finance authority. The Senate Subcommittee on African Affairs received testimony of Julia Bloch, USAID's Assistant Administrator for Food for Peace and Voluntary Assistance, to the effect that Ethiopia's December food crop was "excellent" and that the PMGSE might have been profiting from food aid because of low levels of commercial imports during the three

Working at Cross Purposes 73

previous years (U.S. Senate 1984a:52-54). The implication was that the famine was a regime food system problem rather than a nature-based one. During the next few months, action in the House was geared toward assessing high-level problems of the impact of U.S. foreign policy on African countries and the human rights situation in several regions of Africa. At this level of problem assessment, perceptions of Ethiopian conditions were partly colored by ideological outlook. The report of a mid-1983 study mission released in March 1984 (U.S. House 1984a) revealed a rift between left and right wings of the House Committee on Foreign Affairs. The study mission generally neglected Ethiopian regime factors in concluding that an opportunity existed for a diplomatic "dialogue" with the government (U.S. House 1984a:16). Congressman Solomon's dissent stressed human rights violations and Mengistu's tirades against the United States as a bar to improvement in U.S. relations with Ethiopia (U.S. House 1984a:58-59), although Congressman Wolpe's mid-1983 visit to Ethiopia, which sparked Soviet inspired anti-American media campaigns in Ethiopia (Wolde Giorgis 1989:131), received little attention. The human rights situation in Ethiopia was the subject of further debate in joint hearings held by the House Subcommittee on Human Rights and International Organizations with the Subcommittee on African Affairs (U.S. House 1984b).

Throughout this period, mass-based organizations and actions heightened the sense of famine problems in Ethiopia. PVO and direct mass influence on problem assessment was considerable, but whether it was the driving force behind U.S. government donations, as has been frequently asserted, is questionable. Among the most controversial aspects of the U.S. response is the role of the media in mobilizing aid (Kaplan 1988). Much has been made of the role of an October BBC film in arousing the U.S. government (cf. Gill 1986), and media attention on famine problems in Africa have been hailed as the great force behind U.S. aid to Ethiopia. The events behind the decisions of leading U.S. media to spotlight the Ethiopian famine (described by Boyer [1985]) fed into policy makers' actions to require further governmental action rather than ideological debate.

All of this is not to say that normative order had been completely imposed on the relief effort by this time. As food aid began to flow into Ethiopia at the end of 1984, the assessment of problems changed in focus. Rumors of diversions had been reported in Europe, and USAID reports to Congress on problems relating to commodity control had reported sales of donated edible oil delivered to the World Food Programme (U.S. Senate 1984a:65).

Mid-year assessments of need were provided by House Resolution 1096 (HR-1096). House hearings on "World Food and Population Issues— Emergency Assistance to Africa" (U.S. House 1984c) received testimony on assessments of food needs by USDA, USAID, and international organizations (i.e., the UN Food and Agriculture Organization and the World Food Programme), including estimates of Ethiopian food deficits. Ethiopian problems relating to getting food into rebel areas were discussed in closed session (U.S. House 1984c:29,78). Militaristic dimensions of the famine and relief operation remained a problem of administration rather than a question for policy formation. For example, a 4 October 1983 report that the CIA was providing "training, arms and financial assistance" to "friendly" military forces in Ethiopia did not produce a congressional response (*Newsweek* 4 October 1983). But Congress was concerned with curbing the use of food power, both by the administration and by the PMGSE.

Almost in normative fashion, fact-finding led to policy analysis. Holding hearings allowed experts to analyze the problems of Ethiopian food system development and famine (e.g., on the resettlement program) and to examine administration policies. It also supported a rational basis for building constituencies for proposed policy decisions. Normative order of a sorts was reestablished as problems with logistics and with the coordination of food aid returned to the top of the agenda. The secondary harvest in Ethiopia failed in early 1984, and the number of people at risk of starvation was estimated to have increased to 6 million (U.S. House 1984c:56). Accountability for U.S. food aid distribution was described as a taxpayer mandate by the administration, and Congress raised similar concerns in reference to the Ethiopian situation.

This process of incorporating policy objectives and interests of constituencies commenced with congressional hearings on the African and Ethiopian famines held in late July 1983 by the House Committee on Foreign Affairs (U.S. House 1983a). These hearings followed the Ninth World Food Council Ministerial (held 27-30 June in New York). At one level, these hearings revolved around Ethiopian food problems in general and transport specifically, an early indication of the sharp focus of U.S. food aid policy on Ethiopia. Even before this phase got underway with the hearings on African famine, USAID had already committed $4.75 million to Ethiopian famine relief. Articulating Ethiopian famine in terms of U.S. policy problems and assessing the level of need for food aid constituted the initial phase of a prolonged cycle of U.S. policy formation. U.S. policy concerns were altered during the transition from the emergency to the stability phases of the famine relief effort. During the emergency phase, defined as the period of time during which famine deaths could not be prevented even with food supplies donated from abroad, U.S. policy was focused on establishing a presence, urging the Ethiopian government to take action, and then opposing the resettlement program. During the stability phase, marked by the reduction of famine deaths due to the flow of foreign food aid, the U.S. posture changed to one of maintaining a position in Ethiopia for continuing to provide aid.

Notes

1. One measure of how far the revolutionary sentiments and the military regime have parted is that Mesfin Wolde Mariam's (1984) historical study of Ethiopian famine was removed from bookshelves in Addis because it drew parallels with the 1983 - 86 famine (See Korn 1986a). The motivation for such a move could have been nothing other than to prevent the formation of civilian opposition and relief groups, a real possibility since Mesfin Wolde Mariam was the head of the famine investigating committee after Selassie.
2. See, Order No. 93 of 1974.
3. The UN Disaster Relief Organization (UNDRO) appeal and its request for food aid in April 1983 was one pressure outside the administration-congressional setting which had a substantial impact on U.S. policy for problem identification in Ethiopia.

III

Famine Relief Operations

4

Moderating Extreme Strategies During the Emergency Phase: Radicalism, Humanitarianism, and U.S. Prohibition of Aid for Resettlement and Development (1984-85)

By mid-1984, famine in Ethiopia had reached the emergency phase, which prevailed until the last quarter of 1985.[1] Mortality during the period attributable to famine—when mortality attributable to the Ethiopian government's resettlement program is included—is now estimated at 1 million or more. Military activities and stagnating agricultural production resulting from political and economic interference pushed more and more peasants into famine. During this period, over a quarter of a million MT of food, over one-half of which was donated by the U.S. government, was distributed for famine relief purposes by humanitarian agencies. Relief operations mounted by the RRC were constrained by military actions and by the political programs of the Ethiopian government and Workers' Party of Ethiopia, which launched a massive population resettlement program that was not in actuality a policy for famine relief.

Formation of U.S. policy during the emergency phase focused largely on the logistical arrangements for delivering food to people in need in the northern regions, while prohibitions on developmental assistance advanced efforts to consolidate opposition to the resettlement program. The food distribution system established by donor governments, UN agencies, and PVOs to counterbalance the RRC's system served to implement norms of

80 Reluctant Aid or Aiding the Reluctant?

conflict and cooperation to replace the dual distribution system. U.S. objectives, in particular, strengthened the mandate for relief while weakening the resettlement and political programs of the Ethiopian government.

Famine and Relief During the Emergency Phase

Mortality rates are the defining characteristic of the famine, although data limitations require the use of secondary criteria for measuring the emergency phase. The weakest died in their villages and on the way to distribution centers where no one was counting. But a relatively coherent sense of the pattern of the famine may be formed. Estimates of the mortality curve during the emergency phase are represented in Figure 4.1. The estimated mortality curve is based on several sources of death rates and on estimates derived from other measures of food system collapse. A U.S. House Select Committee on Hunger estimate of the death toll between March and November 1984 alone was 300,000 (see Shepherd 1985a:5); 200 or more died each day at the relief camps,[2] escalating to a high of 16,000-17,000 per week around December 1984, according to the former commissioner of the Ethiopian RRC (Wolde Giorgis 1987:18). Over 1 million people are estimated to have died between October 1983 and October 1985 (Wolde Giorgis 1987:16). It is reasonable to expect that the mortality curve would be bell-shaped, with the declining slope fitted to the shape of the downward curve of people registered in shelters (see table 6.7), a sensible interpretation in light of the fact that abandoning farms and migrating to shelters is one of the final responses to the onset of famine (cf. Wood 1976). Deaths through the end of 1985 due to resettlement raised the level of mortality toward the end of the famine, on the basis of mortality attributable to the program estimated to range from 50,000 to 100,000.

It is far more difficult to estimate the regional distribution and structural contours of famine deaths. Although the regional movement of famine from northwest to southeast may well be part of a long historical pattern, explanations for the regional distribution of famine during the emergency phase have policy origins: further deterioration of food production due to military, political, and economic policies. Regional estimates of famine conditions during 1984-86 may be derived from the number of persons determined to be at risk of famine and the registered shelter populations at camps and food distribution centers. RRC estimates of the number of people affected are presented in table 4.1, which also sets forth estimates of the number and percentage of persons at risk by administrative region and per capita procurement, showing the relationships between people at risk and other measures of food system collapse.

Food shortages in these regions increased for the most part because of two policy factors. In the rebel regions and war zones, the relationship between

Moderating Extreme Strategies 81

military action and the inducement of famine was particularly close. Throughout the emergency phase, famine was concentrated in the northern highland areas, near the battles between the troops of the Ethiopian government, the Eritrean secessionists, and the Tigrayan autonomists. Other causal factors relating to political and economic conditions were also pronounced in adjacent areas. In other regions, Ethiopian food system collapse was more directly responsible for the malnutrition that escalated into famine-based mortality. This is apparent in the peripheral famine areas in the south (cf. Turton 1985) and the west that were not part of any war zone but in which famine conditions later intensified. Famine later moved into the east and southwest, partly through the disruption of and interference with food production through the implementation of Ethiopian agricultural policy, and partly through the villagization program.

Relief strategies adopted by the Ethiopian government and relief agencies under the supervision of donor governments were also regionally-targeted.

TABLE 4.1
Persons Affected by Serious Food Shortages and Changes from Previous Years
1984-86

	1984	1985	1986	1985 Percent of Total Affected	1985 Percent of Pop. (Region)	1985 Percent of Pop. (Total)	1981/82 Per Capita Procurement (kg)
	(in '000)						
Arsi	21	82	20	1.0	4.9	.19	39
Bale	53	193	99	2.4	19.2	.46	9
Eritrea	877	827	650	10.3	30.6	1.97	-
Gamo Gofa	80	106	152	1.3	8.5	.25	-
Gojam	35	76	0	1.0	2.3	.18	31
Gonder	325	363	341	4.5	12.5	.86	11
Hararghe	279	875	1520	11.0	21.1	2.08	-
Ilubabor	-	20	102	.3	2.1	.05	.03
Kaffa	-	58	90	.7	2.4	.14	1.5
Shoa	204	852	709	11.0	8.9	2.03	6
Sidamo	355	533	442	6.7	14.1	1.27	.2
Tigray	1300	1400	1000	17.5	58.1	3.33	-
Welega	-	23	116	.3	1.0	.05	5
Wollo	1821	2587	1547	32.4	71.7	6.16	5
Total	5350	7995	6788	-	-	19.03	7.3

Sources: RRC (1985d); USAID/E (1987:1) for 1986 and Eritrea, 1984 and 1985. Percent of population calculations based on 1984 estimates (see table 3.2).

The relationship between the infusion of food aid and the tapering off of the mortality curve is not entirely clear. One credible analyst has suggested a minimalist relationship between the two, arguing that death rates began to decrease in late 1984 before massive food aid distributions began (Cuny 1989). Even if this is true in terms of timing, it may well be that the tapering off of mortality rates was partly due to systematic internal responses to foreign aid commitments as much as actual distribution of food commodities. For example, moderation of Ethiopian government policies may well have been in response to foreign donations. Moreover, without the aid commodities from foreign donors, stability in relief operations would not have been achieved by the end of 1985, and it is likely that another emergency period would have been precipitated.

Relief operations were responsible for the distribution of over 800,000 MT of food throughout Ethiopia through the end of 1985 (USAID/E 1986). While reliable data on the disposition of donated food are not available—at either the regional, subregional or any lower administrative level—estimates of U.S.-donated commodities may be made. However, estimates of the amounts

TABLE 4.2
Monthly Food Distributions During the Emergency Phase

	Food Distributed (MT)	Beneficiaries Reached
1984	44,500	2,970,000
1985		
January	46,500	3,100,000
February	49,000	3,250,000
March	51,000	3,400,000
April	52,000	3,470,000
May	70,000	4,491,000
June	66,700	5,211,000
July	68,400	5,802,000
August	77,400	6,488,000
September	80,100	7,120,000
October	65,700	6,012,000
November	69,200	6,007,000
December	68,700	6,203,000
Total	809,200	63,524,000
1985 Monthly Average	63,725	5,046,167

Source: USAID/E (1986).

Moderating Extreme Strategies 83

of U.S. food distributed in northern (Eritrea and Tigray) and non-northern regions during FY1985 are difficult to make. During the emergency phase, approximately one-third of U.S. food was distributed in the regions of Eritrea and Tigray, while the remaining two-thirds were distributed in other regions. The basis for these estimates is discussed in chapter five.

During the emergency phase of the famine, Ethiopian famine policy was radicalized under the WPE's control. Ethiopian government operations were directed toward other concerns, reflected by the decision to redistribute massive populations through the resettlement program. Western aid for famine relief was provided in the conventional manner, although donors, especially the United States, placed significant restrictions on aid donated to Ethiopia. Conflicts between donor governments and the government of Ethiopia over food distribution associated with the resettlement program and relieving famine in the war torn regions of the north were initially non-negotiable. Eventually, compromises were worked out, although conflicts continued to shape the execution of the relief operation, including the regional targeting of food aid and the monthly levels of food distributed. Monthly food distribution totals are provided in table 4.2, indicating the increasingly steady rates of distribution during the emergency phase. By September 1985, over 80,000 MT of food were being distributed to reach over 7 million beneficiaries, the highest level during the emergency phase. Up to that month steady increases in the amount of food distributed and beneficiaries reached were evident as relief operations were being firmly put into place.

Ethiopian Government Operations in Controlled and Rebel Regions

Prior to the mobilization of the Workers' Party of Ethiopia in October 1984, the activities of Ethiopian authorities contributed to the further collapse of regional food systems and stifled the development of emergency distribution systems as famine conditions developed all over the country. Because of the regional variations in Ethiopian policies, reasons for the deterioration in the food situation in other regions between 1984 and 1985 are diverse. Military and political operations conflicted with the relief operations of the RRC as well as foreign agencies. There is no conclusive evidence that economically-driven procurement and tax programs were moderated during the emergency phase. In the rebel regions, military actions were doubtless the primary reason for the deepening food shortages.

Military offensives and recruitment into the armed forces continued through the emergency phase, exacerbating food needs and interfering with relief operations. Between May 1984 and December 1984—i.e., during the middle of the emergency phase of the famine—the Ethiopian government recruited 240,000 new "fledgling soldiers" into its military forces, in three separate batches. Recruitment was pursuant to the National Military Service Proclamation and was partly inspired by the EPLF's capture of Barentu (Clapham 1988:110). The largest Ethiopian government offensive against the EPLF in a decade was launched in June 1985 in an effort to recapture Nakfa. The heavy fighting lasted for five months, involved 200,000 troops and an estimated $1 billion in weapons, and resulted in an estimated 14,000 dead and wounded (Kaplan 1988:52, 68). There was also heavy fighting in Tigray during the spring of 1985 (Kaplan 1988:41). Disruption of civilian activity also escalated, particularly in Tigray, where the Ethiopian government had less extensive control, and in the war zones of Eritrea. Military and relief operations of rebel groupings—including the EPLF, TPLF, and OLF—also intensified during the period.

Outside of the war regions, political and ideological operations continued to pre-empt food security and famine relief measures. The second COPWE congress had proclaimed the "maturity in social and ideological matters" achieved by social and political organizations, and announced the inauguration date of the WPE as September 1984 (Clapham 1988:235). Central economic planning continued to reflect the kind of policy making from the top down that is characteristic of the "mature" society of socialist orientation, which is implemented regardless of the needs down below. The deficiencies of central planning in terms of distribution are clear from the fact that even though the party had penetrated nearly all of the countryside under government control, the Ethiopian Domestic Distribution Corporation (EDDC) had distribution centers in only 46 of 577 districts by 1985 (Clapham 1988:160). In contrast, there was no shortage of procurement agents and centers. Whether procurement and other economic policies and programs were moderated during the famine is not clear. Procurements certainly did not cease in response to famine conditions. Increased government spending for military activities created the need for increased revenues and food to service the swelling military ranks as well as to subsidize the urban populations who surrendered their currency to finance the war efforts. In food surplus-producing regions, there is evidence that procurements continued (Goyder 1988). In food deficit regions, the evidence is less clear. It has been asserted that in 1983/84 only 62.7 percent of the AMC quota was achieved, with "total purchases falling to 70 percent of the preceding year. In the famine year of 1984-85, purchases at 1,148,000 quintals were no more than 30 percent of the 1982-83 figure, and quotas ceased to have any meaning" (Clapham 1988: 169). These figures may be assessed by comparing the targets for AMC procurements given in table 3.3 with actual procurements, indicating only a small relationship between the two. Moreover, AMC raids on private markets and

Moderating Extreme Strategies 85

their exceeding quotas in favor of what agents are actually able to procure (Clapham 1988:169) cast doubt on the accuracy of official procurement figures.

Even if procurements had not further squeezed peasant producers, smallholders were not freed from the other economic and political constraints that would have been required in order for them to increase their production. This political-economic capturing was reflected in the new Ten Year Plan's commitment to increasing the number of households in producer cooperatives. The goal was to increase membership from 83,150 households (1.2 percent of the total) in 1983/84 to 4,100,000 (52.7 percent of the total) in 1993/94 (Clapham 1988:118). The villagization program was to provide the foundation for these increases. In the controlled region of Hararghe, where the program was first implemented during 1985, villagization dealt a severe blow to agricultural production.

Before the arrival of foreign food aid donations near the end of 1984, RRC distributions were clearly insufficient for the purpose of relieving the famine. By October 1983, over 143,000 MT of food had been donated, including 7,500 by the Soviet Union (ADAB 1984:55). RRC operations and performance during the early part of the emergency phase were also characterized by a lack of PMGSE support. Worse than the indifference the Ethiopian government displayed was the interference of the PMGSE with relief operations in order to advance military and political objectives. Not only did the government fail to increase RRC funding for relief operations after requests in July 1983 and March 1984 (Wolde Giorgis 1989:127, 134), but Assab port was closed to incoming food supplies from November 1983 to April 1984 to allow military equipment to enter (Pateman 1988:171). RRC estimates of assistance requirements were announced in conjunction with appeals for external aid in March, September, and November of 1984; the RRC commissioner also made trips to Europe and the United States to solicit aid (Wolde Giorgis 1989). Among the most controversial of the RRC appeals were those associated with the March 1984 Assistance Requirements, which were broadly disputed within and without the government and were eventually reduced by 50 percent. The October 1984 donors conference produced a major conflict between the RRC commissioner and the charge d'affaires of the U.S. government, largely over the U.S. response.

Operations of Ethiopian authorities in the countryside were largely limited to political consolidation, coercive agricultural procurement policies, and institution-building efforts implemented through the politicization of PAs' functions. The WPE-inspired resettlement program was also a device for achieving political consolidation and an ill-conceived investment program for future economic development. It was also one of the major factors affecting the responses of donors and the externally-supported distribution system rivalling the RRC's.

The Workers' Party of Ethiopia and Resettlement

Drawing upon the radical strategies for problem solving typical of professed socialist regimes during a raging famine and widespread scarcity of relief items, the WPE decided upon a massive resettlement program shortly after its formation and recognition of the famine in October 1984. Party control of decision making under Mengistu extended to state agencies and eventually down to PA levels. Rather than devote its energies and resources to providing relief and rehabilitation assistance to potential victims, following Party commands the Ethiopian government seized the opportunity to radically transform the population distribution in the northern and southern regions of the country. The ideological inspiration for resettlement was reinforced by Eastern bloc aid and advisors. Mengistu himself met with ambassadors from the Warsaw Pact countries in October to solicit aid for the program (Korn 1986a:127). Resettlement was arguably a famine relief policy, in that it was directed toward regions among the most ravaged by famine (RRC 1985c). Overpopulation and deforestation were claimed by the government to be responsible for the famine in the northern regions, and were viewed as problems that could be resolved by forced removal of inhabitants. The program formulated in the fall of 1984 during the severest period of the famine called for the induction and relocation of a total of 50,000 households from the Tigray and Wollo regions by the end of the year. The second phase was to expand the program to relocate another 320,000 households during 1985-86, this time including residents of Shoa and Gonder (Sivini 1986:224).

Resettlement played an ambiguous role in altering death rates during the emergency period of the famine. Viewed in the most positive light as a famine relief policy (as imputed to it by, e.g., Clarke 1987), resettlement certainly prevented those evacuated from the north from registering increases in the mortality rates in their native areas. While resettlement did not directly cause famine deaths in the regions of origin, fear of being selected for participation diminished opportunities and incentives for food production. Population resettlement also decreased the cultivated areas in the north, thereby heightening the portions of the deficit attributable to production declines (cf. USAID/E 1987b:4). Unsuccessful producers were also discouraged from seeking timely aid because of fear of being inducted into the program. Indirectly, therefore, resettlement may have increased the risk and experience of famine in the north. Deaths did occur, however, in the course of conscripting and transporting resettlers.

Moderating Extreme Strategies 87

To the extent that forced removal reduced mortality rates in the northern regions of origin, the effect of resettlement may be more accurately conceptualized as allocating death rates to different regions in the south. As will be seen below, the massive death rates during the transit process and in the regions of resettlement more than offset the deaths reduced by evacuation of the north.

Viewed in the less favorable light of a political program, resettlement deaths were caused directly and indirectly by state sponsorship of the long-range migration of conscripts to the south. Directly, the program caused widespread deaths during the resettlement process and in the regions of settlement. The selection, transport, and settlement of resettlers has been described by Peter Niggli (1986) in his study on behalf of Berliner Missionswerk and others (e.g., Survival International 1986), clearly documenting the brutality involved. Some evidence has been provided that resettlement caused famine in the resettlement regions of the southwest (U.S. Senate 1986b:52). Clay and Holcomb (1985:99) concluded that 50,000 to 100,000 people may have died through July 1985 as a result of the resettlement program. Other reports (e.g., Magistad 1987) have regarded this as an exaggeration, but estimates of mortality that are based on official resettlement figures support the larger numbers (see Sivini 1986).

Wollo was the region of origin of most resettlers, while Welega was the region of resettlement for nearly one-half of the persons resettled. Table 4.3 provides data on the number of individuals resettled by region of origin and region of resettlement throughout the 1984-85 period prior to the moratorium, or at least the winding down of resettlement during early 1986. Two apparently contradictory hypotheses have been advanced to explain the dynamics of the program and resettler selection in particular. First, removal of oppositionist elements who might sympathize with the Tigrayan People's Liberation Front (TPLF) has been asserted to be the PMGSE's primary objective for resettlement. Testimony collected by Clay and Holcomb (1985) included reports of respondents who fled to Sudan from western Tigray for fear of capture, as well as respondents who escaped from resettlement areas in the south.

A second hypothesis is that the goal of Ethiopian policy was to resettle loyalists from the north in order to further colonize the south and dilute the effectiveness of the Oromo Liberation Front (OLF). In this sense, resettlement might be associated with traditions for consolidating central authority while controlling linkages between ethnicities and other groupings. The program has been described as a neocolonial venture for putting Amhara people from Tigray or Oromo from Wollo into territories occupied by the Sidama and Oromo in Welega regions (cf. Clay and Holcomb 1985). Expansion of the Ethiopian empire from its origins on the northern plateau had demographic no less than policy determinants, which makes efforts to describe

88   Reluctant Aid or Aiding the Reluctant?

Mengistu's policies for resettlement as within the tradition of classical Ethiopian colonization of the south difficult to support. In contrast to the military entrepreneurial penetration encouraged by the voluntary assumption of risks under the Imperial governments' programs (cf. McClellan 1984:666-671), the Mengistu regime implemented a policy of coerced movement partly as a form of punishment. Push factors must be particularly strong to overcome the strong attachment of Ethiopian peasants to their land before migration results.

It is unlikely that the resettlement program rescued very many Ethiopians from famine conditions. Individuals on the brink of famine death would be unlikely to have survived the crude transportation arrangements made for resettlement, much less the regime of the work brigades formed to clear land or to labor on the state farms envisaged for the resettlement sites.

Whatever the objectives, higher death rates resulted from the transport of resettlers and the conditions they found in the resettlement areas. Even in the major resettlement areas, inadequate food supplies, water, medicine, shelter, and other necessities were provided (see Niggli 1986; Survival International 1986). Even though many of the resettlers were transported through Addis, the administration apparently had a blind eye to actual needs. The program was administered as a body-moving operation, without attention to the physiological needs of those transported, much less to the human basics essential to survival.

In practice, the resettlement program during the famine was indicative of

TABLE 4.3
Resettled Populations by Regions of Origin and Resettlement as of January 1986
(Percent of target in [ ])

	Region of Resettlement				
	Welega	Ilubabor	Kaffa	Gojam	Total
Region of Origin					
Tigray	21,367	45,715	22,634	---	89,716
	[14.24]	[10.16]	[90.54]	---	
Wollo	220,636	72,226	48,768	29,839	371,469
	[63.04]	[72.23]	[65.02]	[11.93]	
Shoa	11,279	28,275	6,669	54,858	101,081
	---	---	[13.34]	[21.95]	
Total	253,282	146,216	78,071	84,697	562,266

Source: Sivini (1968:230).

Moderating Extreme Strategies 89

the PMGSE's willingness to exercise total power over the peasantry. The fact that the policy origins of the resettlement program had to do with population control and nothing to do with famine relief (Wolde Giorgis 1989:290), suggests the ideological basis for the asserted relief purposes of the program. In rhetoric, the WPE's resettlement program was a continuation of policies initially formulated in the early 1970s and which had been recommended by USAID and other donors but which had never encouraged coercive recruitment. By the end of 1980, the RRC already managed 40,000 resettled households (Sivini 1986:216). Prior to losing control of the program to WPE officials, it designed four resettlement strategies reflecting cost calculations: conventional settlement, catchment rehabilitation, spontaneous (low-cost) settlement, and integration settlement (RRC 1985b:165-166). Each strategy varied in terms of the amount of resources invested (Malhuret 1985:29).

Even though the WPE's resettlement program seems to have been motivated by a desire to undermine rebel forces and to relocate loyalists, actual operation of the program might well have led to the failure of both objectives had there not been an exceptionally shrewd assessment of the balance of forces in the regions of origin, of the loyalty of resettlers, and of the farming skills of those selected. While such criteria were included in selection instructions (Jansson 1987:65), the better explanation of the program's operation distinguishes the respective roles of implementation and command in Ethiopian food policy. There are other reasons to believe that selection of resettlers to fill quotas set from above was almost random. Given the military administration of the countryside, it is reasonable to expect orders from above to be followed by those in administrative positions below. On the other hand, gaps in command are almost universal in the underdeveloped world. While policy commands devolved almost exclusively through Party and military hierarchies, they were not uniformly obeyed and there was some policy initiative at the regional level. Further evidence regarding the level of decision making involved in implementing peasant policies during the famine is provided by action at the refugee camps and food distribution centers (e.g., the regional handling of the cholera epidemic at Ibnet [cf.Korn 1986a]) and the villagization program, which will be discussed below). Even if unsuccessful, the authorities' desires to break up support for insurgents and to prevent the formation of alliances between the TPLF and the OLF in the northwest, especially in Wollo, was made clear in its military strategy and aid distribution patterns. Likewise, the Ethiopian authorities had a strong desire to exploit the resources of the southeast regions of resettlement through controlled work units. But quotas set from above appear to have led to coerced selection below (Sivini 1986:225-226), regardless of the personality characteristics of those selected. The wide variety of tactics used to lure persons suggests that bodies alone were required. The fact that there was no resettlement of Eritre-

90 Reluctant Aid or Aiding the Reluctant?

ans also cuts seriously against the hypothesis that the sole rationale was to undermine insurgency in the regions of origin. Interviews in Sudan with refugees from Tigray who managed to escape from resettlement camps support this view, indicating that less than half of the resettlers were from TPLF-held areas. Similarly, the fact that the TPLF organized emigration movements pre-empted implementation of this policy by the Ethiopian authorities (Clay and Holcomb 1985:79, 42). Poorly drafted orders from above seem to have been implemented by cadres below, with numbers rather than personalities being the key target.

Whether government and Party authorities intended deaths to result from the resettlement program raises important questions about the general character of Ethiopian policies during the famine. Allegations of genocide have been broadly made, and if supportable, have major implications for conceptualizing Ethiopian policy and the U.S. response. Famine relief as an excuse for relocation is a relatively recent ploy, although a common tool for achieving genocidal ends has been the deportation of unwanted populations for resettlement or extermination. The Turks in Armenia, the Soviets, Nazi Germany, and Kampuchea under Pol Pot, all used programs for involuntary migration to achieve their purposes. Mortality resulting from implementing the Ethiopian program has been estimated to have ranged from less than one percent to 10 percent of the people involved per day, amounting to 50,000 to 100,000 deaths by mid-1985 (Clay and Holcomb 1985:99) and from three to 11 times the normal Ethiopian mortality rate of 2.2 percent (Sivini 1986:233).

The failure of central institutions to control regional administrators and to prevent massive deaths raises presumptions of recklessness if not deliberation in causing deaths. In recruiting resettlers, the use of force and the threat of death for resistance has been documented (e.g., Niggli 1986). The captive, prison-like settings of many holding areas was consistent with malevolent ends, as were the inhuman conditions and general disregard of human needs in the transport phase. "Upon arrival, the dead were removed on stretchers while the others were marched out between rows of soldiers and loaded onto buses" (Survival International 1986:22).

Absence of conditions for sustaining life at the sites of resettlement suggests that the government did not intend, or at any rate had no reasonable basis to believe, that the participants would survive. Appropriations for preparation of resettlement sites were grossly inadequate, so that maladjustment to the sites was predictable. Given that cost estimates for the program greatly exceeded actual expenditures, it could be inferred that authorities were not greatly concerned about measures of success relating to the survival of resettlers. Indirectly as well, the diversion of Ethiopian resources away from the famine during its peak, and the disturbance in northern economies caused by fear of recruitment, increased the death rates attributable to affirmative

Ethiopian government policy. In addition, the program contributed directly to the creation of refugee populations in Sudan, resulting in the destruction of group identities.

Acquiring personnel to form state or collective farms in the south was likewise an explicit goal of the program. With the resource shortfalls, the Ethiopian government's apparent expectation was that foreign donors could be relied upon to provide funding. As will be shown below, Eastern bloc countries donated substantial aid to the resettlement program while Western donors (except Canada and the EEC) perceived the resettlement program as a misguided policy under the circumstances.

It may be that political control was the prerequisite for implementing these population redistribution policies. The more radical resettlement program in Tigray may have obviated the need for villagization, which began elsewhere early in 1985. But like Tigray, there was no villagization program implemented in Eritrea, even though there was no resettlement program implemented in that region either. Socialist institutions for population control generally, but especially the resettlement and villagization programs, were also to have production functions. The potential developmental impact of the resettlement program elicited a broad spectrum of international viewpoints on development policy. The resettlement program has not been cost effective, and no camps have yet become self-sufficient. Villagization was also generally believed to lead to decreased agricultural production in the short term (Survival International 1988:3).

While the future productivity of the programs might have been in dispute, the poor manner in which they were designed and implemented diminished the credibility of the Ethiopian government. It also revealed its limited commitment to relief operations during the emergency phase of the famine. Policy makers in the United States were relatively quick to perceive the abuses involved in resettlement, evident in the congressional request for a presidential determination that Ethiopia was engaged in a deliberate policy of starvation. Even though the determination was negative, the strong message for moderation it delivered may have had some effect on the relief effort and the eventual moratorium placed on the resettlement program.

Funding Decisions and Formulating U.S. Objectives

While mobilization of an initial response to the Ethiopian famine was hampered by information shortfalls and lack of consensus, formulating a program for famine relief was even more constrained. The primary pivot of U.S. policy was divided between attempting to advance its objectives—largely by countering Ethiopian military, resettlement, and collectivization policies—and simply keeping programs operational in the field. Coordinating

92 Reluctant Aid or Aiding the Reluctant?

the diverse interests represented in the macropolitics for U.S. food aid policy in Washington with the expansion of relief operations in Ethiopia during the emergency phase presented further policy challenges.

Three structural characteristics of donor status defined the formulation of U.S. objectives for the famine relief effort. First, macropolitical controls over the disposal of food aid commodities were more important than the surplus status of commodities for emergency purposes,[3] although the domestic politics of efficiency imposed economic constraints on foreign donations. Second, the influence of the foreign policy establishment and the allure of identifying political openings in food-scarce nations continued to provide motivation for famine relief. Finally, humanitarian agencies and the PVO lobby were a third source of macropolitical influence, by which the politics of need was urged to take precedence over the domestic politics of efficiency and foreign policy objectives.

In Washington, U.S. objectives for Ethiopian famine relief were articulated in terms of policy options, but were defined by the competing prescriptions of macropolitical interests. The foreign policy establishment was divided between Reagan Doctrine enthusiasts and those opposed to involvement with Ethiopian development efforts but who hoped that U.S. food aid would attract moderate elements in the PMGSE to the West. Humanitarian interests largely won out, thanks to the assistance of media coverage and allied constituencies. Economic cost considerations were thrown into the balance between these foreign policy and humanitarian forces.

The "natural history" of the formation of U.S. policy provides some evidence of the influence of macropolitical interests and the roles of their constituencies. Policy decisions were made in the process of accessing congressional funding vehicles, subject to foreign assistance guidelines and the range of choices available for programs. U.S. objectives in Ethiopia evolved from:

1. a deep political opposition of the U.S. government to the PMGSE prior to the mobilization phase, a position fostered by the foreign policy establishment; to
2. support of famine relief activity on humanitarian grounds during the emergency phase, largely due to the lobbying efforts of relief agencies; to then
3. conceding to some U.S. role in the rehabilitation of agriculture and Ethiopian food system development during the stability phase, a concession to relief agencies and political moderates; and finally to
4. further movements for sanctions against Ethiopia in response to the government's policies during the famine, with a return to diplomatic stalemate, buttressed again by the foreign policy establishment.

Funding Decisions and Vehicles

Legal vehicles for PL-480 appropriations resulting in donations to Ethiopia were produced during the process of passing through annual cycles of legislation. In addition to regular PL-480 appropriation bills, two other public laws were approved during FY1984 (both emergency supplemental appropriations) and two during FY1985 (one the African Famine Relief and Recovery Act of 1985 [AFRRA] and the other an emergency supplemental).

Approximately $3.106 billion was appropriated for African famine relief between FYs1984 and 1986. Of these funds, the Ethiopian share was large.[4] A total of $487.8 million was allocated to famine relief in Ethiopia, including $428.7 million in food aid and $59.1 million in nonfood aid. The food aid represents 13.8 percent of total U.S. PL-480 Title II appropriations during the period. For FY1984, $23.1 million was allocated to Ethiopian famine relief, an amount which rose to $293 million during FY1985. For FY1986, $172 million was allocated to Ethiopia (USAID/E 1987).

Three kinds of funding vehicles were used in the formation of U.S. policy for African and Ethiopian food aid. First, regular PL-480 appropriations covered programs such as the regular Title II program that had long been in operation in Ethiopia and was reinstated in 1983. Second, emergency supplementals were approved: two for FY1984 to build upon the reinstated Title II program, and another for FY1985. The FY1984 supplementals led to a third kind of vehicle: a substantive piece of legislation culminating in the African Famine Relief and Recovery Act of 1985 (AFRRA).

Emergency supplementals and the African Famine Relief and Recovery Act. Initially, additional funds for PL-480 commodities to be donated to African famine relief were appropriated through emergency supplementals. For FY1984, in addition to the original $650 million appropriated for PL-480 Title II, $150 million was appropriated for supplemental emergency Title II assistance to Africa (U.S. House 1984c:32). The emergency amount was appropriated through two separate supplemental appropriations. The first made $90 million available as approved on 30 March; the second made an additional $60 million available as approved on 2 July. The first FY1984 supplemental to be approved, PL 98-248, was introduced as House Joint Resolution (HJR) 493 on 9 February for $150 million, passed the House on 6 March, and was approved by President Reagan on 30 March for $90 million. The second FY1984 supplemental followed on the footsteps of the first: PL 98-332 was approved by President Reagan on 2 July 1984, appropriating an additional $60 million. The shortfalls in the earlier supplemental were therefore delivered by the second.

94 Reluctant Aid or Aiding the Reluctant?

It was only at the end of 1984, when emergency food for Ethiopia began to flow heavily, that a substantive vehicle for assistance was created. At the apex of U.S. food aid policy was the African Famine Relief and Recovery Act of 1985 (AFRRA), which authorized the appropriation of up to $175 million for assistance to Africa. Later, the FY1985 emergency supplemental appropriated over $795 million to run through FY1986. As a result, in FY1985 a total of $1.447 billion was appropriated for African famine assistance. Regular FY1985 Title II appropriations were $650 million. The 1985 supplemental approved on 4 April appropriated an additional $795 million for emergency relief, including the $175 million authorized by AFRRA and approved on 2 April 1985. During FY1985, Ethiopia received $293 million, or almost one-quarter of the total funds appropriated for African famine relief during the period. After the AFRRA, there was some uncertainty about the future involvement of U.S. food aid in Ethiopia. Title II appropriations for FY1986 totalled $785.7 million. During this period, Ethiopia received approximately $172 million in assistance, bringing the total of U.S. donations to Africa for 1984-86 to $3.106 billion and donations to Ethiopia to $488 million.

During this time, changes in the appropriations process had substantive policy impact. Supplementals get hearings only in appropriations committees, not in substantive committees. This is part of the reason that HJRs 492 and 493 were almost stranded during FY1984 by concerns extraneous to African and Ethiopian famine relief—i.e., domestic policy concerns (low-income energy assistance) and extraneous foreign policy issues (aid to the Nicaraguan contras). During FY1985, the appropriations process broke free of the constraints of the regular appropriations process, and substantive policy lines were crossed to produce a large constituency for relief. Congressional constituencies in the Senate Committee on Foreign Relations and the House Committee on Foreign Affairs were able to give fuller hearing to the substantive foreign policy and humanitarian questions involved.

Supplementals and substantive legislation displayed differences in institutional settings and the structure of the decision making involved. Creating the special funding authority of AFRRA during FY1985 allowed Congress to increase the level of appropriations and to assert a stronger substantive mandate over foreign aid. This vehicle largely defined the foreign orientation of the U.S. famine relief effort in Ethiopia. Domestic policy constituencies thereafter exerted their influence primarily through the politics of efficiency and during the controversies arising from the monetization of PL-480 aid as Section 416 commodities.[5] Finally, after the summer of 1985, with appropriations complete for FY1986, concerns turned toward clarifying the objectives of U.S. aid with respect to problems with the Ethiopian authorities. A reversal in policy direction forestalled hopes for subsequent appropriations and included proposals for a trade embargo and other sanctions.

Moderating Extreme Strategies 95

Institutional setting of decision making. Funding decisions for Ethiopian famine relief were made in the context of ideological conflict between the Left and the Right, which collapsed into compromises between the administration and Congress. USAID Administrator M. Peter McPherson was the principal administration spokesperson in most of the congressional hearings held precedent to funding decisions. Within USAID, the most important bureaus in the Ethiopian famine relief operation were: the Office of Foreign Disaster Assistance (OFDA), which handled the nonfood aid; the Bureau of Food for Peace (FFP), responsible for Title II donations; the Office of Private and Voluntary Cooperation (OPVC), which liaisoned with PVOs; the Africa Bureau; and, the Bureau for Refugee Programs, which had been the bureau of origin of IGETSU.

In Congress, the House clearly had the broader, numerically larger constituency even though it was less powerful in making foreign policy. The House Select Committee on Hunger, authorized in February 1984, was able to consolidate the hunger lobby and organize its forces in Congress. It was able to control many hearings (see U.S. House 1983a:144), and held joint hearings with the Foreign Relations Committee (U.S. House 1984c). The breadth of House constituencies meant that support extended further outside the halls of Congress proper, including many PVOs involved in the relief effort.

The Senate had a more powerful, yet sometimes narrower, base of constituencies. It also had a smaller leadership base for African food aid, including such influential figures as Senators Edward Kennedy and John Danforth. There was no Senate equivalent of the House Select Committee on Hunger, and the dispersion of Senate Committees and Subcommittees with an interest in the famine situation and its relief was broader as a result. The attachment of nongermane Senate amendments to proposed legislation during FY1984 is evidence of lack of coalition and consensus. But important leadership was provided after Senator Richard Lugar assumed the chair of the Senate Foreign Relations Committee—the first hearing he held was on Ethiopia (Swenson 1986).

Humanitarian coalitions outside of the administration played a major role in mobilizing and consolidating support for Ethiopian famine relief during 1983-86. The INTERACTION consortium of relief agencies, formed in the fall of 1984 as a result of a merger of two private agency groupings, provided services to its members while strengthening their collective interests and representation in Congress. During the famine period, PVOs were much more organized and active in policy formation than they had been, since several agencies had objected to the dependence of food aid levels on the size of Commodity Credit Corporation stocks prior to the 1966 amendments to PL-480, favoring instead levels based upon levels of need determined to exist in recipient countries (Hadwiger 1970:358). The organizational role

96 Reluctant Aid or Aiding the Reluctant?

INTERACTION played, and the centralized group it formed (the African Emergency Subcommittee), created linkages with both the U.S. government and UN organizations (Borton 1986:19) on the one hand, and with masses and the media, on the other.

Media and masses were also independently instrumental in keeping government attention on the Ethiopian situation, both through fund-raising activities and through pressure on congressional representatives. November 1984 (which was also the time of bilateral negotiations) appears to be the time when most media coverage occurred. This is corroborated by an analysis of *The New York Times* that found 12 articles on Ethiopia in November 1984, including four on the front page. The Ethiopian famine was the subject of numerous articles in other newspapers, and was the cover story of *Newsweek* during that month. The key role of celebrity mobilizations in funding relief programs has been attributed to the lack of political leadership (Borton 1986:38), but in light of the timing and relative size of public and celebrity donations, too much emphasis seems to have been placed on the latter, as private donations were dwarfed by governmental donations. The ability of the masses to withstand media blitzes and donor fatigue also appears to have been underestimated in view of the fact that the big cultural fund-raisers occurred six to 12 months *after* the high point of media coverage of the famine.

Complexity in the institutional setting for decision making was one factor postponing a consensus on Ethiopian famine relief policy. The struggle for constituencies and the mix of domestic and foreign policy interests in Congress during funding decisions are illustrated by the fate of legislative proposals. On 9 February 1984 the administration, the House, and the Senate made bids for policy solutions for African famine generally. In the House, legislation was introduced for a $300 million supplemental appropriation under Title II of PL-480, as well as $50 million for emergency assistance under the Foreign Assistance Act. A similar bill in the amount of $150 million was introduced in the Senate. The administration's request for supplemental aid totalled $90 million.[6] Less than two months later, the supplemental was approved, but not until the House, Senate, and administration engaged in processes of compromise.

Conflict over decision making was especially obvious during events leading up to the hearings held on HR 1096 (eventually passed as the AFRRA), often taking the form of a tete-a-tete between the administration and Congress but involving party politics as well. During early FY1985, four major food aid proposals were before Congress, including:

1. Senate Resolution (SR) 423 (a proposal of Senators Kennedy and Robert Kasten introduced to replace an earlier proposal for the AFRRA and later approved as the AFRRA);

in the House, two proposals including:

2. House Resolution (HR) 100 supported by Congressmen Wolpe, Ted Weiss, and Mickey Leland for authorizations and appropriations, and
3. House Resolution 699 supported by Congressmen Marge Roukema and Silvio Conte), which resulted in HR 1096 by way of compromise; and,
4. the administration's plan.[7]

During hearings on HR 1096 in February 1985, congressional representatives quizzed USAID officials on Ethiopian relief efforts. The USAID report provided a succinct summary of policy concerns regarding: Ethiopian refugees in Sudan and Somalia; the speed of the food approval process; non-cooperation by the PMGSE, including its denial of access to parts of the country and the priority it was giving to unloading military supplies; and abuses in the Soviet- and Libyan-supported resettlement program. On the positive side, the report noted that the PMGSE was no longer imposing import duties on relief goods and that the formerly assessed administrative charge of $1.50/ton for such items had been dropped (U.S. House 1985a:190). Informally, Congressmen Conte, Weiss, Wolpe, Roukema, and Leland met over the congressional recess to form a coalition around HR 1096 in order to move it toward presidential approval (*Congressional Record*, 26 February 1985: H665). As it turned out, the House version was vetoed but the Senate version was approved shortly thereafter.

By July 1985, after the FY1985 supplemental appropriations were authorized, the problem of relief changed from food needs to nonfood needs (as reflected in U.S. House 1985c). Blankets and transport as well as remedies for the treatment of disease, became the critical items. McPherson reported food pileups in the ports servicing Ethiopia, the need for trucks to transport it to the interior, and the unwillingness of Ethiopian authorities to maintain the efforts they had exerted during the first four months of 1985 (U.S. House 1985c:5). Famine in the north, the northern initiative, and the Ethiopian government's response were the focal points of debate. McPherson testified to the problems in government-held areas *as well as* in areas not controlled by the government, dispelling some of the notions that USAID acted ideologically rather than problematically.

Although the administration was exercising greater control over information for decision-making purposes, it had no monopoly over it. Senate hearings in February 1985 followed from the conclusion of Senator Kennedy's delegation to Ethiopia the preceding December (U.S. Senate 1985a). On the one hand, these hearings were geared toward mobilizing support for Kennedy's bill for supplemental appropriations for FY1985. On the other, they provided a forum for airing the administration's proposal and building

98 Reluctant Aid or Aiding the Reluctant?

senatorial support. In addition to sponsoring missions to Ethiopia, the House Subcommittee on Hunger's staff issued monthly reports which were widely circulated.

Congress's outside sources of information and policy influence were evident in the way PVOs lined up behind versions of House bills and negotiated on their behalf (especially over AFRRA). CARE and CRS had supported the larger Representative Hall bill for FY1984 appropriations (U.S. House 1984c:137). Bread for the World had found the administration's request for the $90 million FY1984 supplemental "woefully inadequate," and challenged its method of computing food needs (U.S. Senate 1984a:81, 82). PVOs also sided with the left wing of the House's assessments of Ethiopian food needs in FY1985. During FY1985, HR 1096 was endorsed by INTERACTION as a coalition as well as by several individual PVOs (U.S. House 1985a:104).

The coalition between PVOs and Congress was not unilateral or uniform. A proposed Lewis Amendment to the Foreign Assistance Act would have required PVOs to raise 25 percent (as opposed to the current 20 percent) of their budget from private sources in order to be eligible for U.S. donations. Whether there was a punitive intent behind the proposal, such as disrupting their coalition with the left wing of Congress, or an economic one is not clear (U.S. House 1985e:87). But INTERACTION objected to the proposed Lewis Amendment, raising arguments about funding burdens and invoking the language of a PVO "partnership" (U.S. House 1985e:87).

Congressional attempts to monitor and earmark food aid were problematic from an administrative point of view. Congressional competence to monitor aid levels was tested throughout the relief period. Congress also attempted to oversee the budgetary authorities for aid (particularly for Title II and OFDA). An early controversy arose between Representative Wolpe and Assistant USAID Administrator Bloch over whether the Title II program was shrinking or growing. Accounting for internal transport costs and the change from the disaster account to PL-480 (McPherson in U.S. House 1985a:75) likewise raised questions of a budgetary nature in Congress. The U.S. Senate (1984a:28-30) had expressed earlier concern about the "reprogramming of $50 million" under the FY1984 appropriations. Funding problems also resulted from the forward authorization and appropriation of the AFRRA and the FY1985 supplemental, which provided funding through the end of FY1986. As early as December 1985, questions arose in the House over how much USAID had left from the FY1985 funds (U.S. House 1985e:24, 47).

Between 2 and 30 October 1984, allocations to Ethiopia included $39 million for shipment of 80,432 MT of food, one-fourth of which was delivered through the cross-border operation to Eritrea and Tigray, as well as another $6.4 million for medicine and air transport (The White House 1984).

Moderating Extreme Strategies 99

During the first two months of FY1985, two-thirds of the 300,000 MT committed to Africa were for Ethiopia (U.S. House 1985e:55). By mid-January 1985, $370 million had been approved for Ethiopia for FY1985 (U.S. Senate 1985a:31). Implementing U.S. objectives in Ethiopia as food aid flows increased involved close scrutiny of three aspects of the relief operation by sponsors in Washington: logistical arrangements for providing aid, assuring that aid was reaching the northern regions, and controlling the use of U.S. aid with respect to the Ethiopian resettlement program. Legal restraints on U.S. aid to Ethiopia had an effect on the mobilization of aid during the emergency phase and placed restrictions on activities with potential developmental impact. Macropolitical constituencies rallied to their favored positions on the underlying issues, but efficiency considerations and the neutrality concerns of international norms for famine relief also had an influence.

U.S. Relief Objectives and Program Choices

During the emergency period, moderating PMGSE programs was the overriding objective of U.S. policy, with some uncertainty as to the roles that rehabilitation of agriculture and disciplining the Ethiopian government should play. Early objectives were to get food aid appropriated, committed, delivered, and transported to Ethiopian famine victims. Humanitarian idealists hoped U.S. policy would bifurcate its objectives, putting the substantive Ethiopian policy problems to the side and proceeding with aid to famine victims. Logistical arrangements provided objectives on which substantial agreement could be reached more readily than could problems stemming from the need for aid in the war zones of the northern regions and U.S. policy regarding the resettlement and villagization programs. Legislative restrictions on developmental assistance to Ethiopia set the outer bounds for U.S. program choices regarding these latter programs, reinforced by U.S. foreign policy and political objectives.

Logistics. Early U.S. policy objectives were to acquire an administrative presence in Ethiopia and exert some positive influence over the relief operation. However, even in the best of circumstances, USAID's food aid planning involves a delicate balance between decision making in Washington and in the field. In emergency situations and in hostile environments such as Ethiopia, the difficulties are heightened. Being thrust into the midst of famine alongside many other sources of famine relief policy with a small staff, few resources, and limited support from the administration in Washington, USAID's ability to effectively compete for control over the planning of the famine relief operation and distribution of PL-480 commodities was severely hampered. This administrative dilemma, as well as the political antipathy of the United States toward the PMGSE, may explain the pace of the U.S. government's response.

Between 1979 and the onset of the 1983-86 famine, USAID's Ethiopian operations had been nearly eliminated, with its small PL-480 regular Title II program being administered out of the regional mission in Nairobi. It was not until October 1984 that the PMGSE agreed to permit a USAID staff of five permanent employees, who arrived during the first quarter of 1985. USAID also employed 50 temporary duty employees for short-term work during the course of the relief effort as well as a number of contract employees (USAID/E 1987:12). Presumptions that the United States "entered the battle in Ethiopia from a position of strength" in 1985 (Smith 1987:32)—whether in terms of relieving famine or vis-a-vis the Ethiopian government—are untenable in this situation. USAID planning was almost always one step behind the RRC, from initial perceptions of the famine to adjusting to its spread as time wore on. USAID's small staff was certainly not in a position of strength with respect to the Ethiopian government. USAID also relied on the UN Office for Emergency Operations in Ethiopia's (UNOEO/E) food needs assessments at the outset, which ultimately were based on RRC estimates (cf. Borton 1986).

The relatively late start of the United States may have been mitigated by the greater efficiency of the U.S. program: There was less of a delay between the allocation of aid and the distribution of commodities and other resources for the U.S. program than there was for many European programs. The European Court of Auditors found that the time lag between decision and delivery of EEC food aid to Ethiopia extended to a maximum of 19 months (Gill 1986:70), while the response time of the United Kingdom's programs in Ethiopia ranged from six to 32 weeks from initiation to arrival (Borton 1989:235). U.S. aid for African famine relief programs in FYs1984 and 1985 required about six months to deliver commodities after USAID in Washington received a mission's request (U.S. G.A.O.1986:2).

U.S. food aid clearly became one of the major forces behind Ethiopian famine relief. Congressional concern over logistical arrangements for delivering and distributing food aid for Ethiopian famine relief was directed toward exercising its oversight functions, and it held hearings to obtain information from the administration on the progress being made. The State Department took a retracted posture in the struggle to wage a relief effort. This was perhaps required by diplomatic relationships, necessary to preserve the U.S. foreign policy position, and useful for maintaining a minimal level of PMGSE openness to food aid, but it was probably detrimental in the short term to USAID's strategy for working out logistical arrangements. Congressional deference to the administration in food aid policy reached its peak in the targeting of food aid. Congress did not participate in negotiating the bilateral aid agreement and may not have known it was being considered. Congressional recognition of administration competence no less than food power factors have been responsible for this.

Throughout the emergency phase, USAID in Ethiopia (USAID/E) was busy monitoring the emergency situation, processing PVO requests for commodities and other aid, and attempting to comply with directives from Washington (USAID/W). An adjustment process coordinated the perceptions and priorities of USAID/W and USAID/E. One of the key outcomes of these negotiations between the field and headquarters was the final adjustment of commodity allocations to PVOs for each fiscal year.[8] These allocations were doubtless based on a wide range of considerations, including regional operations of PVOs, the intensity of famine in those regions, and abilities of PVOs and others to distribute with accountability.

Northern aid. Interference with relief in the northern war regions soon became the compelling and overriding concern of policymakers in Washington. When negotiations for a cease-fire failed, the northern initiative (the Food for the North initiative, or FFN) and cross-border feeding operations launched from Sudan were the two U.S.-supported programs aimed at alleviating problems in these war zones.

In many ways, the cross-border policy was a compromise. Cross-border operations started in April 1984, but the difficulty of logistical arrangements was discouraging (U.S. Senate 1984b:29-31). USAID lawyers also had some concerns about the "legal ramifications" of the cross-border operation (*New York Times* 14 March 1985), reflecting normative considerations in providing support to rebel-held areas, and presumably also about intrusions into Ethiopian sovereignty over traffic crossing its borders. These concerns were expressed by the charge d'affaires in the U.S. Embassy in Addis Ababa in the following terms:

> Despite profound political differences with the government in Addis Ababa, Washington avoided involvement with the insurgent organizations and held to its long-standing policy of support for the territorial integrity of Ethiopia. AID dealt only with the Western private voluntary agencies, who in turn handled all necessary arrangements with REST and ERA. This mechanism did not offer absolute assurance against American relief food falling into the hands of rebel soldiers, just as the United States could not be absolutely certain that food it gave the RRC would not be diverted to improper use. (Korn 1986a:136)

U.S. aid for the cross-border operation was low-profile for two reasons. First, more overt aid would have been likely to antagonize the Ethiopian government. For this reason, the U.S. embassy preferred not to know anything about it (cf. Gordon 1986). Ethiopian officials protested cross-border operations and made "vague threats, but these were never translated into action" (Korn 1986a:137). Second, by keeping cross-border aid at a low visibility level, the probability of right wing groups' escalating such aid into support for "anti-Marxist" liberation movements under the mandate of the Reagan Doctrine was diminished (cf. Clark 1986:30-31). The small amount of U.S. aid provided to the relief organizations of the rebel organizations in the north, and the large amounts of aid provided outside of the rebel-held areas in the regions of Tigray and Eritrea, both highlight the weakness of assertions that U.S. policy in the north was driven by the Reagan Doctrine's military objectives.

Similarly, the FFN initiative which began in the spring of 1985 called upon U.S.-based PVOs to distribute additional amounts of food in the northern war regions of Eritrea and Tigray. As early as March 1984 CRS had expressed its hope to expand its program "northward in Northern Tigray and in Eritrea" (U.S. Senate 1984a:74). The hope to expand the CRS program in Mekelle to Northern Tigray and Eritrea—where the nutritional status of people was suspected to be even worse—was reported by CRS Director Kenneth Hackett to the Senate Subcommittee on African Affairs (U.S. Senate 1984a:70-71).

While a compromise was made in policy for providing aid to the war zones of the north, no such outcome resulted in the case of resettlement to the south, partly because there were no proponents of the resettlement program within Congress or the administration. Villagization was presumably not a concern of policy makers in Washington, because there was no effort made to restrict U.S. food aid from being used to implement this program.

Resettlement and villagization. The resettlement policy of the Ethiopian authorities, and the most appropriate form of response by the United States, was a later concern of Congress and the administration. If food power factors were ever exerted, it was in formulating U.S. objectives on this issue.The administration had expressed opposition to the program as early as December 1984 in a State Department briefing conducted by USAID Administrator McPherson (U.S. Department of State 1984c), but resettlement did not receive a congressional hearing until late 1985 and was not perceived as a definite "challenge to American policy makers that cannot be ignored" until it was the subject of Senate Foreign Relations Committee hearings in March 1986 (U.S. Senate 1986a). The resettlement issue was raised but was not a real concern to Congress in the hearings on the problems of population movements and refugees associated with the famine held by the Senate in February 1985 (U.S. Senate 1985a:23). The inhumane handling of an apparent cholera epidemic prompted USAID responses to the PMGSE's forced evacuation of the camp at Ibnet during 28-29 April 1985. During the 1986

Senate hearings, controversy arose because of reports of brutality in the selection and transportation of resettlers, but not necessarily because of the conceptual merits of resettlement as a developmental strategy.

Part of the reason for the late formulation of U.S. objectives regarding resettlement was that opposition to the program was not uniform. In the private voluntary sector, the resettlement issue nearly split the INTERACTION coalition, as some members were opposed to it while others were supportive of the program (Whitaker 1987). Conservative members of Congress sponsored and passed a provision in the International Security and Development Cooperation Act of 1985 that required President Reagan to determine whether the Ethiopian regime was "conducting a deliberate policy of starvation." If so determined, then the act required that a trade embargo be imposed. A social science tete-a-tete that occurred during House hearings held in October 1985 on the issues underlying the request for a Presidential Determination (U.S. House 1985d). Two diverging viewpoints on the program were represented. There was wide disagreement among the witnesses, who included two Ethiopianists (Harold Marcus and Edmond Keller) and a human rights activist (Jason Clay). Marcus testified that the Ethiopian government was trying to "fulfill the most basic human rights of survival," Clay that the government was engaging in a deliberate policy of starvation, and Keller that while there was no official policy of starvation the Ethiopian government was making some bad policy choices.

In its justification for determining that the Ethiopian regime was not conducting a deliberate policy of starvation, the administration referred to the perceived success of leverage and the threat of an embargo. Although the resettlement program was characterized as "inhumane" and as one that had diverted needed transport and logistical resources away from the relief effort, donors were believed to have "pressured" Ethiopia into several actions to enhance the relief effort. These included: agreeing to expansion of food distribution in the war zones in the northern regions, reducing the pace of the resettlement program, and more humane treatment of people evacuated from relief camps (U.S. House 1985d:174-175).

In later Senate Committee on Foreign Relations hearings, the Director of Cultural Survival (Clay) prevailed as the social science expert called upon to testify on the question of human rights violations stemming from forced removal of people in Ethiopia. Abuses in the selection, transport, and resettlement of persons were documented. The outcome of these hearings on resettlement was captured by Assistant Secretary of State Alan Keyes, who indicated the need to "carefully monitor" the use of U.S. food resources "so as not to support the program that involve[s] those abuses" (U.S. Senate 1986a:15). Preventing the use of U.S. aid to support and subsidize the resettlement became the key U.S. policy objective, but proved to be difficult to achieve. Subsequently, more detailed criticisms of the resettlement program were advanced, providing momentum for the movement for sanctions against the Ethiopian government that emerged during the stability phase of relief operations. In addition to calling for the provision of adequate land and support for resettlers, the director of USAID's Drought Coordination Staff expressed several objections to the Senate Subcommittee on Foreign Relations in March (U.S. Senate 1986a:44). In February 1986 Congressman Roukema introduced a resolution in the House calling for: suspension of the program until the end of the drought, termination of any coercive recruitment, and permission to media and international observers to access resettlement camps.

A "moratorium," or at least suspension of the resettlement program due to insufficient resources to continue it, was put into effect in early 1986. This temporary moratorium by the Ethiopian authorities may suggest that food power had been used effectively by the U.S. government, but it has also been asserted that U.S. criticism had no effect on the decision to place a moratorium on the program's operation (Jansson 1987:68).

For the most part, the United States was able to restrict its aid from going to the resettlement program on human rights grounds. Another argument for barring U.S. assistance was that it was developmental in nature—however defective in design and implementation—and prohibited by legislative restrictions on U.S. foreign assistance from being applied to resettlement programs. As relief operations stabilized, the purposes to which U.S. aid was being applied even outside the rebel regions and resettlement areas became somewhat clearer, especially in the context of the villagization program. This program, first implemented during the famine period in the Hararghe region, was supposed to reorganize peasants into collective villages, supposedly to provide basic social services. Somewhat surprisingly, restrictions on developmental assistance were not an absolute bar to rehabilitation programs or to PVO assistance with the villagization program.

Prohibitions on Developmental Assistance

Legal guidelines for foreign aid also played a role in the formulation of U.S. objectives, both in terms of restricting funding decisions and in limiting the policy choices for aid programs. Most significant was a series of legislative restrictions on foreign aid that prohibited the United States from providing developmental assistance to Ethiopia, notably the Hickenlooper Amendment to the Foreign Assistance Act and related sanctions. The Hickenlooper Amendment (section 301(d)(3) of the Foreign Assistance Act of 1962) prohibited the United States from providing aid to governments that nationalize assets of U.S. citizens. The Brooke Amendment (section 518 of the Foreign Assistance Appropriations Act of 1985) provided for similar prohibitions in the case of countries which failed for a period exceeding one year to repay loans or to make payments for military equipment purchased.[9]

These restrictions have been interpreted by some as having interfered with the response of the United States to the famine emergency as well as having influenced U.S. funding decisions and program choices. Clearly, it was harder for USAID to mobilize resources for famine relief in Ethiopia because there was no in-country staff. But the reduction of the USAID presence in Ethiopia was due as much to Ethiopian government action as to suspension of aid because of Hickenlooper. The generally critical General Accounting Office report on the U.S. response did not include Hickenlooper among the factors involved in the sluggish pace of early U.S. government decision making. Instead, direct assessments of U.S. government foreign policy concerns delayed initial approvals, concerns which included a reluctance to be exploited by Ethiopian government policies or to provide support to them (U.S. G.A.O. 1985a:5-9).

Conflicting interpretations of the Hickenlooper Amendment's applicability to Ethiopian famine relief, and issues regarding the need for waivers, arose throughout the famine relief period. The conflicts in interpretation and policy recommendation were most apparent in the diverging pronouncements of the administration and Congress. Throughout the relief period, the administration was persistent in its position that no waivers of Hickenlooper were required and that USAID did not "need additional legislation or waivers to provide the necessary assistance" (McPherson in U.S. House 1985a:107). In Congress, on the other hand, there was a fair amount of debate over the applicability of Hickenlooper and whether waivers were required. Considerable controversy developed over the interpretation of the scope of the Hickenlooper Amendment. The issue of the effect of Hickenlooper was raised in the Senate (U.S. Senate 1985a) and in the House, where Representative Wolpe requested a waiver to "ensure that there are no complications in providing [emergency aid] particularly in Ethiopia." USAID Administrator McPherson declined to support any waiver of the Hickenlooper and Brooke Amendments for emergency supplementals during House hearings, denying that there was any need for a waiver (U.S. House 1985a:107).

Hickenlooper had a direct effect on the conflict that arose between the administration and PVOs distributing U.S. food over the type of aid to be provided. PVOs were in favor of assistance that would go beyond providing emergency aid for the famine through distributing food commodities. Several U.S.-based PVOs distributing relief commodities in Ethiopia had had developmental programs in Ethiopia prior to setting up emergency famine relief programs, or used their relief programs as the foundation for future developmental activities. INTERACTION was of the view that a broad definition of relief and rehabilitation objectives should be adopted that would include substantial aid to Ethiopia (U.S. House 1985e:27). Opponents of this viewpoint objected on the basis of Hickenlooper and Brooke Amendments, arguing that they prohibited any aid not strictly for relief purposes. Drawing the line between relief and developmental assistance became one of the most critical issues for aid policy. Programming assistance in the form of emergency relief while avoiding developmental impact took a central position in policy implementation.

Indirectly, therefore, the Hickenlooper Amendment may have had an effect on famine relief activities under PL-480. First, assessing food needs required that USAID distinguish between the emergency and structural portions of Ethiopia's food deficit. The United States could provide food aid to address the emergency but not the structural food deficit requirements that stemmed from Ethiopian food policy decisions. Second, PVOs were required to ask questions about whether the assistance they were requesting in response to the famine was for relief—and therefore legitimate for funding by the U.S. government—or whether it was for development—and therefore prohibited. Proposals of some PVOs were turned down because they were "not sufficiently limited to immediate relief but involve[d] rehabilitation and recovery" (U.S. House 1985e:26-27). USAID's contributions to UNICEF's cash-for-food program were threatened on developmental grounds (*Manchester Guardian* 4 January 1985). Even so, aid that could be effectively used, despite being developmental in nature and strictly prohibited, might be finessed as rehabilitation and permitted by U.S. officials.

The dilemma of segregating emergency relief from developmental assistance was resolved by a compromise that permitted aid for "rehabilitation." According to McPherson, the Hickenlooper Amendment was interpreted to mean that aid did not preclude providing seeds. Nor did it preclude providing aid for building wells for drinking water (although observers have indicated that wells for irrigation were deemed developmental and that USAID would therefore not provide aid for them). Even the donation of trucks for food transport was permitted—in the fall of 1983, delays in donating trucks partially attributable to Hickenlooper were eventually circumvented by an agreement whereby title to U.S. government-donated trucks passed to the UN rather than the Ethiopian government. By defining aid activities as being for rehabilitation, the differences between relief and development assistance were blurred and the impact of Hickenlooper on the relief effort was diminished.

Subsequently, the AFRRA of 1985 authorized a waiver of the applicability of Hickenlooper's prohibition of assistance to Ethiopia (U.S. Senate 1985b:7). The Brooke Amendment did not go as far as prohibiting disaster assistance by virtue of a waiver of Hickenlooper contained in Section 491 of the Foreign Assistance Appropriations Act, of which it was a part (U.S. Senate 1985b:6).

Moderating Extreme Strategies 107

Despite the Senate report's language, this authorization of a waiver was not entirely pragmatic. The report stated that even though "legal opinions have deemed both Public Law 480 and disaster assistance to be exempted from the Hickenlooper prohibition, the committee has included a specific waiver of 620(e)(1) in order to assure the most expeditious handling of any assistance provided to Ethiopia" (U.S. Senate 1985b:7). As has been noted, the administration had used the development prohibition in reviewing PVO requirements, and absolute barriers seem to have been raised (see Leland, U.S. House 1985f:49). But on 8 May 1985, a telegram from the State Department to the U.S. Embassy in Addis Ababa indicated that aid could be used for "relief, rehabilitation and recovery projects," including a long list of permitted activities (Gill 1986:116). However, USAID was permitted "to contribute to development projects [in Ethiopia] only from money appropriated under the African Famine Relief and Recovery Act of 1985" (*New York Times* 9 May 1985).

Despite the focus on legislative restrictions, there were also deeper reasons for prohibiting or at least restricting development assistance to Ethiopia. These were raised by USAID Administrator McPherson, who claimed that it would not be "prudent" to provide developmental assistance to Ethiopia without assurance that it would be "effectively used" (U.S. Senate 1985a:40). Aid for resettlement was strictly prohibited as a developmental program no less than on humanitarian grounds. This underlying conflict between providing immediate aid for famine relief and providing aid for developmental purposes—as well as the restrictions of the Hickenlooper Amendment surfaced over U.S. support of PVO operations. In the Ethiopian situation, the U.S. government was hard pressed to avoid running afoul of legislative prohibitions on developmental assistance, while continuing to rely on PVOs—the only viable agents—to distribute emergency famine relief commodities. The potential for end runs on Hickenlooper restrictions was heightened by this situation, particularly through USAID funding of internal transport expenses. By early 1985, CRS had "committed a very substantial amount of privately contributed moneys to development projects in Ethiopia" (McClosky in U.S. House 1985b:32). An estimated $30 million were earmarked by the agency for agriculture, water and sanitation, and health and medicine programs for Ethiopian rehabilitation (U.S. House 1985c:115). USAID's position was that this money should have been used to offset transportation costs, rather than requesting additional USAID money for these purposes. In effect, the position was that USAID was indirectly underwriting Ethiopian development by relieving PVOs of transport costs so that they could invest their money in developmental projects instead.

As a result of this flexibility, it is not clear whether prohibitions stemming from the Foreign Assistance Act effectively stifled the transfer of develop-

108 Reluctant Aid or Aiding the Reluctant?

ment resources to Ethiopia. Even if it had, critics of U.S. policy have typically assumed that prohibitions on developmental aid had adverse effects on relief operations. This assumption must be reviewed in light of evidence that development activities sometimes conflicted with relief. Moreover, development work sometimes placed obstacles in the way of relief activities. Competition between food for relief and food for development was apparent in certain aspects of WFP and EEC activities. One problem stemmed from the fact that transport operations for food destined for food-for-work projects conflicted with the need for transport of relief food (WFP 1985:30-31). A related problem noted with respect to EEC food aid was that much of it was locked into food-for-work projects and the Ministry of Agriculture rather than into the RRC for relief (Goyder 1988:90). The reluctance of one missionary agency (SIM, International) to become involved with relief activities for fear of sacrificing its proselytizing functions has already been mentioned. While the United States officially avoided this dilemma by prohibiting developmental assistance, as distribution systems merged, the distribution of U.S. food aid commodities had a developmental impact. U.S. aid contributed to the expansion of RRC operations and credibility, accomplished indirectly through USAID funding of PVO operations and directly through the bilateral program. U.S. objectives for segregating relief from development were also subverted through the support of PVO activities, which strengthened distributional infrastructure and PAs in particular.

Notes

1. The rationale for setting the end of the emergency phase near the end of 1985 includes the better harvest in the fall of 1985, the decline in shelter populations, routinization of food distribution, and the predominance of dry over wet feeding.
2. In Korem, for example, death rates varied from 100 per day in October, 1984 (totalling tens of thousands by November [Hancock 1985:94]), to 23 in a day in December (Patinkin 1985:15).
3. After the 1966 amendments to PL-480, commodities for foreign donation under Title II were no longer required to be of surplus status. Significant procurement policy changes allowed the Secretary of Agriculture to determine the availability of commodities for foreign donation regardless of Commodity Credit Corporation determination of a commodity's being in surplus.
4. For FY 1985, Ethiopia was the second largest aid recipient in Africa, behind Sudan. Some of the Sudan aid was directly related to Ethiopian famine, providing relief to refugees from Eritrea, Tigray, and the resettlement areas, and fueling cross-border feeding operations from Sudan into northern Ethiopia.
5. These programs were reviewed on a case-by-case basis, and by April 1985 several Title II programs included a monetization component (U.S. House, 1985b:6).
6. On 10 July 1984, the Administration's Emergency Food Aid Initiative was

Moderating Extreme Strategies 109

released (The White House 1984). It was based on President Reagan's request that the National Security Council review the African famine situation and make recommendations (U.S. House 1984c:63). The initiative was presented by McPherson to the Senate (U.S. Senate 1984c:12 - 13) and the House (U.S. House 1984c:10 - 13). It called for a five-step plan, including: prepositioning of grain, a $50 million fund, financing or payment of transport costs, creation of a governmental task force, and establishment of an advisory group.

7. On 3 January 1985 the administration released its plan for a food and aid program called the African Hunger Initiative. McPherson presented this program to the Senate in February (U.S. Senate 1985a:27, 32 - 37). This initiative called for: $268 million for Food, $25 million for Refugees, and $25 million for OFDA.

8. See, for example, the U.S. Department of State (1986) telegram of March 1986 announcing USAID/W's final FY 1986 allocations.

9. Additional sanctions prohibiting developmental aid were extended to the multilateral setting by the Gonzalez Amendments to legislation authorizing U.S. participation in several multilateral development and lending institutions. The Gonzalez Amendment to the International Development Association Act of 1962 permitted the imposition of Hickenlooper-type sanctions through U.S. action in the World Bank, requiring executive directors of the United States "to vote against any loan or other use of Bank funds" to such countries. In 1976, a similar amendment was inserted into legislation approving U.S. participation in the African Development Fund (Vandevelde 1989:134 - 138).

5

Merging Donor and Recipient Policies for Emergency Food Distribution

Donor reactions to the Ethiopian resettlement program and policies in the northern region reinforced a dualism in food distribution operations which revolved around conflicts between humanitarianism and political objectives. However, positing a strict segmentation between emergency programs sponsored by Western aid agencies for relief, and a coercive program for resettlement (and later villagization) administered by the RRC (see, e.g., Korn 1986b:6) would be too simplistic. Nevertheless, there are important elements of accuracy in such a dualism, even though these distribution systems overlapped considerably and eventually merged substantially. This dualism evolved in part out of donor and recipient policies, but also out of the policy responses of donor nations and the diplomatic jockeying that occurred on the ground in Ethiopia. As food distribution proceeded, a gradual merging of donor and recipient policies and operations became evident.

This merger occurred in the transition from the emergency to the stability phases of the famine and relief operations. As food distribution programs evolved during the emergency phase, RRC- and PVO-based systems pursued their own targets. While movement toward normative distribution patterns were encouraged by U.S.-based PVOs, the RRC's political-military mandate and its inability to serve beneficiaries in the rebel-held areas required foreign agencies to take the initiative. Gradually, donor and recipient government operations developed a division of labor, coordinated by the UNOEO/E and implemented for the most part by NGOs and the RRC. PVO operations were considerably strained by their position as norm-bearing organizations caught between the often conflicting initiatives of donor and recipient governments.

112 Reluctant Aid or Aiding the Reluctant?

PVOs and Evolution of Dual Food Distribution

Food distribution programs of PVOs based in the United States (i.e., with international headquarters in the United States) played a major role in the relief effort, attempting to serve both donor and recipient governments. While depending on the recipient government for operational support and permission to operate in the first place, they depended substantially on donor governments for funds and food. As elements of the principal system for merging donor and recipient government policies, PVOs also acquired independent bases of power in Ethiopia. PVO coalitions and groups served to heighten the independence of PVOs from both donor and recipient governments. This allowed them to challenge the authority of both donor and recipient governments. Whether their positions are best viewed as autonomous, or they are to be seen as shifting their loyalty from one government to the other, is important. International organizations affiliated with the UN (especially UNOEO/E and WFP), and other international agencies, took on quite important functions and added a further dimension of complexity to the institutional relationships

TABLE 5.1
Contributions of Donors to Food Distribution Systems, 1985-86

	Commodities Donated (MTs)		
	To RRC	To NGOs	RRC Share (%)
Donor			
United States	50,000	729,748	6
EEC [a]	304,790	252,418	55
Canada	75,472	55,922	57
Other OECD [b]	47,434	64,546	42
Warsaw Pact [c]	24,003	930	96
Other [d]	57,315	15,145	79
Total [e]	559,014	1,118,709	33

Source: USAID/E (1987:38-38A).

a. EEC also includes bilateral donations of member governments.
b. Other OECD includes Australia, Austria, Finland, Iceland, Japan, New Zealand, Norway, Sweden, and Switzerland.
c. Warsaw Pact donors include Bulgaria, Czechoslovakia, German Democratic Republic, Hungary, and Poland.
d. Other donors include China, India, Iran, Israel, Libya, Pakistan, United Arab Emirates, Yugoslavia, Zimbabwe, and several other minor donors.
e. Does not include 98,331 MT from WFP and private donors.

forged by the U.S. food aid program.

The division of functions in food distribution that evolved between donor and recipient governments was partly built upon the pre-existing division of responsibilities for estimating food needs and securing funding for operations. Responsibility for estimating food aid requirements and soliciting aid for relief fell primarily on the recipient government, although conferences for soliciting and donating aid were also organized by donor governments and international agencies. Recipient government functions were initially controlled by the RRC, but the WPE (and its Central Committee) later asserted control over their execution. Institutionally, as programs merged, the RRC's loss of control was not simply transferred but diffused through infrastructural systems developed by donors and their operating agencies.

Pledging and earmarking aid for Ethiopian famine relief were donor functions. Donors held various conferences at different sites—including Geneva and New York—and attended donor conferences and diplomatic meetings in Addis Ababa (see Korn 1986a). In formulating their own aid programs, donor governments also earmarked aid for particular purposes, prescribed special regional distributions, and in the case of most Western donors, included prohibitions on using their aid for the resettlement program.

Diverging policy priorities reflected in executing these functions also produced a division of labor among donors for food distribution. In terms of donation strategy, policy and funding decisions were implemented through food distribution programs administered by either PVOs or the RRC. Donor groups and their respective contributions to the RRC system and international distribution systems operated largely by PVOs are represented in table 5.1. Patterns of foreign donations channeled into the RRC and the international famine relief systems provide the clearest evidence of the dual system for food distribution. Overall, 33 percent of food aid donated during 1984-86 was targeted to the RRC system. U.S. donations were heavily concentrated in PVO operations, and virtually all Warsaw Pact country aid and commodities were donated to the RRC, while other donor groups had more balanced donation patterns.

The RRC Distribution System

As the bearer of primary responsibility for famine relief in Ethiopia, the burden for planning appropriately fell on the Ethiopian government and its relief agency. For the PMGSE, famine relief was closely tied to the regime's objectives for building power throughout the country. The PMGSE's objectives in distributing emergency food aid were to advance the war effort and the resettlement and villagization programs, and to build state-controlled socialist institutions generally. Food distribution programs operated by the

114 Reluctant Aid or Aiding the Reluctant?

RRC were shrouded in some mystery, especially in connection with the policies of collectivization, resettlement, and villagization implemented during the famine, but also by the constant military activities of the Ethiopian government. At the outset, some planning authority had been delegated to the RRC bureaucracy—more by default than by affirmative grant—but not without Party supervision. Former RRC Commissioner Dawit Wolde Giorgis's confessions (1989) about the relief effort require corroboration, but until obtained they must stand as the principal source of information about the Ethiopian government's controls over food distribution. Bureaucratic reshuffling, radicalization of the resettlement program by central authorities, and other power initiatives demonstrated the limits on RRC authority.

Reliance on outside aid further limited the potential for RRC independence, even though the RRC undertook some direct distributions, made repeated attempts to control foreign agencies, and was supported in its famine relief program by ties to external agencies and resources. One explanation of Ethiopian policy has been advanced by the director of a French agency involved in relief and development: Its "aim" for allowing Western agencies into the country was to "make the West pay for the resettlement scheme and help pay for the war effort in the north" (Brauman 1986a:68). A similar line of reasoning could be applied to PMGSE expectations for implementing the villagization program throughout the country.

Four different approaches of the RRC to famine relief and food distribution are distinguishable, reflecting different magnitudes of RRC control, subordination to state or party objectives, and commitment to power principles. First, in areas without any real threat of insurgency, where the regime wanted to maintain its control, RRC operations resembled the surface structure of any famine relief organization (i.e., distributing food on the basis of need and operating without deep intervention in the political economy of the locale). In parts of the south outside the resettlement areas, for example, the RRC seems to have distributed food in a neutral manner without a clear power purpose (cf. Turton 1985; see also Jansson 1987) and relatively free of PMGSE or WPE supervision.

In regions where the regime was committed to deep intervention in local political economies and food systems, two quite different RRC approaches to food distribution were evident. One approach was taken in the northern regions of Eritrea and Tigray where civil war conditions prevailed (and to some extent perhaps the far east of the Ogaden and pockets of Oromo territory in the east and west), where military objectives of conquest and power building substantially displaced neutrality. A great deal of controversy arose over the capacity of the RRC to distribute food in rebel-held areas. To promote military victory over insurgents, selective relief policies and food distribution practices were implemented, providing aid to loyalists only, restricting relief agencies in their operations, and requiring proofs of loyalty from beneficiaries in order for them to receive food. Efforts were undertaken to assure that the distribution of food in the government-held areas was as strictly controlled by military and Party authorities as possible.

Another approach was closely related to the RRC's resettlement mandate and practices. Where the Ethiopian government's need to control food was greatest for achieving its objectives, its administrative competence was often weakest. Prior to the arrival of foreign food commodities, the RRC was heavily involved in resettlement activities, and it continued to insist on classifying the resettlement program as an operation for famine relief (see RRC 1985c). RRC cooperation with the Office of the Nationality Problem, which directed the resettlement program, generally pre-empted RRC's relatively moderate plans. RRC relief activities in the northern regions were observed to deviate substantially from normative famine relief principles. As has been noted, these included selecting strategic locations for distribution centers, using relief as a tool for luring peasants and conscripting them into military service and resettlement, and thereby disrupting the civilian bases of support for opposition groups. In the regions of resettlement, the RRC had a very poor administrative infrastructure for food distribution, much less for development.

Similar to the resettlement strategy was a fourth approach, aimed at strengthening military support: centrally-controlled Peasant Associations and collective institutions, largely controlled through villagization programs. This was implemented during the emergency phase in the southeast and subsequently through all of the country except for Eritrea and Tigray. In Hararghe, and later in nearly every other administrative region of the country, food aid distribution was oriented toward building the regime's power by strengthening PAs through the villagization program. In many regions, villagization was both a causal factor in famine, because it prevented peasants from farming, and an effective infrastructure for distributing relief commodities and building central controls. Remnants of a traditionally "disorganized," nomadic peasantry, difficult to control and subject to movement and organization by rivals such as the OLF, and memories of Somali invasion were close to the surface and provided partial motivations for the program. The second rationale for villagization—i.e., to strengthen institutions for providing basic social services to peasants—has not been substantially fulfilled in either Arsi or Hararghe regions at least (Cohen and Isaksson 1987:457-458).

The rise and fall of the RRC's status in the Ethiopian political economy during the famine was one of the most critical developments during the relief operation. Prior to the mobilization of aid in 1984, the RRC administered 193 food distribution centers, as well as shelters and reception centers. These relief centers were distributed throughout the administrative regions as indicated in table 5.2 (ADAB 1984:47). It is clear that the RRC initially had some independence from the PMGSE and its governing bodies. It was in the vanguard in publicizing the famine, conducting fund-raising appeals, and supervising private organizations' food deliveries beginning in 1983. The RRC was able to receive grants directly from donor governments, giving it control over extensive external resources. As the Central Committee began to assert its power over the RRC and delegated supervisory responsibilities to Politburo members, a political agenda displaced neutral relief criteria. Ethiopian authorities attempted to impose a series of staffing controls over PVOs, limiting the number of foreign nationals on their staffs in order to increase the number of Ethiopian nationals. Implementation of these restrictions was largely unsuccessful, as some PVOs were able to maintain large expatriate staffs in their Addis Ababa headquarters and in the field. But the RRC also resisted retrenchment as its share of food aid commodities donated from abroad diminished and as its development mandate was withdrawn in favor of other Ethiopian government agencies (such as the Ministry of Agriculture). The RRC's authority was further eroded from within by Ethiopian Embassies' approval of PVO staff visas without RRC consultations (Jansson 1987:22).

Installing foreign programs for famine relief, particularly those supported by U.S. aid, clearly competed with the RRC. USAID strategies for implementing U.S. policy and its interactions with PVOs clearly invoked the

TABLE 5.2
RRC Distribution Sites and Shelters, 1983

Region	Distribution Sites	Shelters
Hararghe	50	8
Wollo	30	2
Eritrea	23	4
Bale	16	-
Sidamo	16	-
Tigray	15	4
Shoa	14	-
Gonder	13	3
Gamo Gofa	11	-
Kaffa & Ilubabor	5	1
Welega	-	-
Total	193	22

Source: ADAB (1984:47).

Merging Donor and Recipient Policies 117

processes of negotiation typically involved in international relief operations. Limiting U.S. assistance to famine relief operations served to segregate PVOs somewhat from the Ethiopian authorities, especially with respect to the resettlement program. The fact that most donors, excluding Canada, the EEC and the Eastern bloc, were unwilling to support the resettlement program further depleted the resources available in the south. The RRC was generally alone in planning for the stockpiling of food in the areas of resettlement (cf.Harris 1987). According to one report, during the first half of 1985 the RRC withdrew food from Wollo—one of the regions hardest hit by famine— in order to stockpile food outside Addis Ababa and critical military areas in Eritrea and Tigray (Kaplan 1988:29). As stability was reached in famine relief operations, the RRC- and PVO-based systems merged. Involvement of the Soviet Union in food distribution was minimal until implementation of the resettlement program began. When it did begin, the Soviet presence further separated the RRC system from that of the major Western donors and the United States.

U.S. Aid and PVO Operations

Despite the diversity of Ethiopian objectives for food distribution, distribution of U.S.-donated commodities partially meshed with Ethiopian policy in the case of all four RRC approaches. Even though USAID had limited capacities in Ethiopia, U.S. food aid donated under the authority of PL-480 evolved into the dominant source of commodities and funds for famine relief, followed by the EEC and its member governments. This is clearly demonstrated by the amounts of aid provided between 1985 and 1986 by major donors, as listed in table 5.3. The U.S. program alone resulted in the distribution of over 800,000 MT of U.S. food commodities to over 7 million beneficiaries during the period between May 1983 and the end of FY1986 (USAID/E 1987:iii). Adding other Western and Eastern bloc aid brings the total to nearly 2 million MT. Because U.S.-sponsored operations were among the most important contributions to food distribution, they served to reinforce Ethiopian government policy, even while initially promoting a dualism in relief. Remedying perceived deficiencies rather than controlling overall relief operations was USAID's strategy; as a result, it reacted to pre-existing recipient government programs and procedures. A gradual transition from crisis to stability in food distribution operations resulted in changes in USAID planning.

Total U.S. donations and proportions of total donations by fiscal year (and by phase of the operation) are listed in table 5.4. The volume of U.S. aid for Ethiopian famine relief grew dramatically between FYs1984 and 1985 and then dropped off somewhat during FY1986. Steady and sustained growth in

118 Reluctant Aid or Aiding the Reluctant?

the quantity of food distributed and the number of beneficiaries reached is apparent throughout 1985 and 1986; a slight decline occurred in both after a peak in September 1985, and aid levels fell sharply in January 1986, again gradually increasing through the end of the year.

PVOs starting up operations in Ethiopia for PL-480 commodity distribution programs were required to make a wide range of programmatic adjustments, including recruiting and establishing personnel, coordinating field operations with in-country and international headquarters, acquiring and delivering equipment, and building relationships with USAID, the RRC and Recipient Institutions (RIs) in order to facilitate distribution of food to individual recipients. Three distinct modes of adjustment were apparent among U.S.-based PVOs starting up operations in Ethiopia. First, some organizations with a prior presence in Ethiopia expanded their operational capacity for distributing PL-480 commodities. The exemplar of this mode was Catholic Relief Services (CRS), which had operated a regular Title II program in Addis Ababa since the 1950s. Even though it was small at the time of the outset of the famine, by 1986 more than 4,200 people were implementing the

TABLE 5.3
Major Food Aid Donors and Donor Groups, 1985-86 [a]

Donor	Commodities Donated MTs	Percent of Total
United States	779,748	46
EEC [b]	557,208	33
Canada	131,394	8
Other OECD [c]	111,980	7
Warsaw Pact [d]	24,933	1
Other [e]	72,460	4
Total [f]	1,677,723	

Source:USAID/E (1987:38-38A).

a. The Soviet Union led donors in "nonfood" aid during the period.
b. EEC also includes bilateral donations of member governments.
c. Other OECD includes Australia, Austria, Finland, Iceland, Japan, New Zealand, Norway, Sweden, and Switzerland.
d. Warsaw Pact donors include Bulgaria, Czechoslovakia, German Democratic Republic, Hungary, and Poland.
e. Other donors include China, India, Iran, Israel, Libya, Pakistan, United Arab Emirates, Yugoslavia, Zimbabwe, and several other minor donors.
f. Does not include 98,331 MT from WFP and private donors.

Merging Donor and Recipient Policies 119

TABLE 5.4
U.S. Aid to Ethiopia, FYs1984-86

Fiscal Year	Food Aid Amount (MT)	Food Aid Value ($ million)	Nonfood Aid ($ million)	Total Aid ($ million)
1984	41,343	23.09[a]	0	23.09
1985	446,642	249.06	44.05	293.11
1986	340,423	156.54	15.06	171.60
Total	828,408	428.686	59.11	487.80

Source: USAID/E (1987: 14-17); Korn (1986a: 186-87).

a. Includes $4.2 million for ocean transport.

program CRS was operating with its Joint Relief Partners (JRP) (CRS 1986:4). WVRO had also had a presence in Ethiopia since 1971, operating famine relief programs near the southern border with Sudan (WVRO nd:14) prior to distributing PL-480 commodities. Although not a cooperating sponsor, SIM, International had been operating in Ethiopia since 1927 and did distribute some PL-480 food it received from U.S.-based PVOs (such as Lutheran World Relief through its 2,700 churches [SIM, International 1986]). In contrast, among non-PVOs with a previous presence in Ethiopia, the League of Red Cross Societies (LICROSS) and the International Committee of the Red Cross (ICRC) expanded the relatively small Ethiopian Red Cross Society (ERCS) staff to over 600, raising the number of delegates from 18 to 28 in 1985 (ERCS 1985:29).

A second mode of internal adjustment involved transplanting PL-480 programs operated by PVOs into other recipient countries and adding staff from other countries. Rather than building from within, or starting from scratch, this mode transferred operational structures from other contexts to the Ethiopian setting. CARE, for example, imported a nearly ready-made PL-480 program from India to start up its Ethiopian operations, including a staff with expertise, pretested transport and inventory procedures, and proven distribution strategies. Of course, the problems with institutional transplants generally applied to the strategies derived from these structures and adopted for Ethiopian famine relief. Being inexperienced with governments implementing command programs may have hampered CARE's staff.

Finally, a third mode was characterized by building operations from the ground up.[1] In the case of Save the Children Federation (SCF)—which had neither a previous PL-480 program in operation in another context nor other programs in operation in Ethiopia—internal structures for distributing commodities had to be built. This mode probably undercut the operational philosophy of the PVO, at least provisionally, because it was required to rely on other organizations to perform its tasks. SCF did not have cooperating sponsor status during its first year (1985) and had to rely on CARE's expertise and status at the outset. CARE provided staff and logistics for setting up SCF's secondary distribution system—an inventory monitoring and reporting system—and other assistance (see CARE 1986a). SCF had to design a training manual and program for its primary distribution staff (SCF 1985a), whereas more experienced PVOs were able to rely on professional relief workers and general expertise to train Ethiopian nationals in their employ. In this situation, SCF probably had less legitimacy for negotiating with donor and recipient governments. SCF's formal agreement with the PMGSE to "assist the RRC to recruit and pay 10 to 15 teams [of Relief and Rehabilitation Assistants] to enroll families" for food aid eligibility may reflect this weakness. Prior to acquiring cooperating sponsor status, SCF presumably had negotiated indirectly with USAID as well. SCF began operating independently in 1986.

Aspirations—as well as operational bases—of U.S.-based PVOs were especially important for two related reasons. First, these factors were certain to effect the PVOs' cooperation with other agencies and governmental authorities as well as their willingness to evaluate their own performance. Second, distributional aspirations in conjunction with program operations provided a baseline for their performance and their compliance with PMGSE and U.S. initiatives. The PVOs' conception of their "purpose" (including religious, humanitarian, and developmental mandates) provided organizational principles outside the strict control of donor and recipient government agencies.

Contrary to their actual operations, aspirations of U.S.-based PVOs in providing famine relief present little evidence of being tools of either donor or recipient governments. Instead, they expressed the often developmental goals of agencies also in the business of providing disaster relief. A noticeable "chauvinism" marked the outlook and operations of several PVOs. At least one CRS official was convinced that it had the very best program, indeed the only competent program in Ethiopia, directly attributing its ability to operate on a large scale to its presence and operation in Ethiopia since the 1950s (Swenson 1986). Other PVO officials generally expressed the belief that they each had the most humane operational philosophy and, while they were not often heard to disparage their fellow agencies, they believed themselves to be much more humanitarian in function than USAID and were not reluctant to assert this belief.

Among the major U.S.-based PVOs, CRS (in collaboration with its partners in Church Drought Action Africa/Joint Relief Partners [CDAA/JRP])

Merging Donor and Recipient Policies 121

had the most ambitious aspirations, aiming at country-wide distributions, except in Arsi. CDAA/JRP's distributional responsibilities centered on Eritrea and Tigray. CRS distributed food in Hararghe, Gonder, Gojam, and Bale, while its partners (Ethiopian Catholic Secretariat [ECS], Ethiopian Evangelist Church Makane Yesus [EECMY], and Lutheran World Federation [LWF])handled distributions in the other regions. It clearly drew upon its expertise in providing famine relief. During the emergency phase, CRS distributed over 225,000 MT of food, including food distributed through the CDAA/JRP programs, and it had the largest program, distributing 402,000 MT of commodities during the entire FY1983-86 period. As has been noted, CRS was the most vocal in its opposition to USAID—hardly evidence of being a tool of U.S. food power.

In contrast, SCF had the most carefully circumscribed plan, limited to the single awraja of Yifat na Timuga in northern Shoa. Its aspirations were based upon the community development ideals of the organization, rather than any expertise in famine relief. This would have important consequences for its program, which distributed just over 17,000 MT during the emergency phase and over 40,000 MT through the end of FY1986. While its modest size and objectives may have allowed it greater independence from USAID, it was heavily dependent on other organizations.

WVRO was much more ambitious than SCF and nearly as ambitious as CRS partly because of its reputation of being willing and able to work with communist regimes (Bolling 1982). Its previous presence in Ethiopia, as well as its experience with famine relief, accounted for its ability to distribute over 43,000 MT of food during the emergency phase and almost 82,000 MT during the famine period. But shortfalls in its performance of distribution functions, especially in the Food for the North initiative, were partly attributable to reliance on the Ethiopian government for transport.

CARE occupied a middle position among U.S.-based PVOs, limiting its food distribution operations to two administrative regions (Hararghe and Sidamo) and distributing over 33,000 MT during the emergency period and 107,000 MT of food during the FY1984-86 period. But CARE also took over wider functions in the overall U.S. food aid program. It monitored RRC distributions under the bilateral agreement, provided start-up assistance to SCF, and provided at least part of the initiative for the swap component of a seed program for agricultural rehabilitation. On the other hand, CARE was assigned by the RRC to Hararghe, where villagization of the predominantly Oromo population began and proceeded most rapidly, partly because of CARE's support.

Compared to U.S.-based PVOs, the International Committee of the Red Cross (ICRC), as a specialized international organization, distributed over 62,000 MT of PL-480 commodities. Its operations were concentrated in the

122 Reluctant Aid or Aiding the Reluctant?

most sensitive areas (Jansson 1987:47), where its mandate and expertise were tested. However, it was not required to negotiate with the RRC because it operated through the Ethiopian Red Cross.

At one point in time, there were 49 different international agencies in operation (Wolde Giorgis 1987). Despite the wide range of aspirations and operational philosophies of PVOs, conflict between relief agencies was far less than that between donor and recipient government policies. Disagreements over strategy and competition over regions was evident, yet formal and informal coalitions among all kinds of institutional actors were formed,[2] indicating that cooperative arrangements were not precluded.

USAID exercised its aid functions through substantive initiatives both in Washington and in the field, as well as through its budgetary power over the allocation of commodities and funds to PVOs and other organizations. U.S. policy was implemented by USAID through two types of strategic decisions. The first type involved substantive initiatives for relief policy, including those associated with the major role USAID played in PL-480 aid appropriations, commitments, and allocations for Ethiopian famine relief purposes in the first place. Second, USAID had authority to target PL-480 Title II commodities to PVOs and other recipient organizations ("cooperating sponsors") with responsibilities for distribution. USAID's supervision of this aspect of the implementation process was accomplished initially by reviewing and approving plans submitted by recipient organizations for providing famine relief. As required by USAID regulations, Food for Peace (FFP) plans and Annual Estimates of Requirements (AERs) were submitted to the USAID Food for Peace Office. AERs were required to contain estimates of the number and type of recipients, the size of proposed distributions, and the number of feedings per month for a specified number of months (USAID/W 1986a:Ex.E). For USAID, expectations about PVO performance must have been formed on the basis of more general familiarity with PVOs and their operations. PVOs had to meet registration requirements for operating guidelines and accountability standards in order to receive a preference for PL-480 aid (USAID/W 1984b:11). But it is likely that expectations were obtained through past performances (Borton 1986) and—especially in the case of new cooperating sponsors—through negotiations in the field over details of the AER.

Virtually all of the U.S. donations were outside of the RRC system and over 75 percent of PL-480 commodities were donated to U.S.-based PVOs. The bilateral agreement concluded between the U.S. and Ethiopian governments in 1984, accounting for 50,000 MT (only about 6 percent of U.S. donations), was more symbolic than strategic, although it tested the RRC's ability to perform in a normative fashion. Table 5.5 shows the proportion of U.S. aid that was allocated to U.S. PVOs, international organizations, the

RRC, and others during FYs1984-86. Even though they commanded so many resources, PVOs were unable to achieve the measure of independence that many had expected.

Approving requests was a complex process involving negotiations between USAID and cooperating sponsors in Ethiopia as well as in Washington.[3] USAID assessments of requests were based on infrastructural capacities of agencies as well as equity considerations. Targeting cash grants for nonfood aid to PVOs under various budgetary authorities allowed USAID to exercise more direct control. Table 5.5 also shows the allocation of cash grants to PVOs during the emergency and stability phases of the relief operation. Grants covered inland transportation costs incurred by the distribution of commodities through PVO programs. They also provided for nonfood aid needs through USAID's Office of Foreign Disaster Assistance (OFDA). OFDA grants reflected the wide range of nonfood aid required by the relief effort, ranging from blankets and medicine to equipment for drilling wells.

PVO operational independence from donor and recipient governments was less apparent. Most U.S.-based PVOs had programs affected by one or more of the policy objectives of the Ethiopian government. Needs assessment and planning—including assessing transport requirements and availability, distribution facilities, staffing needs, and threats posed by rebellions—undermined the development of normative food distribution operations. Disagreements

TABLE 5.5
Allocation of PL-480 Commodities and Nonfood Aid to Distributing Organizations, FYs1984-86
(Percentages in [ ])

	Food Aid (MT)	Nonfood Aid ($'000)
U.S.-based PVOs	637,483 [77]	50,980.73 [86]
International Organizations	106,237 [13]	7,158.27 [12]
RRC	50,000 [6]	475.00 [.2]
Others	34,688 [4]	491.54 [.8]
Total	828,408	59,105.54

Sources: USAID/E (1987:14-16); Korn (1986a: 186-187).

over needs assessments were rampant between USAID and others involved. To estimate food needs, the UNOEOA issued monthly status reports that were widely relied upon by donors and operational agencies, including USAID until it established its own system. Just as PVOs received their regional assignments from the RRC (Brauman 1986b), so they often relied upon the RRC's assessments of need. U.S.-based PVOs often relied on RRC assessments and rarely conducted their own needs assessments.[4] They also were required to comply with USAID reporting requirements to continue to obtain funding approval for further operational support. Whether the normative dimensions of a food distribution system were dissolved by the contradictory objectives of donor and recipient governments is the most important issue involved. But the policy objectives of the Ethiopian and U.S. governments varied across regions, and RRC and PVO programs reflected this diversity.

Variations in Regional Competence and Undermining the RRC System from Within

Along with Party and central government policy determinants of RRC operations, another overlapping factor responsible for donors' refusal to channel aid through the RRC's food distribution system was the regional variation in the RRC's ability to perform. Throughout the famine, technical and administrative limitations converged with military and political priorities in the regions of rebellion and control.

Particularly during the emergency phase and in the rebel regions, the provision of relief was often tied to the dynamics of nationalism. Ethiopian authorities clearly had a much stronger stake in these developments than did the U.S. government or other bilateral or multilateral donors. Operations of rival relief organizations in areas outside of Ethiopian control, especially in the regions of Eritrea and Tigray, fueled the conflict and competition between authorities and liberation movements. Ethiopian authorities of course refused to admit any lack of control over any area within the country, and through the resettlement and villagization programs attempted to extend control to the south and east while tightening control throughout the countryside.

In response to the Ethiopian performance during the emergency phase, the U.S. government continued to implement its cross-border policy but also concluded a government-to-government agreement with the RRC for bilateral distributions of food aid. USAID also expanded its in-country distribution programs in the northern regions and throughout the country. These programs established a strong U.S. presence for relief operations in Ethiopia and, while falling short of a normative system for distributing food commodities, helped

Merging Donor and Recipient Policies 125

to establish an infrastructure for stabilizing the famine and continuing food aid operations.

Ethiopian Performances

Rival claims to control over territory, particularly in the rebel regions, served as the foundation for claiming responsibilities, developing capabilities, and nurturing organizational motivation for providing aid to persons within the jurisdiction of Ethiopian authorities and rebel organizations. Even in regions with less organized insurgencies such as Hararghe and Wollo, the lack of Ethiopian government control precluded or interrupted food distributions.

Food had clearly not been getting into the northern regions in sufficient amounts to offset increased needs. Allegations that Ethiopian authorities were using food as a military and political weapon accompanied assertions that the Ethiopian government was doing all it could to prevent food from getting into rebel-held areas, using its control of truck fleets, ports, and conscription to restrict food to loyalist areas. Ethiopian government interference with moving commodities into rebel-held areas was coextensive with maintaining military partitions and trenches in Eritrea, and with retaining its control of the major towns in Tigray. Moreover, military actions and bombing operations included villages, civilian populations (Dines 1988:148-149), and even five relief camps in rebel-held parts of Eritrea (Kaplan 1988:69).

Evaluating estimates of the proportion of aid going to government- and rebel-held areas involves one of the most controversial dimensions of the relief effort. Suspicion was cast over the reliability of distributions in government-held areas by reports of the diversion of EEC-donated food to the military, and by the food-for-arms program (Pateman 1988:175). Even though the Ethiopian government never admitted its lack of control over areas in the north, there was broad recognition of the control exercised by the rebel organizations. According to the RRC's commissioner, Tigray was the least accessible region for the RRC, with less than 40 percent of the affected population being within its reach. Only 60 percent of the Eritrean population in need was capable of being reached by the RRC (Wolde Giorgis 1989:237-238).

By mid-1985, estimates of the proportion of people in need being reached by the Ethiopian government were released by the UN and the International Committee of the Red Cross. Apparently, the numbers were accepted by the U.S. government. According to these estimates, 80 percent of the population needing aid in Tigray was being reached by the RRC, while in Eritrea the proportion was 76 percent (U.S. House 1985d:181).

These figures were hotly disputed by the relief arms of the Eritrean and Tigrayan rebel forces, about whom far less is known. But at least one observer with firsthand knowledge has claimed that these relief agencies were "just as efficient as the RRC" (Kaplan 1988:27). The Eritrean Relief Association (ERA) of the EPLF was established in 1975. By 1983, it had gained some amount of cooperation from 120 international agencies and ran 10 camps in Eritrea holding some 65,000 people. It also distributed over 16,000 MT of food to 600,000 people (Pateman 1988:167). In Eritrea in 1984, the ERA claimed that there were over 1 million people in need of assistance in the parts of the region under its administration. Two-thirds of these people were claimed to be in the highlands (Firebrace and Holland 1985:91). As the famine intensified, the number of people affected and the amount of food distributed by ERA increased. The RRC estimated 827,000 to be in need in Eritrea in 1984, notwithstanding the fact that the RRC had no access to most parts of the region (Firebrace and Holland 1985:97). In 1984, with 1.25 million people affected, ERA distributed almost 25,000 MT of food, which increased to 1.75 million people and 88,000 MT in 1985, and then decreased to 1.5 million people and almost 80,000 MT of food distributed in 1986 (Pateman 1988:180). The Relief Society of Tigray (REST), on the other hand, had a later start as the relief wing of the TPLF and had far fewer resources. In late 1985, the TPLF claimed to control 85 percent of Tigray (U.S. House 1985d:208). REST's strategy seemed to emphasize evacuation of civilian populations in Tigray toward Sudan, which diminished its food distributions in the zones of fighting and recruitment for resettlement.

RRC distributions were affected by access to regions, transport conditions, and its own operation. Regional RRC officials also varied in terms of their competence in relief activity, subordination to political and military orientations of the Regional First Secretaries of the WPE, and strategies for controlling the level of insurgency and agricultural conditions in their regions. The worst scenario was exemplified by the forced evacuation of food aid beneficiaries at the Ibnet camp. This incident raised questions about Ethiopian government authority and responsibility for relief operations, the authority of the RRC official in charge apparently having been overrun by military and Party officials. Although former RRC Commissioner Dawit Wolde Giorgis (1987) indicated that the order came from a regional authority as a counterinsurgency move, at the time there was some question as to whether Mengistu knew of the order to require beneficiaries to leave the camp.

RRC activity was focused on the northern regions of origin and the southern regions of resettlement, to the detriment of relief needs in northern areas and elsewhere. In the north, transporting resettlers and food supplies to the regions of resettlement drained the relief effort of these items. Suspicion was cast on RRC distributions by the use of food aid to lure recipients into the resettlement program, which has already been mentioned. More significant in terms of delaying the stabilization of a food distribution system for relief was the program's diversion of resources away from the relief effort. The organizational, transportational, and food resources committed to removing Ethiopians from the north deprived those left behind of resources to survive the famine. Similarly, the threat that resettlement presented to resettlers was seized by the rebel movements, who perhaps saw a threat to their organizations and civilian bases as well. There was a fundamental disagreement between the EPLF and the TPLF on evacuating refugees from their regions to Sudan. The TPLF's response to the famine and resettlement program was to escort people to Sudan, based on its decision in September 1984 to create a "pipeline" to that country (Clark 1986:11). The EPLF disapproved of this strategy, partly because of its potential ruthlessness (Clapham 1988:212).

During the stability period, it was less the diversion or withholding of food that was the defect in Ethiopian performances than it was the use of food to compel the formation of villages. Although the RRC lost its exclusive jurisdiction over villagization in 1984, food distributions in the villagization areas were coordinated in time and place with the villagization process.

U.S. Responses

Even if there had been agreement on levels of need, divergences arose over how to satisfy the needs, in what order, and on whose initiative. In U.S. policy problem assessment, there was a temporary shift from estimating food needs to assessing regime problems associated with the war, famine, and resettlement program, and then to evaluating how to exercise control over food distribution. This is reflected in the September 1984 hearings held by the Senate to assess the "lessons of 1984 and the prospects for 1985" for food aid in Africa (U.S. Senate 1984b). Early on, regime factors associated with several logistical problems in providing famine relief to Ethiopia were identified. According to USAID Administrator McPherson's testimony, confusion over how much food was needed had been created by the lack of cooperation on the part of the PMGSE, which had not performed a crop assessment requested by FAO (McPherson in U.S. Senate 1984a:14, 31). The problems with the PMGSE supported the need felt by some congressmen to "push the Ethiopians" because the Ethiopian government was not committing the necessary resources to transportation (U.S. Senate 1984a:229).

One of the earliest concerns of the United States was the fact that the RRC was using political criteria for establishing operating distribution centers in the north, and failing to allow, much less conduct, food distributions in and around the rebel-held areas in Eritrea and Tigray. Such concerns were buttressed by the relief arms of the rebel movements whose operations came to rival those of the RRC and PVOs in the rebel-held areas.

To counteract PMGSE restrictions on food distribution in the north, U.S.

initiatives included cross-border feeding operations; expansion of feeding programs in the north through the bilateral and PVO distributions, including distribution in rebel-held territory; support of cease-fire arrangements; and, refusal to participate in the resettlement program. In contrast, U.S. policy regarding the villagization program during the stability period was not clearly formulated or implemented.

Cross-border operations. Some of the earliest U.S.-distributed food in Ethiopia was distributed in the north after being transported across the Sudanese border. U.S. involvement in cross-border operations was not strictly controlled by USAID in Ethiopia. CRS reported in March 1984 that over 17,000 MT of food had been moved across the Sudan border in the previous eight months (U.S. Senate 1984a:74). According to the ranking official in the U.S. Embassy in Addis at the time: "In April 1984 AID contributed 5,000 MT of grain to a private organization working with the Relief Society of Tigray and the Eritrean Relief Association [but the] United States took care to have no dealings with REST and ERA" (Korn 1986a:136). USAID made a further grant of 23,000 MT for delivery via Sudan in mid-November 1984, and another substantial allocation that December (Korn 1986a:136-7). Cross-border aid to ERA and REST via LWF—as well as the northern initiative for aiding beneficiaries in rebel-held areas—attempted to remedy the PMGSE's lack of control and failure to provide aid in these areas. These operations were conducted by grants to Lutheran World Relief, Mercy Corps International, and the ICRC; from the Sudan side, only ERA, REST, and ICRC were also operational in Eritrea and Tigray (USAID/W 1987). CARE had been asked to participate in cross-border operations from Sudan but had refused (Smith 1987:37).

The U.S. government's decision not to support REST and ERA after Vice-President Bush and USAID's administrator visited Sudan in March 1985 was apparently based on a misinterpretation of the RRC commissioner's statement regarding the RRC's ability to distribute food in Eritrea and in Tigray (Pateman 1988:178).

The bilateral program. A "sharp change in policy" (*Africa Report* January-February 1985:39-40) resulted in the negotiation and conclusion of a bilateral aid agreement near the end of 1984. Negotiations held in Washington over the bilateral distribution program led to a formal agreement on 2 November 1984. It is interesting to note that there was no public congressional discussion of the bilateral, perhaps a sign of deference to diplomatic initiatives of the administration. Ethiopia was declared a friendly country in 1984 in order to meet legislative requirements so that the bilateral program could be authorized (U.S. G.A.O. 1985b:5). This direct government-to-government agree-

Merging Donor and Recipient Policies 129

ment was concluded after sufficient assurances were received that the food aid would be used in accordance with the overall policy objectives of the United States.

The Department of State-USAID transfer authorization that resulted provided for the donation of 40,000 MT of wheat and their cost of transportation. The authorization was amended to include 10,000 MT of corn-soy-milk and their associated transportation costs.[5] The substance of the agreement included provisions regarding distribution criteria, a Plan of Distribution, and reporting requirements, all in accordance with USAID regulations. The total amount donated was much less than the 600,000 MT claimed by RRC Commissioner Dawit as needed for the period November 1984-October 1985. Food aid commodities donated through the bilateral were to supplement the donation of 80,000 MT already approved by the United States for distribution by NGOs during FY1985.

While a detailed distribution plan was deferred, the broader dimensions of planning were negotiated and agreed to by negotiators for donor and recipient governments. The U.S. donation of 50,000 MT of food aid commodities was supplemented by an agreement to pay 50 percent of the internal transport costs associated with distribution. Funding for the transport costs associated with distribution showed greater give and take between USAID and the RRC. While USAID agreed to "pay 50 percent of the cost of internal transport [i.e., inside Ethiopia], storage and handling of the 50,000 MT bilateral program— [it was] contingent upon the government of Ethiopia [to identify] the remaining 50 percent from its own [nondonor] budgetary resources or other resources." Port arrangements presented another compromise: The RRC announced termination of its previous requirement for advance payment of port charges. A transport plan was to be developed in conjunction with CARE, which was to provide technical assistance (and also discharge monitoring functions).

While primary distribution details were deferred, aid to resettlement was explicitly prohibited. Relief supplies were to be moved to all distribution sites and beneficiaries selected solely on the basis of need (which satisfied USAID concerns about registration requirements).[6] A subsequent meeting between USAID and RRC staff was held on 15 December 1984 to negotiate the remaining terms of the bilateral. The RRC's distribution plan was "accepted in principle" by USAID (U.S. Department of State 1984b). Its coverage is set forth in table 5.6, which shows the regional distribution of food and beneficiaries: Wollo was to receive nearly 25 percent of the food, with the rest being divided among eight other regions. This plan was revised in February 1985 (U.S. Department of State 1985c), indicating further flexibility in the donor-recipient relationship.

CARE's collaboration was obtained to implement the bilateral program's

130 Reluctant Aid or Aiding the Reluctant?

TABLE 5.6
Planned RRC Distributions of PL-480 Commodities Under the Bilateral Agreement

Region	No. of Beneficiaries	No. of DCs	MTs
Wollo	133,173	14	9,988
Shoa	70,053	10	5,254
Hararghe	69,760	3	5,232
Eritrea	66,667	5	5,000
Sidamo	53,654	5	4,024
Gonder	46,667	4	3,502
Tigray	40,027	7	3,000
Bale	26,667	4	2,000
Gamo Gofa	26,667	5	2,000
Total	533,335	57	40,000

Source: RRC Distribution Plan (1985b).

distribution policy. CARE provided assistance both in formulating the plan and in monitoring the distribution of commodities. It had agreed to this role in order to express and demonstrate confidence in the ability of the RRC to perform, but CARE also faithfully furthered U.S. objectives. Despite the discovery of the diversion of 1,000 MT of food to resettlement areas, apparently by mistake, and the redirection of another 7,000 MT to Distribution Centers (DC) in need of food but not in the distribution plan, the RRC's performance under the bilateral was considered "generally good" (USAID/E 1986).

Northern distributions and Food for the North initiative. The inability of the RRC to serve rebel regions also inspired the Food for the North initiative. FFN had developed out of proposals supported by the U.S. government for diminishing, if not resolving, the military conflicts contributing to famine inducement in the northern regions. One proposal for resolving distribution problems in the north was to negotiate a cease-fire agreement. In November 1984, the Democratic Caucus of the House passed a resolution for a ceasefire, calling for a "joint U.S.-Soviet overture to the Mengistu government and the guerrillas" (Shepherd 1985a:8). A major humanitarian food lobby organization—Bread for the World (BFW)—had strongly encouraged the administration to take diplomatic initiatives to stop the war and to obtain a cease-fire in Ethiopia (U.S. Senate 1984a:88).

A second, more realistic proposal was to create some kind of safe passage for food commodities. There was general agreement on the need for safe

Merging Donor and Recipient Policies 131

passage concessions on the part of both the PMGSE and the insurgents (U.S. House 1985a:61, 29, 58). Leland and others had spoken with Ethiopian Foreign Minister Goshu Wolde about safe passage after being declined an audience with Mengistu. In February 1985, Senator Kennedy proposed a "mercy corridor," which McPherson also believed could be effective (U.S. Senate 1985a:38). By July 1985, McPherson had indicated that it appeared that the PMGSE was ready to allow some additional food into the northern regions (U.S. House 1985c:6). This northern initiative was perhaps the relief effort's one diplomatic achievement (see Gill 1986). Negotiations for the FFN initiative had been initiated as early as late 1984 by Congressman Jim Wright. These negotiations involved contacts between Vice-President Bush and Ethiopian Foreign Minister Goshu Wolde. High-level talks between Assistant Secretary of State Chester Crocker, U.S.Ambassador-at-Large Vernon Walters and Ethiopian Foreign Minister Goshu Wolde had been held in October 1984 and, following further negotiations in March 1985, had resulted in an agreement (Korn 1986b:5) which allowed relief agencies to provide increased levels of aid to people in rebel-held areas (Shepherd 1985c:25).

CRS and WVRO were the U.S.-based PVOs involved in the FFN initiative, with responsibilities for food distribution in Eritrea and Tigray, respectively. Expansion of their operations in these regions was considerable, reflected in the increased amounts of food distributed and beneficiaries reached. These levels increased from 12,000 MT of food for 280,000 beneficiaries in FY1985 to proposed levels of nearly 35,000 MT for 500,000-670,000 beneficiaries in FY1986. In Eritrea, CRS's FFN program, which was implemented by the Ethiopian Catholic Secretariat, distributed 5,000 MT to 180,000 beneficiaries from three distribution centers during FY1985. Its FY1986 program expanded to over 25,000 MT (including 4,000 MT carried over from FY1985) to serve 400,000 beneficiaries, often at half rations. In Tigray, WVRO's FY1985 FFN program distributed just over 8,000 MT of food, although its beneficiary base was reduced to 100,000 and its distribution center to one because of the RRC's objection to WVRO's working through the International Committee of the Red Cross. Its FY1986 FFN program was increased to over 12,000 MT to reach 270,000 beneficiaries, but distributions never began at three of the five planned distribution centers. Except for the component in the town of Axum administered by the Ethiopian Orthodox Church, the program was terminated in April 1986 after two WVRO relief workers were killed by the TPLF in Alamata (USAID/E 1986).

Population redistribution. The United States had limited capabilities for reaching the war-torn regions of the north. While the U.S. government was apparently satisfied that its aid was sufficiently segregated from the resettlement program, little concern was officially expressed about the impact of U.S. food aid on the villagization program. This program had the objective of bringing massive numbers of peasants from scattered villages and homesteads throughout the country into collective villages under the control of villagization committees. As late as March 1986, it was admitted that the United States did not have much information on the villagization program, and the director of USAID's Drought Coordination Staff promised to provide a later report on villagization in Ethiopia (U.S. Senate 1986a:41). There was a general understanding that villagization was causing formerly self-sufficient regions to become food deficit regions (U.S. Senate 1986a:11).

In view of the U.S. response to Ethiopian performance on a variety of relief issues, food distribution was a matter of conflict rather than cooperation. Expecting PVOs to mediate the conflicts that arose would have been unrealistic. But their role in merging the RRC system with the U.S.-supported system for food distribution was important. Whether it amounted to imposing normative order over relief operations or involved catering to donor and recipient government commands is less certain.

**Accommodations Between Donor and Recipient Policies:
A Norm-Bearing PVO Distribution System?**

Donor and recipient controls over PVO operations and food distribution were not absolute. Several observers have identified the UNOEO/A as a norm-enforcing organization in the Ethiopian relief effort (e.g., Borton 1986; Jansson 1987). For the distribution of PL-480 commodities, U.S.-based PVOs were most likely to have exerted a normative influence. These agencies distributed over 75 percent of PL-480 food aid and received the bulk of nonfood aid donated by the United States (see table 5.5). Table 5.7 describes the distribution of U.S. food during the emergency and stability periods of the relief effort, estimating the amounts of food distributed in the northern regions of Eritrea and Tigray and in the non-northern regions. It is estimated that approximately one-third of U.S.-donated food distributed in Ethiopia (i.e., not including cross-border aid) went to the northern regions of Eritrea and Tigray, although that proportion probably decreased somewhat during the stability phase.

Because of the strong role of the PVOs, donor and recipient government agencies rarely confronted each other directly, although ideological skirmishes were frequent. Relations between USAID and RRC were "tense" at times—USAID restrictions and auditing requirements irritated the RRC while problems with visas caused irritation for USAID (Jansson 1987:21). In some areas, U.S. famine relief programs served as a challenge to Ethiopian government policy; in others they reinforced that policy; while in yet others they may have served to temper the regime's approach.

Merging Donor and Recipient Policies 133

TABLE 5.7
Estimated Amounts of U.S. Food Distributed in Northern and Non-Northern Regions by Phase of Relief

	Emergency Phase		Stability Phase	
	Northern	Non-Northern	Northern	Non-Northern
PVO-Program				
CARE		33,008		74,000
WVRO-Regular		35,120		31,464
WVRO-FFN	8,100		7,174	
SCF		17,401		23,000
CRS-Regular [a]	1,000	10,869	1,200	11,583
CRS-Emergency	27,038	13,521 [b]		
CRS-FFN	9,000		27,424	
CRS-MC		4,654		4,654
CDAA/JRP [c]	54,000	107,194	35,612	71,223
ICRC [d]	46,154		13,500	
LICROSS		11,610		10,000
RRC [e]	10,000	40,000		
WFP [f]	973	9,000		
EOC [g]			4,463	
FHI				6,960
Totals	156,265	282,377	89,373	232,884

Source: USAID/E (1986)

a. Proportion for FY1985 extrapolated to FY1986.
b. Based on estimate of two-thirds going to northern regions.
c. Based on average of one-third going to northern regions roughly estimated from distribution details.
d. All distributed in conflict areas, including Wollo, Gonder and Hararghe.
e. Based on proportions given in bilateral distribution plan for original 40,000 MT.
f. Distributed through RRC; proportion derived from bilateral distribution plan.
g. All food assumed to have been distributed in northern regions.

Even though the U.S. government had a strong interest in retaining some control over these commodities donated for relief, PVOs provided the potentially normative patterns for U.S. food aid distribution in Ethiopia. Donors like the United States asserted their own objectives for famine relief, earmarking food for specific regions and attempting to circumvent PMGSE controls. U.S. policy formation was largely directed toward retaining some control over food and nonfood aid donated to the relief effort, especially at the level of primary distribution where Ethiopian government controls had the most potential for abuse. Interaction with U.S. famine relief operations had a moderating effect on the RRC's relief operations and contributed to a substantial merging of dual food distribution systems in many parts of the country.

While international standards and practices played important roles in the relief operation, norms of the PVO community certainly do not provide a complete explanation for the operation of food distribution. Being the special province of PVOs, logistics provided them with some faith that the techniques of relief would adequately circumvent efforts to interfere with relief operations. Due in part to their unwillingness to make hard "political" decisions, representatives of these agencies had an idealistic faith that apolitical activities engaged in under the aegis of humanitarianism would result in the best of all possible futures for Ethiopian beneficiaries of food aid programs.

Whether PVO activities exercised a normative effect depends on whether they diminished the potential conflict between U.S. government and PMGSE objectives. PVOs were certainly neither powerless nor totally responsive to donor or recipient government commands and initiatives, in many ways determining their own course of action. When recipient and donor governments are in disagreement over the fundamentals of relief and development—as was the case for the U.S. and Ethiopian governments—the stress on PVOs involved in famine relief escalates. Controversial host government action tests the loyalty and responsiveness of PVOs to both donor and recipient governments, their respective headquarters, and the individual beneficiaries of their programs. The expectation that PVOs would exercise independent authority was one functionalist justification for the division of labor between USAID and PVOs in food distribution. In Ethiopia, conflict over PVO operations resulting from competition between USAID and the RRC for control of or influence over PVOs was noticeable and particularly disruptive from a normative standpoint. Such arrangements created new authority and accountability problems, which themselves became a source of conflict between donor and recipient governments.

Clearly, it is inaccurate to conclude that PVOs were mere agents of U.S. policy. A deep conflict arose between USAID and CRS, which is peculiar since CRS was the distributor of by far the largest amounts of PL-480 food commodities, and USAID had originally wanted all PL-480 commodities to be distributed through the CRS coalition of agencies, but this desire for a monolithic structure was successfully resisted. CRS had the largest PL-480 program, yet it was the PVO most outspoken in its criticism of U.S. policy. Disagreements over the level of the Ethiopian food deficit led to an early dispute between the two: In CRS's view, USAID had seriously underestimated the amount of food needed; CRS's estimate was closer to the RRC estimate and was based on an independent assessment performed by a private firm (Tekul 1986; Dwyer 1986; see also INTERTECT 1986). In many ways, CRS appeared sentimentally closer to the PMGSE and RRC than to the United

Merging Donor and Recipient Policies 135

States and USAID. A memo from a ranking CRS official in Addis to another referred to the author of this book as someone who might be gotten to "toe our [CRS's] line against [US]AID."

USAID controls over PVOs seem to have been exercised to minimize dilution of the requirements of regulations for PL-480 programs rather than to maximize power accomplishments based on political objectives. A sense of modesty prevailed in USAID, which had a technical rather than a political agenda for requiring conformance with regulations. Whether the planning documents of PVOs were normative instruments or something quite less is important to assessing the autonomy of PVOs vis-a-vis USAID. USAID purported to control PVOs by reviewing their proposals for aid. While the contents of PVO plans conformed to requirements, there was a great deal of variation among them in terms of the amount of detail, definitiveness of distribution strategy, overall indicators of future performance, and preparation for likely pitfalls. CRS's plan for FY1986 included a request for 225,743 MT of PL-480 commodities, to be distributed to well over 1.5 million recipients (CRS 1986). According to the supporting documentation for SCF's FY1986 request for 42,000 MT, food was to be distributed to beneficiaries at 280 Distribution Centers (DCs), each serving an average of 250 families (SCF 1985c). WVRO's plan for FY1986 was to distribute 130,000 MT of U.S. food (WVRO 1986a). In fact, it appears that plans provided only the broadest contours of PVO-anticipated operations, and provided little *in themselves* as a base for USAID predictions of performance.

Loose delegation was USAID's strategy, apparent from its toleration of diversity in PVO operations. Gaps in USAID mechanisms for control were evident in PVO plans and operational philosophies. The bifurcation of USAID and PVO roles in terms of diplomatic and technical areas was evident in PVO ideology as well as that of USAID. The head of one PVO portrayed their role as including responsibility for assuring that food aid programs were "technically sound" and carefully planned (U.S. House 1984a:103). USAID generally did not recognize a PVO role in planning, even though PVOs asserted the desire for one (Borton 1986:vii-viii). But, by excluding them from such roles, PVOs were also freed to pursue their own objectives and those of other donors in the course of distributing U.S. food aid commodities.

Whether Ethiopian authorities were able to turn the resulting dilution of U.S. policy objectives to their advantage depended in part on the character of PVO initiatives. RRC control over U.S.-based PVOs was considerable, and was problematic for USAID when it created conflicts between PVOs and USAID. RRC influence is undeniable because PVOs were required to capitulate somewhat to the demands of the host government and its agencies in order for their program to survive. The fact that some U.S.-based PVOs were able to delay entering into formal agreements with the PMGSE until late 1985

(USAID/E 1987:7) indicates a looseness in recipient government control over the planning function. Similarly, implementation of RRC restrictions on expatriate staff (RRC 1985b) was largely unsuccessful, as some PVOs were able to maintain large expatriate staffs in headquarters and in the field. CRS and WVRO had expatriate staffs of 15 and 125 respectively (*Christian Science Monitor* 5 October 1985). SCF's program highlighted training of staff to carry on without expatriates. CARE seems to have had the smallest per beneficiary staff at the country headquarters level. The RRC had a great impact on PVO activities, providing estimates of need (partly based on its Early Warning System), approving programs and distribution sites for PVOs in various regions, and, on at least a few occasions, determining where PVOs were to distribute commodities. It also set restrictions on PVOs and had major involvements in transport, logistics, and dispatching commodities for distribution. The RRC exercised control over PVO entry and areas of operation, staffing and movement of staff, distribution of commodities through ports, rail and road, and screening of beneficiaries in many regions. Although the RRC was able to relieve some of the planning burden of PVOs by supporting the processing of visas and supplying travel permits (see CRS 1986:13), it also added burdens by creating restrictions.

For the most part, U.S.-based PVOs were adept at conforming to RRC requirements. Contrary to several other relief agencies, U.S.-based PVOs avoided being subjected to criticism or having programs terminated over conflicts with the RRC and PMGSE. Medicins Sans Frontiers' program was terminated after it had loudly voiced its objections to the resettlement program,[7] and it acquired a pariah status among PVOs (Jansson 1987:77). Criticism of the RRC was rarely aired by PVOs. No doubt many feared PMGSE retaliation. But there was an ideological sympathy with the RRC among many. PVOs with secure bases in Ethiopian society or in political sympathy with the recipient government may have had increased operational independence from the donor government, or have been more resistant to Ethiopian government controls. However, the Christian Relief and Development Association (CRDA), an Ethiopia-based consortium of relief and development agencies, was very close to the RRC, some believing that it was too close (Goyder 1986).

The converse of this agility of U.S.-based PVOs was of course that they would be poor agents of U.S. substantive policy interests when push came to shove. Virtually all PVOs declared Ethiopian development to be one of their own objectives or a mandate from other donors—a direct conflict with U.S. policy. U.S.-based PVOs did not appear to have pushed for moderation of the PMGSE's resettlement and villagization policies, which at the very least had contributed to the famine and created some obstacles to relief efforts. One

Merging Donor and Recipient Policies 137

WVRO official reported: "We've put years into Ethiopia. We cannot in good conscience sacrifice all that work to make a grand political point. We are guests of that [PMGSE] government and our entire program rests upon their approval" (Keating 1986:77). While USAID was in sympathy with the cautious posture of PVOs vis-a-vis the Ethiopian authorities, the agency also regretted their failure to strongly advocate moderation (McPherson in U.S. House 1985a:191).

Attributing independence to PVO operations would be as mistaken as viewing them as dependent organizations. Overall, it appears that PVOs fulfilled a diplomatic function in their food distribution strategies instead of establishing a strictly normative system. They performed a power broker function in which they traded strategic advantages between donor and recipient governments. This is evident from the conflict over resettlement aid and the setting of relief criteria, which were the most volatile questions in food distribution operations. Prohibition of U.S. aid to the resettlement process was one of the firmest targets of U.S. policy, and there is some evidence that the U.S. government exercised some leverage over other donors (Cuny 1989). It is almost certain that USAID opposition to the resettlement program powered PVO opposition to it as well. One observer argued that this was possible because of PVO dependence on U.S. commodities (Jansson 1987:67), but U.S.-based PVOs generally attempted to stay clear of the resettlement program. Those operating in the northern regions of origin (especially CRS and WVRO) had agendas based on traditional notions of relief directed toward providing food to those in need and rehabilitating regional food systems, which made the concept of donor restriction at least theoretically acceptable to them. Even so, they appear to have been somewhat implicated in the program by relieving Ethiopian authorities of relief responsibilities. The CRDA had some operations in resettlement regions in the southwest, and U.S. aid also supported PVO operations in areas targeted for villagization.

Conflict over setting criteria for relief aid at the regional level was evident in the cross-border operations and the FFN initiative, and was largely a reaction to the Ethiopian government's deficiencies. Cross-border aid to ERA and REST via LWF, and the northern initiative for aiding beneficiaries in rebel-held areas, attempted to remedy the PMGSE's lack of control and failure to provide aid in those areas. While CARE refused to participate in cross-border operations, apparently out of fear of sacrificing its in-country food distribution program, the FFN initiative involving CRS and WVRO was directed toward balancing eligibility requirements to include people in rebel-held areas.

At the individual level, conflicts over beneficiary status intensified as the

138   Reluctant Aid or Aiding the Reluctant?

relief operation was stabilized. PVOs, like USAID and often the RRC as well, were reactive agents unable to take a policy command role, instead being forced to respond to Ethiopian government policies and Party initiatives. Ethiopian authorities were able to consolidate their control over food distribution and institution building.

Notes

1. Borton (1986:2) notes that several U.S.-based agencies were built specifically for the African famine relief effort. SCF's Title II program was built for the Ethiopian effort.
2. For example, the CRDA consortium, the CDAA/JRP coalition headed by CRS, and the relationships between ICRC/LICROSS and the ERCS.
3. The process of drafting plans and negotiating operational details between PVOs and USAID occurred both in Washington and in Addis Ababa. Although the U.S. G.A.O. (1985:11-12) report indicates that requests for emergency food aid were developed in the recipient country, a fair amount of input was provided by headquarters in the U.S. Proposals were frequently sent directly to Washington, then pouched to Addis Ababa for the necessary USAID/E endorsement (U.S. House 1985a:173). Correspondence between USAID/W and a PVO concerning its allocation of seed for the seed-swap program reflects the dialectic involved (see USAID/W 1986b).
4. CARE performed an initial survey of eight awrajas in Hararghe prior to setting up operations (Narula 1986). SCF performed a joint assessment with RRC before accepting assignment to Yifat na Timuga in Shoa (SCF 1986a). CRS commissioned an independent assessment of the food situation in Ethiopia in December 1985 (see INTERTECT 1986).
5. The wheat was valued at $6.68 million and transportation costs estimated to be US$3.4 million; the corn-soy-milk was valued at $3 million, and the transportation costs estimated to be an additional $1.55 million. AID No. 663-XXX-000-5640, dated 11 December 1984, was amended by Amendment No. 1 to AID No. 663-XXX-000-5640 dated 27 February 1985.
6. The preceding description of the bilateral is based upon USAID/W (1984a).
7. Two versions of the events leading to the termination of MSF's program have been recited. One is that it was "thrown out" by the Ethiopian government; the other is that it withdrew (Clay 1989:264). It is interesting to note that the reputation and operations of MSF in famine relief have been questioned, and U.S.-based PVOs reacted strongly against MSF (see, for example, Jansson 1987:26, 77).

6

Stabilization of Relief: Consolidation of Ethiopian Control and Collaboration of Donors in Food Distribution and Development (1985-1986)

By the end of 1985, relief efforts had become considerably stabilized. Food aid continued to be required in order to forestall famine conditions, but famine deaths had slowed significantly as the capacity for distributing aid had become firmly established. PVO operations continued to support the RRC system for distributing food; tertiary and secondary distribution mechanisms were coordinated with the assistance of UN organizations.

While the consolidation of food distribution systems was substantially responsible for the stabilization of relief operations, institutional conflict persisted between donor and recipient governments and PVOs. This was most evident in the criteria adopted for beneficiary status and the principles by which primary distribution was accomplished. The achievement of normative order was partially displaced by political and military agendas of the Ethiopian government. A similar dynamic prevailed over the institution-building efforts undertaken by Ethiopian authorities and PVOs. U.S.-based PVOs were unable to resist the consolidation of control by Party authorities and Peasant Associations that had been accomplished by the villagization program that was implemented throughout the countryside.

Stability in Food Aid Needs and Relief Operations

The emergency phase of the famine wore to an end as a result of two factors: Levels of need diminished as a result of relaxed procurements and improved harvests, and operating agencies established reliable mechanisms for distributing food to people in need. As reflected in table 6.1, RRC estimates of the number of people affected by serious food shortages declined in all regions between 1985 and 1986 except in Gamo Gofa, Kaffa, Ilubabor, Welega, and Hararghe. Significantly, regions with increased numbers of people in need were all located in the resettlement areas in the southeast, except Hararghe, which was the first region to experience widespread villagization. Death rates due to famine had significantly declined, although they had not been eliminated.

Stability in tertiary and secondary distribution was achieved by around mid-1985 (cf. Kaplan 1988:27), reflected in the pattern of food distribution shown in table 6.2. Stable amounts of food distributed and beneficiaries reached (at the average rate of over 60,000 MT and nearly 5 million

TABLE 6.1
Persons Affected by Serious Food Shortages, 1985-86, and Changes from Previous Years
(in '000)

	1985	1986	Percent Change 1985-86
Arsi	82	20	-310
Bale	193	99	-95
Eritrea	827	650	-27
Gamo Gofa	106	152	43
Gojam	76	0	-
Gonder	363	341	-6
Hararghe	875	1520	74
Ilubabor	20	102	410
Kaffa	58	90	55
Shoa	852	709	-20
Sidamo	533	442	-21
Tigray	1400	1000	-40
Welega	23	116	404
Wollo	2587	1547	-67
Total	7995	6788	-18

Sources: RRC (1985d); USAID/E (1987:1) for 1986 and Eritrea, 1984 and 1985.

TABLE 6.2
Monthly Food Distributions During the Stability Phase, 1986

	Food Distributed (MT)	Beneficiaries Reached
January	37,800	3,776,000
February	41,100	4,110,000
March	45,800	4,560,000
April	44,600	4,457,000
May	50,300	4,775,000
June	63,300	5,570,000
July [a]	72,500	4,491,000
August [a]	78,000	6,488,000
September [a]	81,500	7,120,000
October [a]	72,500	4,491,000
November [a]	72,500	4,491,000
December [a]	61,500	5,570,000
Total	721,400	59,899,000
1986 Monthly Average	60,117	4,992,000

Source: USAID/E 1986.

a. Estimated from USAID's estimates.

beneficiaries per month) indicate that control over the distribution systems had been acquired.

But the transition from the emergency to the stability phase posed new challenges for USAID, the RRC, and PVOs. They were most apparent in changes in the *type* of aid required, donated, and distributed between 1984 and 1986. A change in the proportion of nonfood aid to food aid was evident, contributing to the transition from emergency to rehabilitation program operations. In the earlier period, nonfood aid had been associated with emergency needs, and the overriding concern was to move food inland from the ports. In the later period, it was associated with rehabilitation, and the concern regarding criteria for beneficiary status at the primary distribution level became more critical. Although not going so far as to encourage development—even after the Hickenlooper claims had been settled—policy changes by USAID and minimization of Brooke Amendment restrictions permitted a wide range of rehabilitation activities.

For U.S.-based PVOs to make this transition smoothly depended upon their ability to adapt operations to the changed field conditions and to adopt new strategies for responding to USAID's initiatives. The contrasting amounts

TABLE 6.3
Shares of U.S. Food Aid and Nonfood Aid to Ethiopia, FYs1985 and 1986
($'000)

	FY1985	FY1986
Food Aid	249.1	156.5
Nonfood Aid	44.0	15.1
of which for Rehabilitation	.5	8.2
Total	293.1	171.6

Source: USAID/E (1987:14-17).

of food and nonfood aid allocated to U.S.-based PVOs and international organizations are set out in table 6.3. Although nonfood aid is not a larger proportion of total aid, more than one-half of nonfood aid during FY1986 was for agricultural rehabilitation; during FY1985, nearly all nonfood aid was for activities relating to food transport.

In the case of the RRC, a dramatic decrease in the amount of direct food donations likewise required changes in program operations. Food aid donated directly to the RRC for distribution declined significantly between 1985 and 1986, from 365,000 MT to 273,000 MT. Nonfood aid donated to the RRC declined even more dramatically, from $49 million in 1985 to $8 million in 1986 (USAID/E 1987:38-39).

Institution-building policies and programs contributed to the achievement of stability in relief operations and provided the foundation for rehabilitation activities and developmental programs. With the RRC's developmental mandate being restricted, Party controls over PVOs were intensified. It was one thing to allow PVOs some autonomy in distributing food for relief purposes, but to allow them to engage in rehabilitation and development activities without Party supervision could have challenged Party authority and provided an opening for nonrevolutionary institutions to develop.

Expansion of PVO Operations

Even though U.S. government donations of food aid commodities and nonfood aid were channelled primarily through PVOs and international relief agencies, initially at least the injection of external aid also served to strengthen RRC programs. Despite WPE and PMGSE efforts to control the overall direction of the relief effort, the growth in RRC staff and its resistance to retrenchment indicate that the RRC likewise acquired some operational

Stabilization of Relief 143

authority and autonomy.

Stabilizing the movement of commodities from donors to the recipient country and then to beneficiaries at food Distribution Centers (DCs) depended very much on strengthening the RRC mandate. Developing a reliable and efficient system for moving relief commodities from ports inland was a major factor in the transition from the emergency to the stability phases in relief. This system involved a fairly clear division of labor between donor and recipient governments at the tertiary and secondary levels of distribution. Logistically, tertiary distribution required that donors or their agents (e.g., PVOs) schedule food shipments, and that the recipient government prepare for the arrival of food aid commodities.

Commodity movement at the tertiary level—especially loading at donor ports and discharge at recipient ports—is of major significance. The leverage rhetoric used by many observers and commentators implying that donors used food power by simply refusing to ship food is far too simplistic. Coordinating procurement and shipping operations in donor countries with the food needs in recipient nations involves a complex administrative machinery. On the loading side, a wide range of administrative problems were identified by a U.S. G.A.O. (1986) study, despite which the U.S. program was determined to have performed quite well. The constraints on cargo capacity and the discharge features of ships heightened problems with logistical arrangements at the ports. Actual performance, and the fact that the United States diverted shipments *to* Ethiopia (U.S. G.A.O. 1986:13), renders untenable the assertion that the United States used its position as a food donor nation in a coercive fashion.

On the discharge side, "port discharge rates, seasonal constraints, [and] competition for berths" were critical performance factors (U.S. House 1985c:109). Four ports were utilized by U.S.-based PVOs (in addition to some air transport in the crisis period): Assab and Massawa in the region of Eritrea, Djibouti in the Republic of Djibouti, and Mombassa in Kenya. The PMGSE controlled the ports of Massawa and Assab through its Maritime Transit Authority, and a PMGSE planning committee supervised daily operation of the ports (CRS 1986:24). But there was little indication that the PMGSE's control of Assab and Massawa led to total control of all food aid shipments. At other ports, especially Djibouti, PMGSE control was unlikely, partly because of a lack of administrative power.[1] Numerous violations of normative principles, such as the United Nations Institute for Training and Research (UNITAR) (1982) rule requiring waiver of commercial documentation requirements and duties for relief shipments, were reported. Other PMGSE misconduct at ports included the assessment of duties on relief shipments and giving priority to nonrelief items such as cement and military equipment. There were reports of delay on the rail from Djibouti as well as

144 Reluctant Aid or Aiding the Reluctant?

Ethiopian discouragement of using ports other than Assab (which may have been due to PMGSE interest in using Assab, which had some of the highest port charges in the world).

Disputes over the ability of the Ethiopian government to absorb aid commodities often confused estimates of need levels with discharge capacities. Attributing delays or shortfalls in foreign donations to absorptive capacity constraints alone is far from satisfactory; but donors were reluctant to ship food without assurances that it would be quickly and properly discharged and not be wasted in the ports or diverted from relief purposes. Port congestion did create a considerable obstacle to relief. Bottlenecks at the ports of arrival were probably the largest aggregate determinants of shortfalls in flows of commodities inland, especially after food began to arrive in massive quantities at ports around January 1985. In June 1985 there were again reports of extensive congestion at Djibouti (Korn 1986a:139).

Eventually, UN coordination of shipment arrivals was imposed. This required concessions on the part of donor and recipient governments, as well as the UN Disaster Relief Organization (UNDRO) and World Food Programme (WFP), whom many had expected to take over the task. The UN Office for Emergency Operations in Africa (UNOEO/A) came closest to being a "relief dictator" in being able to impose a normative system on food transport.[2] Headed by the administrator of the UN Development Program, its operations in Ethiopia (UNOEO/E) were commanded by Assistant Secretary General Jansson, who had directed UNICEF's operations in Kampuchea. Its aim was to "mobilize" relief efforts with a "minimum of bureaucracy" (*UN Chronicle* 1985:4). It took over the other UN organizations and displaced UNDRO (Franklin 1986), filling a vacuum created partly by bureaucratic in-fighting among UN organizations (Gill 1986). UNOEO/E has generally been credited with a very good performance (Borton 1986:9-15). Its success may be measured by the steady pattern of U.S. government food arrivals shown in table 6.4. There was a surge in arrivals after January 1985 and steady rates thereafter in the pattern of deliveries to Ethiopia. This system was either consistent with donor and recipient governments' objectives, or had a normative status immune to their objections.

Again, flexibility and UN coordination rather than recipient or donor government determinism prevailed in patterning secondary distribution. The Ethiopian government had the clear advantage in controlling commodity dispositions in the process of moving food from ports to points of primary distribution. Moving commodities from ports inland to points of further distribution involved a host of constraints localized in the social structure of the recipient nation and the activities of PVOs operating there. Donors were left with attempts to influence the process in the field through their own initiatives and those of their operating agencies. U.S.-based PVOs adopted a variety of strategies for moving U.S. commodities to DCs, combining several means of transport and warehousing facilities for the purpose, including airlifts and more traditional land-based transport. Airlifting food in the northeast during the crisis period was a "very substantial operation" covering several months (U.S. House 1985e:13). Two major airlifts—Operations Tesfa and St. Bernard—took place in the early months of 1985 (Brandenburg 1986:401). Two schools of thought on food airlifts diverged: on the one hand, on cost considerations and the relative inefficiency of airlifts; on the other hand, on the fact that encouraging airlifts may have reduced incentives to forge more effective land transport systems (Kirch 1986). While the amount of food airlifted to beneficiaries was small in proportion to total aid, it was essential for relieving famine in some of the nearly inaccessible highland areas in the north and east. Coordination between food and nonfood aid was also necessary. For example, airlifting food to Makelle after it had been cut off from the port of Massawa by clashes between Ethiopian and rebel forces along the road (The White House 1984) was facilitated by a $100,000 grant to TransAmerica. Airlifts involved a fair amount of international cooperation as Soviet, British, and German planes were used to deliver food of the U.S. government and other donors.

TABLE 6.4
Arrival of U.S.-Donated Food in Ethiopia, 1985-86 (in MTs)

Month	Year	
	1985	1986
January	21,004	61,917
February	61,698	46,344
March	21,587	4,201
April	15,501	25,404
May	49,714	38,968
June	30,423	22,722
July	47,360	17,410
August	67,676	51,052
September	26,196	5,110
October	52,584	33,473
November	34,872	5,064
December	30,804	-
Total	459,419	311,665
Monthly Average	38,285	25,972

Source: USAID(1987: 82-83)

146   Reluctant Aid or Aiding the Reluctant?

Moving commodities over land also invoked a wide range of PVO resources and strategies. Of the 783,000 MT of U.S.-donated food—including private donors—to arrive for distribution in Ethiopia during 1984-86, 379,000 MT arrived in Assab (48 percent), 224,000 MT in Massawa (29 percent), 173,000 MT in Djibouti (22 percent), and 7,000 MT in Mombassa (1 percent). The flow of food inland from the ports is difficult to estimate. PVOs used three major supply lines from these ports to their DCs: (1) the main system from Assab port to warehouses in Dessie, Kombolcha, and Nazareth; (2) from Massawa port through Asmara; and (3) from Djibouti port through Hararghe, with the option of forwarding food to Nazareth (cf. USAID/E 1987:29). CARE also transported food for its Sidamo program by truck from the port of Mombassa in Kenya. Table 6.5 shows the food arrivals of four U.S.-based PVOs (CARE, CRS, WVRO, and SCF) by port, and estimates of the amount of food delivered to northern and non-northern regions. These estimates are based on the secondary distribution operations of these PVOs. For its Hararghe operations, CARE moved food from Djibouti port up the rail to Dire Dawa and occasionally other railheads toward Addis. CARE also used the port of Mombassa in Kenya for its Sidamo program (for which it received a special grant from USAID to cover transportation costs). CRS shipped food by rail from Djibouti to Dire Dawa, Nazareth, and Addis. From Massawa, commodities were transported inland by the Ethiopian Marine Transit and Service Corporation (MTSC) to Asmara, and then further inland. From Assab, CRS food was also transported by truck into Wollo. WVRO also used all three ports and inland transport systems. SCF food arrived in Assab and was transported by truck to Effeson in Shoa.

Military involvement in secondary distribution was controversial. In view of the military administration in Ethiopia, it might have been beneficial for the military to have been more heavily involved in moving commodities away from ports, but the threat of greater diversion of food away from the civilian sector prohibited donor approval of such involvement. Suspicions aroused by military involvement and PMGSE priorities focussed substantial diplomatic resources on the question. RRC Commissioner Dawit's concerns about the use of military trucks for transport (USAID/W 1984a) indicate that the issue was not a donor smokescreen. Much of this concern was justified, partly because of findings that in some circumstances the PMGSE paid "its armed forces in food, which the soldiers [sold] to Sudanese merchants, who in turn [sold] it to the relief agencies" (*Africa Report* March-April 1985). A proposal of the U.S. Department of Defense to use U.S. Air Force planes to transport food and supplies was vetoed, largely because of USAID opposition (*New York Times* 9 November 1984).

Acquiring trucks, facilities, and equipment was probably the greatest challenge to PVOs that were transporting food inland to points of primary

Stabilization of Relief 147

distribution. Prerequisites ranged from trucks and warehouses to field offices[3] and housing for staff. During the stability period, PVOs had at least 850 trucks at their disposal, largely supplied by the U.S. government (cf. USAID/E 1987:84). According to its FY1986 plan, CRS and CDAA/JRP in 1986 had 52 operational trucks and expected to lease 60 additional ones (CRS 1986:26). WVRO operated 24 trucks in late 1984 (WVRO 1985a) and 60 in 1985 with plans to lease more (WVRO 1986). SCF registered 21 trucks with trailers plus 30 smaller trucks (SCF 1986). CARE had a total of 38 long-haul trucks. In addition, USAID donated a fleet of 70, CRDA had a fleet 52 which it rotated among PVOs, and the WFP's Transport Operation in Ethiopia (UNWTOE) had a fleet of 250 vehicles as of late 1985. In contrast, variations in the commitment of the PMGSE's fleet of trucks ranged over time from low to high and back to low. During 1983, the RRC had a fleet of 117 trucks for relief transport while the PMGSE registered a total fleet of 6,000 for other purposes (Barnes 1985:7); the RRC fleet reached a high of 999 trucks

TABLE 6.5
Port of Arrival of U.S.-Based PVOs' Food Commodities and Estimate of Regional Distribution (in MT)

PVO	Port of Arrival			Regional Distribution (Estimated)	
	Assab	Massawa	Djibouti	Northern	Non-Northern
CDAA/JRP	197,147				197,147
SCF	33,806				33,806
WVRO	51,063				51,063
Others	96,700			23,602	73,098
CDAA/JRP		141,789		141,789	
WVRO		20,917		20,917	
Others		61,619		61,619	
CARE			102,447 [a]		102,447
CDAA/JRP			46,113		46,113
WVRO			23,120		23,120
Others			7,964	7,964	
Total	378,716	224,325	179,644	255,891	526,794

Source: Estimated from WFP data reported in USAID/E (1987:82-83).

a. Includes 6,784 MT arriving in Mombassa distributed in Sidamo.

148 Reluctant Aid or Aiding the Reluctant?

(USAID/E 1987:84). PMGSE's nondeployment of trucks for relief was manifested by the transport of troops and military equipment to war fronts, training centers, and other destinations instead.[4]

Financial responsibility for transporting commodities raised conflicts between donor and recipient governments, partly because of disagreement over their final disposition. In 1985, USAID had planned to rent 100 trucks from Kenya to move commodities. It was unable to obtain permission from the PMGSE, either because the Ethiopian government wanted money donated instead or because it objected to foreign control of the fleet (U.S. House 1985c:5-6). Despite these and subsequent complications, U.S. officials were willing to admit that Hickenlooper Amendment controversies had also delayed getting the U.S. truck fleet into Ethiopia (Gordon 1986). But this delay was also due to an Ethiopian law providing that trucks used in the relief effort were not to leave the country after the effort wound up but were to become the property of the Ethiopian government, in direct violation of legislative guidelines for U.S. aid. USAID was able to subterfuge this PMGSE policy for reversion of its fleet of trucks to the PMGSE after relief operations had been terminated by donating them to the UN, which had reached an agreement with the PMGSE that excepted its fleet from this policy. USAID then donated a fleet of 150 trucks to the UNWTOE, which, in addition to port coordination, controlled a fleet of trucks for allocation to operating PVOs.

Conflicts between the U.S. government and operating agencies also arose over financial responsibilities for transporting food. The United States reimbursed PVOs for inland transport costs incurred through the distribution of PL-480 commodities. Transport funding rules may have reflected a pragmatic recognition that PVOs are unlikely to distribute commodities unless transport costs are also provided for. Commodity and transport cost decisions tended to be consistent and were approved jointly by OFDA and FFP. In one instance, the manager of CARE's East Africa programs indicated that without transport money, CARE might distribute food donated by the Canadian government rather than PL-480 commodities. USAID received some criticism because it did not have a consistent rule for reimbursing transportation costs during 1985 (Clark 1986), preferring to remain flexible until a 50 percent rule was adopted for 1986 (USAID/E 1987:13). CRS and USAID came to blows over the change in USAID policy for transport cost reimbursements in FY1986. It was asserted by CRS that changing from a 100 percent reimbursement system to 50 percent for financing inland transport for PL-480 commodities would "eat up" the increased donations CRS had obtained from charitable contributions (U.S. House 1985c:59). This change of budgetary procedure also raised the wrath of other critics. Staff of the House Select Committee on Hunger (Clark 1986) argued that it was an attempt of USAID to "enforce the moral-

Stabilization of Relief 149

ity" of PVOs. But USAID also provided grants to PVOs and other organizations to cover many of the nonfood aid costs that were committed through OFDA. OFDA grants reflected the wide range of nonfood aid required by famine relief efforts, ranging from blankets and medicine to equipment for wells. The fact that no complaints were made about nontransport grants subverts suggestions that USAID was partial in making them or in reimbursing inland transport costs.

An adequate system for stocking warehouses was essential to support primary distribution. CARE, for example, had a shortage of food for distribution after January 1986 attributable to shortfalls in commodity deliveries; but stocks on hand and commodity loans from other PVOs prevented the nutritional slide from being too severe (Dunn 1986). Warehousing facilities were critical links in distribution, as the potential for recipient government control over commodity movement was greater at points of temporary storage and primary distribution. Minimal problems were reported at this level, however, partly because local officials controlled many of the warehouses and partly because donor pressure doubtless encouraged the recipient government to make facilities available. There is some evidence that negotiating over warehouses was primarily a field level activity engaged in by field officers of operating agencies (cf. Janardanan 1986).

Warehousing facilities acquired for use by U.S.-based PVOs varied in many respects. In terms of "title-holder," warehouses controlled by the AMC, RRC, military, and local government authorities were used, as were makeshift structures devised specifically for food distribution. There was also considerable variation in the size and quality of warehousing facilities. In early 1986, CRS had a warehousing capacity at the secondary level of 37,000 MT, distributed among Nazareth (12,000 MT), Wollo (10,000 MT), Dire Dawa (6,000 MT), Asmara (6,000 MT), and Addis Ababa (3,000 MT) (CRS 1986:25). This capacity represented less than two months' worth of food commodities, leaving only a small margin in the event deliveries from the ports were delayed. But CRS delegated responsibility for moving the food from regional warehouses to recipients to its operating agencies (CRS 1986:28). WVRO had its central warehousing and dispatching point at Kombolcha, with expanded storage facilities at project sites (WVRO 1986:5). SCF had a 33,700-ton storage capacity in Yifat na Timuga (SCF 1985c:7). Overall, the quality of warehouses was quite high, contributing to the low rate of food loss attributable to inland movement and storage.

Of equal importance in stabilizing relief operations was maintenance of a functioning infrastructure for prompt distribution of food to beneficiaries. Explaining the increase in the rate at which PVOs distributed aid is a hazardous undertaking because many factors came into play.[5] The regional specialization of the PVOs and the geographical, social, and transport condi-

150 Reluctant Aid or Aiding the Reluctant?

tions in their regions shaped the success of their operations. The RRC's role in approving DC locations and beneficiary lists and in dispatching commodities was another important factor. Several measures of the food distribution expansion of several U.S.-based PVOs are depicted in table 6.6. These reflect the increases and fluctuations in the amount of food distributed by CARE, SCF, and CDAA/JRP, as well as fluctuations in the number of beneficiaries reached by WVRO. The distributions of LICROSS are presented for comparative purposes. Steady rates of food distribution are indicated by all measures.

As reliability in supplying DCs improved, more latitude was afforded in monitoring primary distribution to meet eligibility preferences of Ethiopian authorities. Primary distribution was less subject to accountability concerns and monitoring during the emergency phase, largely because constraints

TABLE 6.6
Indicators of Expansion of PVOs' Food Distribution

1985	CDAA/JRP Food MTs	SCF Food MTs	CARE Food MTs	LICROSS Food MTs	WVRO Beneficiaries
February	n.a.	44	n.a.	n.a.	n.a.
March	n.a.	190	257	n.a.	91,450
April	14,712	205	874	n.a.	159,813
May	15,390	610	1,676	n.a.	145,549
June	17,049	691	2,680	n.a.	145,675
July	17,794	2,169	3,659	n.a.	181,077
August	n.a.	2,555	5,565	1,854	199,322
September	18,919	3,274	7,347	4,249	254,773
October	19,580	4,501	6,817	4,531	287,257
November	20,027	n.a.	7,569	4,529	247,437
December	19,454	n.a.	4,716	4,175	n.a.
1986					
January	16,710	n.a.	2,515	2,642	n.a.
February	16,611	n.a.	3,936	2,244	n.a.
March	10,441	n.a.	4,744	2,703	n.a.
April	14,851	426	3,820	2,101	n.a.
May	n.a.	498	5,662	3,200	n.a.
June	17,155	2,454	7,059	3,017	n.a.
July	20,554	1,552	6,752	2,321	n.a.
August	21,792	n.a.	n.a.	n.a.	n.a.

Sources: CDAA/JRP (1986); SCF (1985b); Heller (1986); CARE (1986c); LICROSS (1986); USAID/E (1986).

Stabilization of Relief 151

earlier in the distribution process—i.e., at ports, warehouses, and in transportation to DCs—were of overriding importance. The achievement of relatively normative operations at the secondary level of distribution placed greater strain on operations at the primary level and gave the Ethiopian authorities greater leverage over institution-building activities.

Adherence and Resistance to International Norms

Distributing food for famine relief was in many ways caught between the tension of creating a normative set of entitlements for beneficiaries and working to transform a food system responsible for the famine in the first place. By distributing commodities, U.S.-based PVOs engaged in several processes which affected the political economy of food entitlements; these processes were positioned between normative operations and military-political control. First, setting up DC infrastructures and selecting individual beneficiaries of aid through indigenous Recipient Institutions (RIs) were influenced by the local political economy of the area of distribution; PVO decision making and the mechanics of distribution themselves were affected by the subsistence economies of the locale. Secondly, PVOs managed the food consumption of beneficiaries—both in terms of determining the amounts and sizes of individual rations and also in terms of the rituals for transferring possession to beneficiaries. Thirdly, decisions regarding management of the broader setting of distribution—including continuous assessments of social and political conditions in their operating areas, and maintaining relationships with USAID, other PVOs, and international organizations, the RRC, and other Ethiopian agencies—had an important effect on PVOs' abilities to distribute commodities.

During the stability phase, the infrastructure for determining beneficiary status and the process of primary distribution had been routinized. The greatest conflict between normative distribution operations and the Ethiopian setting of relief occurred in the context of the villagization program. Institution building from traditional bases was largely superseded by adding political power through this program to Peasant Associations (PAs) and Party organizations at the woreda and awraja levels.

Beneficiary Status and Primary Distribution

Both Ethiopian and U.S. government policy objectives were achieved through the institutions which transferred food aid rations to individual beneficiaries. On the surface, primary distribution was a matter of technique. PVOs rationalized the process of distributing food to beneficiaries at DCs so that criteria for beneficiary status were reduced to processing people through

152 Reluctant Aid or Aiding the Reluctant?

checkpoints within the DCs. But this is deceptive because primary distribution also invoked the structure of Ethiopian food entitlements. Adjustments of PVOs to expansion and contractions of beneficiary lists by RRC and local authorities were almost reflexive. Decisions related to managing entitlements included estimating local needs for food aid, selecting beneficiaries and distribution sites, and finally administering distributions to beneficiaries through RIs. Setting criteria for beneficiary status implemented the policy objectives of the Ethiopian government and, to the extent that they were based on need alone, the targets of U.S. policy.

Important differences existed between the emergency and stability periods in the methods and amount of control exercised over primary distribution. During the emergency phase, outside of the broad rebel-loyalist dynamic of the PMGSE criteria, only sporadic controls were exercised over primary distribution. Although the military strategy for starving out the rebels aroused Western donors, there is little evidence that donors were presented with heightened opportunities vis-a-vis the Ethiopian government during this period for subverting this strategy, other than supplying food to rebel-held areas. Refugee camps and large, uncontrolled groups in feeding centers were typical in the emergency phase, which lasted in most areas roughly until late 1985 when shelter populations were reduced. During the spring of 1985, there were 1 million people in and around the shelters of northern Ethiopia (USAID/E 1987:3). As stability was attained, shelter populations decreased, from over 575,000 in April to 70,000 in October 1985. Table 6.7 shows the fluctuations in RRC estimates of shelter populations at five different points in time during 1985 for the most seriously affected administrative regions.

Given the shortage of food commodities on hand for distribution, medical

TABLE 6.7
Registered Shelter Populations, 1985

	February	April	June	August	October	Average
Eritrea	12,000	43,000	26,000	57,000	2,280	28,056
Gonder	-	98,000	108,000	86,800	4,000	59,360
Hararghe	-	20,000	18,000	18,000	11,450	13,490
Shoa	11,000	8,000	7,000	7,000	400	6,680
Sidamo	-	-	2,000	2,000	11,200	3,040
Tigray	81,500	240,275	129,000	117,770	6,490	115,007
Wollo	98,000	166,600	164,600	103,300	34,350	113,370
Total	202,500	575,875	454,600	391,870	70,170	

Source: USAID/E (1987:25).

Stabilization of Relief 153

problems and treatment needs tended to dominate the early scene. Little control could be exercised by DC personnel beyond providing relief items to beneficiaries. Operating agencies had little control over mortality levels. The application of triage principles was the greatest strategic option open to distributing agencies during this phase, but it was a normative system of only the narrowest scope. During this period, decisions were more spontaneous and followed less from organizational principles than from the individual assessments of staff members.

During the stability period, on the other hand, with infrastructures for distribution largely in place, more orderly distributions proceeded at the primary level. PVOs typically distributed food from a more widely dispersed set of DCs, usually with the objective that beneficiaries take the food back to their homes and villages for consumption. Criteria for beneficiary status were among the most divisive and decisive components of food aid operations during this period. Control over determinations of beneficiary status by Ethiopian political institutions was strong but not absolute in all cases. Selection, screening, and registration processes were ultimately controlled by local institutions, but often under the supervision of party authorities near the woreda level. In programs operated directly by the RRC, the minimum criteria were loyalty and residence in approved PAs. In parts of the north, these criteria were occasionally exploited when beneficiary status became a lure for the resettlement program—respondents reported the use of food aid in Wollo as a decoy for resettlement (Niggli 1986:9-14). Similarly, people targeted for villagization were induced to relocate through offers of food aid, as will be described below.

Conflicts between recipient and donor criteria were evident. There was evidence that Ethiopian authorities rerouted distribution of emergency food aid to loyalists. Prerequisites for receiving food aid included beneficiaries having fulfilled their quotas for various programs and made tax payments. Any distributions under PMGSE auspices would ipso facto be precluded from reaching rebel-held territories where levels of need were among the highest. Moreover, DCs in government-held areas in Tigray operated by the RRC "would give food only to those with identification cards [that] indicated membership in a government Peasant Association. Because people from TPLF-controlled areas had no such documents, they were denied food and sometimes beaten" (Kaplan 1988:90). In contrast, the U.S. government was insistent that food be distributed solely on the basis of need, without reference to loyalty to governmental or rebel organizations, and it presumably encouraged PVOs to use some criteria to counteract PMGSE biases against people from areas controlled by rebel organizations.

The beneficiary base of PVOs was a highly constructed set of social relationships formed between PVOs, RIs, the RRC, and Party authorities. PVOs were largely neutral in theory but often out of control in actual practice. U.S.-based PVOs did not often push for control over beneficiary status determinations. Lacking the influence to act as normative agents, they functioned more as diplomatic power brokers between Ethiopian authorities and donor governments. DCs had to be established, beneficiaries had to be selected, recruited, screened, approved, registered, scheduled for particular days for distribution, and finally given possession of the donated relief items.

Establishing DCs for primary distribution involved a host of negotiations at various levels of authority. In general, local cadres of the WPE "were much more important at the local level than the RRC officials" (Jansson 1987:13). In many areas:

> The power structure at the regional level was rigidly clear. The Regional party secretary was supreme and even the regional army commander, usually a major general, was under his control. Then came the chief administrator and only after him the RRC regional representative . . . regional and local party secretaries always had to be kept in the picture and frequently made decisions on relief matters, although that should have been the task of the RRC regional and local representatives (Jansson 1987:32).

Approval of high-level Ethiopian authorities (usually cadres of the WPE or the RRC) was certainly necessary for beginning program operations, but approval of local officials at the awraja and woreda level was also indispensable to making program adjustments. Similarly, maintaining the operational levels of DCs, much less expanding their distributions, required official approval. Management of the beneficiary base, warehousing, and distribution facilities in the face of pressures for alternative demands and uses likewise required close relationships with local officials.

Expanding the number of operating DCs as the stability phase was approached certainly required such approval. While it is difficult to generalize about the process of establishing DCs, the rates of expansion were rapid. By April 1985, the RRC and PVOs were operating 45 shelters, 280 DCs and 180 feeding centers (Wolde Giorgis 1989:228). The growth in the number of DCs operated by several PVOs (including new DCs and the discontinuation of other DCs at various points in time) is described in table 6.8. It can be inferred from these rates that PVOs were largely powered from within and that restrictions on expansion per se could not have been too severe.

Aid Criteria and Rationing

The dynamics of primary distribution—especially the separation of beneficiary selection from actual food distribution—provided the greatest openings for deviations from normative principles in the operation of some U.S.-

based PVO programs. CARE's program in Hararghe, for example, relied upon woreda and awraja PA and Party officials, as well as RRC screening, to approve beneficiaries for food aid. Lists of eligible beneficiaries were initially prepared by PAs and approved by woreda or awraja relief committees. Expansion and contraction of beneficiary lists was believed to be an artificial process, not accurately reflecting need levels. The importance which the authorities attached to controlling beneficiary status was starkly revealed by the imprisonment near Miesso of a CARE employee who distributed food to hungry persons not on the beneficiary list (*Jeune Afrique* 25 February 1987: 36). Some control was exercised by religious institutions in the north, and some PVOs acquired control over eligibility determinations. But CRS could not control beneficiary selection in many parts of Eritrea and left this function to churches operating in the area. More significantly, SCF initially exerted some control over beneficiary selection by conducting house-to-house sur-

TABLE 6.8
Growth in Number of PVO-Operated Food Distribution Centers

	CDAA/JRP	CARE
1985		
March	n.a.	1
April	64	7
May	52	9
June	76	20
July	80	32
August	n.a.	40
September	82	43
October	82	42
November	82	42
December	100	42
1986		
January	100	20
February	84	38
March	n.a.	41
April	74	33
May	n.a.	33
June	86	34
July	97	34
August	97	n.a.

Sources: CARE (1986c); CDAA/JRP (1986).

veys at the village level to determine the nutritional status of beneficiaries. Presumably the ERCS—because of its indigenous base—also had some amount of control over the selection of beneficiaries.

Among personality criteria for beneficiary status, most important was whether potential beneficiaries were rebel-supporters or loyalists, full-fledged PA members, or belonged to a religious community (cf. Clay 1986). For normative patterns in primary distribution to emerge, need-based personality criteria had to be filtered through this preliminary process of eligibility screening, usually by political authorities. In many cases, PVOs had little to do with the mechanics of beneficiary selection. Targeting the "most vulnerable" groups provided some normative criteria. For example, CRS and its affiliated agencies, as well as other PVOs, adopted the following criteria for beneficiary status::

1. Children under five and lactating mothers;
2. Severely undernourished children who are in need of intensive feeding; and
3. Those with no other resources and so affected by famine that they cannot care for themselves (CRS 1986:11).

Other personality characteristics of beneficiaries often included a second set of gender- and age-based criteria. Gender-based criteria were applied indirectly, reflecting the military situation and recruitment needs in the region involved. Males were reported to fear conscription in the militarized regions and were reluctant to seek emergency food aid rations. Similarly, social sector criteria distinguished between rural and urban dwellers, while emergency aid was limited by the RRC and most PVOs to rural dwellers. That sectoral position was not an absolute bar to recipient status was indicated by the pressure applied on CARE by a kebele in Dobba woreda, Chercher awraja in Hararghe to successfully obtain food commodities for its members. Age-graded criteria were especially pronounced during the emergency phase in order to remedy the pattern of deterioration that strikes the young first. corn-soy-milk mixtures and other wet rations were directed toward infants and lactating women.

Some evidence of roughly normative distribution is provided by the rationalization of the process of primary distribution, which became much more pronounced as famine conditions and relief operations stabilized. Scheduling distributions provided openings for microlevel power initiatives largely outside of the control of PVOs. Servicing a large number of beneficiaries from PAs widely dispersed around DCs required staggering distribution schedules. Coordination among PVOs, woreda officials, PA heads, and beneficiaries was necessary for regular distributions to occur. The large, consistent amounts of

Stabilization of Relief 157

food distributed countrywide is strong evidence of such a system. Even though most DCs had routinized procedures for processing beneficiaries through the reception, identification, and transfer stages of primary distribution, some technical problems were posed by such diverse items as containers and packaging which interfered with smooth distribution at the primary level. For example, butter oil packaged in cans required cumbersome opening procedures, and leaking containers of oil caused delays and shortfalls at the primary level. On the other hand, at many DCs, children also acted as entrepreneurs to smooth the process, mining for water in the Sekota, Wollo region (Schellinski 1986), and sewing up wheat sacks and weaving baskets from plastic ties of relief bags in DCs in Hararghe.

Rationing during the stability phase is further evidence of patterning at the microlevel, but raises questions about whether normative or organizational determinants were more important. There was less disagreement about the appropriate size of the ration and more about the best beneficiary unit (i.e., the family unit or the individual). CRS's emergency feeding program was targeted at families with children under five years of age (CRS 1986:43), and it rationed food to the family unit. Dry food rations were for a "normal" family of five, assuming that excesses would find their way into the market (CRS 1986:41). CARE's rationing scheme in Hararghe targeted individual beneficiaries. The ration size was 12.5 kgs of bulgar wheat and 450 grams of oil per beneficiary per month (CARE 1986b), adjusted according to availability. SCF's guidelines were: 550 grams/day or 15 kgs/month for each adult (SCF 1985c:3). USAID sided with agencies targeting individual beneficiaries rather than family units on the ground that when families were larger than the mythical average, they suffered (Gordon 1986). Ration sizes were reduced so that during the first six months of 1986 most beneficiaries received only half rations (USAID/E 1986).

Beyond rationing differences, diversity in distribution styles was evident in the more substantive aspects of PVO operations. Organizational complications involved in primary distribution were at least partially offset by innovations stemming from conflict and compromise among PVOs. Differences in ideological and technical outlooks were offset by loans of commodities and coordination of regional activity. Nutritional surveillance programs were intended to identify areas of greatest food needs. Similarly, concerns about accountability were partly responsive to donor requirements, partly to the internal operating procedures of agencies. Two examples of breakdown may serve to indicate the flexibility of PVO operations. First, CARE did not require registration for its early distributions in Shinele largely because of the nomadic lifestyle of the Somali beneficiaries. Second, CRS's accountability requirements were relaxed in Eritrea because of the absence of administrative authority there other than the clergy who handled the primary distribution.

It would be a mistake to conclude that normative patterns or principles regulated PVO operations or the donor-recipient relationship at the level of primary distribution. Differing values between donor and recipient governments over the camp setting during the crisis period were evident. When large numbers of people were congregated and sheltered around DCs, problems in administration and control arose. Theft and conversion of relief goods were generally not problems in Ethiopian camps. As PVOs attempted to move the DCs outside of emergency shelters, their operations became enmeshed in Ethiopian political institutions. Further expansion of PVOs' operations through the dispersion of their DCs away from original distribution sites strained their infrastructural capacities. As reflected in table 6.8, the number of PVO DCs increased rapidly, indicating an expansion of institutional capacity. The distance of DCs from clusters of beneficiaries and central locations with respect to PAs, rail lines, and roadways was critical. For example, CARE adjusted the location of several DCs in response to local conditions. One DC required travel over a road that ruined the tires of trucks very rapidly, so it was closed and peasants were directed to another DC several kilometers away. In addition, CARE established a DC in between two other very large ones in order to relieve the beneficiary pressure on these. Other PVO operations were similarly affected by local conditions.

Institution Building and Villagization

One of the key areas in which Ethiopian government policy prevailed over U.S. objectives was institution building, and the Ethiopian program for villagization in particular. Expansion of DCs for food distribution may be expected to have gone hand in hand with the building of RI authority in the countryside on the part of the RIs under whose auspices food was transferred to beneficiaries. It was the separation of beneficiary selection from food distribution that created the gap in which Ethiopian institution-building objectives were advanced. Institution building was, in fact, an intended consequence of food distribution during the stability phase, evident in the military partitioning of distribution activities between government- and rebel-held areas, and also in food distributions following implementation of villagization programs. Open conflicts over the institution building involved in food distribution was rare (except in the case of resettlement), but Ethiopian authorities were able to consolidate their control to the detriment of traditional Ethiopian institutions.

Institution building by PVOs

Among the most important operational factors in primary distribution during the stability phase were the relationships PVOs maintained with

Stabilization of Relief 159

indigenous institutions. Even though decisions about primary distribution and beneficiary status were made in an institutional context that PVOs had little control over, advantages were gained in some areas where indigenous institutions were favorably oriented to particular PVOs, especially religious ones. Four kinds of institutions were involved at the primary level of food distribution for famine relief: religious organizations, including churches and parishes of various denominations; "voluntary associations," such as Red Cross societies; specifically military institutions, including governmental units and those of insurgent organizations (such as the EPLF, TPLF, and OLF); and government organizations, including Party groups, the RRC, and Peasant Associations.

It may be in the nature of the aid relationship that something be given in exchange for food distributed. Managing the political economy of food aid entitlements, and the position of beneficiaries within it, involved a variety of quid pro quos. Based primarily on value differences (i.e., power-based versus need-based), conflicting styles of primary distribution were also influenced by local conditions and the structure of food entitlements in different regions.[6] To be sure, U.S.-based PVOs used logistical procedures with a normative content, but they interacted with beneficiaries within the context of an exchange relationship, as will be seen. Quid pro quos operated somewhat differently in each of the four different institutional settings, and some PVOs used work-for-food exchanges to phase out their food distributions programs, except in cases where food-for-work programs were later installed.

Exchange relationships were involved at the institutional as well as individual levels. Relying on institutional infrastructure for primary distribution inevitably, even if not purposefully, strengthened the institutions involved. U.S. policy would have been expected to aim at strengthening insurgent, religious, and voluntary organizations, with the objective of subverting PMGSE-backed institutions, while the PMGSE would have been expected to attempt to strengthen selected branches of political and military organizations. However, the institutional preferences of donor and recipient policies were moderated by other considerations as well. The effectiveness, flexibility, and durability of the entitlements created, rather than the character of their institutional counterparts, were also important to donor and recipient governments. For PVOs, RIs provided an in-country base of power more or less independent of the RRC and USAID, and were likewise strengthened. The degree of independence acquired and the amount of power provided by the RI-PVO alliance depended upon many considerations, including the RI's position in the traditional or modern segment of Ethiopian social structure.

U.S. support of religious and voluntary associations was also a reflection of Western relief philosophies. Religious PVOs had objectives other than relief, including proselytizing and fostering development, which added

160 Reluctant Aid or Aiding the Reluctant?

another dimension to the institutional base for food distribution. The traditional authority of religious institutions was directly supported by a number of U.S.-based PVOs; PMGSE officials clearly had little patience with religious organizations. Many PVOs had a religious mandate, strong religious commitments, and solid religion-based constituencies in their distribution areas. Christian churches and parishes concentrated in the highlands in the north were especially strengthened by the WVRO and CRS programs. The power of priests was doubtless heightened by the food they distributed.

CRS and the other religion-based members of the JRP coalition were strongly connected with traditional religious institutions. CRS's RI in Eritrea was the Ethiopian Catholic Secretariat (ECS), while the Lutheran World Federation (LWF) was connected with the Ethiopian Evangelical Church Makane Yesus (EECMY). CRS derived a good deal of independence from the RRC, and the only real option for USAID was to utilize CRS's relationships with these indigenous institutions to reach beneficiaries. But it was not until July 1986 that an agreement was signed between the Ethiopian Orthodox Church (EOC) and the U.S. government. Incidentally, CRS and RRC also signed agreements with the EOC at about the same time, perhaps indicating a rivalry for formal connections with the Church.

Supporting religious institutions also subverted the PMGSE's desire to exercise strict control over social organizations. U.S.-based PVOs may have tempered the fervency of PMGSE opposition to religious authority in the rural regions. Despite persecution of religious leaders and organizations, PMGSE efforts to undermine religious authority were largely unsuccessful, and numerous observers have noted the continued strength of religion in Ethiopia (e.g., Thomas 1987). WVRO appeared to be more proselytizing in its approach, and rumors circulated in Addis Ababa during the summer of 1986 that WVRO workers had refused to give food to some beneficiaries because they had refused to attend a church service. But nonrelief missionary agencies were less likely to expand their operations into the area of relief. SIM, International, for example, did not want its missionary mandate to be sacrificed by the exigencies of providing famine relief (SIM, International 1986).

The ordinary control of PVOs over food distribution was slackened by the fragility of the PVO-facilitated infrastructures in the northern regions. Extreme geographical conditions and military and rebel activities made relief more difficult. As one CRS spokesperson indicated, it was necessary to dump commodities into churches and hope they were able to distribute it to peasants (Swenson 1986). PVOs could provide minimal accountability under such circumstances. In addition to sacrificing control of distributions, CRS participation in the FFN initiative, and its reliance on priests to monitor the food

Stabilization of Relief 161

distribution program, resulted in a need for closer monitoring (INTERTECT 1986:4).[7]

By involving churches and clergy in food distribution, PVOs distributing U.S. food aid commodities contributed substantially to supporting religious institutions in Ethiopia. It has been noted that one "of the side effects of famine has however been to reestablish links between the mission churches and their Ethiopian counterparts, and thus to give them a measure of protection" (Clapham 1988:155-156).

Whether a similar conclusion may be drawn in the case of voluntary organizations is subject to doubt. LICROSS and ICRC were somewhat in between politics and religion, as voluntary organizations associated with the ERCS served as their institutional base for recruitment of staff, beneficiary selection, and food distribution. Unlike recipient governments in many other relief efforts, the PMGSE discouraged private-side voluntary efforts. Nonetheless, by January 1985 the Ethiopian Red Cross Society was reaching 137,000 beneficiaries with the support of LICROSS and ICRC (ERCS 1985:29). The strength of the Red Cross in Ethiopia should not be underestimated, but membership was lower than it was for religious institutions and much less food was distributed through its DCs. As of 1983, the regional branch membership of ERCS totalled 85,000, with the largest memberships in Sidamo (13,636) and Hararghe (12,375) (see ERCS 1983:9-12). The lesser importance attached to Red Cross societies in the relief effort may also have been due to the fact that the United States had less interest in strengthening the societies since they had fewer connections with U.S. organizations.

Strengthening the military and the status of military personnel through the relief effort was a key policy issue. U.S. government objectives were to keep food out of the hands of the military; PMGSE objectives were for military institutions to limit if not control food distributions in all regions of the country. The indirect support of a military administration and institutions by distribution of U.S.-donated relief commodities was inevitable. Diversion of aid to the military was not so much the problem, although there were occasional reports of such occurrences. As was the case of Western support for resettlement, a much more sophisticated circuitry in Ethiopian political economy routed Western aid to the support of PMGSE militarization. The infrastructure in the north was severely tested by the militarization of the region. Distribution in government-controlled areas of Eritrea and Tigray as well as parts of Wollo were limited because would-be beneficiaries feared conscription (Shepherd 1985b:54). At the secondary level as well, the military (of both the PMGSE and rebel forces) controlled much of the food distribution by their control of delivery systems. According to the CARE employee who monitored the food distributed under the bilateral, PMGSE military check points were in place at regular intervals on roads. There was also military partitioning of parts of Hararghe and other regions, but it was much less tight than in the north (Janardanan 1986).

Military administration went hand-in-hand with food distribution in many parts of PMGSE- and rebel-held areas. In the north, the PMGSE was known to use relief commodities to pay its soldiers, who sold the food to merchants in Sudan, who in turn sold it to the relief arms of the insurgents (i.e., ERA and REST). The positions of ERA and REST are more difficult to assess. Because they were the relief arms of the militarized rebel forces in Eritrea and Tigray respectively, these organizations also had a military interest in food.

Militarism interfered with nonmilitary infrastructural development as well as distribution. Apart from pre-emption of relief, the military also had a direct involvement in most phases of distribution, providing some warehouses, assisting occasionally with local truck transport, and providing security and beneficiary control at primary distribution points. Conducting relief operations in war conditions raised its own problems, and the extreme circumstances in the north especially disrupted ordinary relief operations. Seizures of DCs and raids by rebel troops were not uncommon. The murder of WVRO staff in Tigray and the kidnapping of relief workers in the same region highlighted rebel activity but were less significant than the regular disruption of food production and distribution occasioned by changes in control over regions. Girawa in Hararghe was held by the OLF during at least one day in 1985; it bears an uncertain relationship to CARE's distributional shortfalls during the period. Whether civilian institutions will be able to regulate conflict in the future is doubtful.

While PMGSE military strategy determined in the last instance the parameters of relief distribution, political institutions controlled by the PMGSE also acquired substantial support from the distribution of commodities donated by the United States. In contrast to CRS, CARE and SCF both worked exclusively[8] within the authority of PAs and awraja and woreda relief committees, which have the strongest relationships with the central political structure. PAs in Ethiopia are notorious for their being controlled from above by central institutions and are therefore largely unable to act upon the basis of grass-roots initiatives. There is also substantial evidence of corruption in PAs in their distribution of land under the land reform proclamation. Whether this corruption extended to emergency food distributions is unclear, but U.S.-based PVOs undertook accountability control measures in most regions to minimize the risk of corruption.

In the ordinary operation of food distribution programs, PAs would have been strengthened by increased member recognition of PA authority, and would have supported future obligations of beneficiaries to these units. There is evidence of beneficiaries in Hararghe being required to pay taxes and dues

Stabilization of Relief 163

to PAs before being eligible for relief food (Clay 1986). In this sense, food aid functioned as a transfer payment from donors to the recipient government. In northern Shoa, SCF's tradition of community development work converged with PMGSE objectives. Its training program for indigenous staff was planned to produce a "cadre for longer-term village development work" (Borton 1986:56). Working with PAs, it recruited its local staff through training programs.

But the Ethiopian policy for extending the writ of party and state deeper into the countryside and for redistributing rural populations was implemented through PAs. The villagization program in particular made direct use of U.S. food aid donations distributed by PVOs to encourage participation and to assist in feeding villagized populations thereafter.

Population Redistribution and Villagization: Taking the Upper Hand

In the southern regions of resettlement, the role of U.S. food aid in supporting new institutions was indirect, as aid from other donors was directly used to transport and feed resettlement participants. Operations of resettlement authorities controlled these regions; other agencies had been requested to provide assistance, but PVOs distributing U.S. food aid did not operate in them, nor did many other Western agencies. There is little doubt that U.S. food aid supported the program at least indirectly by relieving the PMGSE of obligations to use its food for relief. In matters of transport as well, assertions that the effects of the resettlement program on relief transport "were marginal" (Jansson 1987:37) are untenable. In most areas, the RRC's DCs in regions of origin operated on different principles than U.S.-based PVOs, and it appears that food was used as a collectivization tool, both in regions of origin and later in regions of resettlement.

In contrast, villagization and distribution of Western food aid commodities were often complementary activities. Villagization during the famine period began in Hararghe under the initiation of the WPE's regional first secretary, not pursuant to central authority (Clapham 1988:90). However, Mengistu's support of the program resulted in villagization becoming national policy after October 1985 and later constitutionalized in the new constitution. The program was rapidly extended throughout the countryside in several phases. After Hararghe, the regions of Shoa and Arsi began the process, followed by Kaffa, Welega, and Ilubabor. After December 1985, villagization began in Gonder, Wollo, and Sidamo (Clapham 1988:174-179). Soon after being affected by villagization, these regions required increased levels of food aid, as the number of people affected by food shortages increased (see table 6.1).

Largely the fait accompli of the distribution of food aid donated by the West, complying with villagization was a prerequisite for food distributions in many areas. Distributions required approval of the RRC, awraja, and woreda PAs, as well as Party authorities who had been closely associated with the program. Most likely, food distributions were also coordinated with the National Villagization Coordination Committees (NVCC) at the PA level and above, and by the Ministry of Agriculture, which houses the Secretariat to the NVCC (Cohen and Isaksson 1987:437).

It is unlikely that villagization would have been accomplished without the benefit of Western aid. PVO involvement with villagization was unwilling. CARE's regional director, for example, commented that while he was "unaware" of any force being used to achieve villagization, neither was he aware of any social services being provided (Narula 1986). Western aid permitted the Ethiopian government to expand the villagization program by allowing food to be used as bait, "luring farmers to participate in villagization," and by picking up "the slack" in food production (Clay 1988:107). The disruption of agricultural production was severe in many areas, and the declines in production subsequent to villagization will continue in the future.

By the end of the famine's stability period, the Ethiopian countryside had been totally revamped. Instead of maintaining their own plots of land, millions of peasant farmers had been gathered into centralized villages. By September 1986 it was reported that over 4.5 million peasants had been villagized; by September 1987 the figure had nearly doubled to 8 million (Clapham 1988:176). Many PVOs were prevented from beginning programs in areas until after villages had been completed; then, their aid was solicited to provide some of the promised services to the villagized populations (Clay 1989:274, 265). The close proximity of many food DCs to new villages strengthened the forces behind the program, as well as the authorities issuing the commands and implementing the program.

It is clear that the villagization authorities anticipated the need for some coercion. Food and promised services were meant to sweeten the program's bitter aspects. In addition, drawing upon traditional religious institutions to assist with villagization was part of official policy, if not part of program practice, as tolerance of religious institutions in new villages was supposed to contrast with their intolerance in resettlement areas. According to the PMGSE handbook on villagization: "It is beneficial, therefore, that religious institutions be allowed to exist, as much as possible, in the villages that are being established . . . *This would make villagization palatable.* (U.S. House 1986:35; emphasis added).

However palatable the level of tolerance allowed for religious institutions may make villagization in the short term, it is unlikely that villagization will facilitate food production as hoped by the Ethiopian authorities. Political control objectives and the diffusion of Party authority throughout the countryside have been achieved to a considerable extent. In this sense, the Ethiopian

Stabilization of Relief 165

government has drawn upon a long tradition of turning foreign aid to its own political purposes. However, the weakness inherent in being a chronic food deficit country and relying on Western food aid to the point of near dependency is a new stage in Ethiopian development that results partly from its Soviet alliance.

Notes

1. But Ethiopian influence in Djibouti should not be underestimated. CARE at one point requested a Party official to urge quicker offloading of commodities at Djibouti port for shipment to the railhead at Dire Dawa.
2. UNOEO/E was phased out in October 1986 (*Christian Science Monitor* 29 October 1986) and replaced by the Emergency Planning and Preparedness Group (EPPG), which continues to operate out of the UN complex in Addis Ababa.
3. In Dire Dawa, the base town for most programs in Hararghe, some agencies operated out of hotel rooms while others managed to obtain larger quarters and built compounds.
4. In Hararghe, the author's vehicle was forced off the road between Jijiga and Harar in August 1986 to permit a convoy of 94 military trucks pass for maneuvers in Jijiga.
5. WVRO was unable to distribute much of its butter oil around August 1986, so USAID authorized a give-away to CARE. It continued to have difficulties performing under the Food for the North initiative. CARE was regularly "short" of commodities, indicating an ability to perform above plan.
6. Oxfam-U.S.'s program in the north for distribution of seeds and oxen, described by McCann (1987), took such factors into account to a much greater extent than did many food distribution programs. Rehabilitation programs by their very nature required preliminary studies of local conditions.
7. CRS also operated in Muslim areas (Tekul 1986). In Hararghe, CRS operated in the center of the region in the awrajas of Webera and Harar Zuria. It is notable that central Hararghe is an area of Christian concentration, reflected by the fact that the church in Kulubi was built by Haile Selassie's father in tribute to a Christian saint.
8. In Hararghe, and probably elsewhere as well, a mixing of bases of authority was seen. Many PA heads were observed to be (Muslim) religious leaders.

IV

Developmental and Sociological Conclusions

7

The People's Democratic Republic of Ethiopia, U.S. Food Aid Policy, and the Future of Food Aid in Ethiopia

The depth of Ethiopia's descent into the fourth world of food insecurity may be measured by the collapse of regional and national food systems, the huge death tolls, and the massive outpouring of Western aid during the famine of 1983-86. Both the famine and the relief effort have major implications for conceptualizing the course of Ethiopian national development and the contributions of external relationships to it. They provide an interesting case for testing the flexibility of the dependency paradigm in the sociology of development.

Drawing conclusions from a single case study is always risky. Limiting conclusions from this famine and relief effort to the central features of Ethiopian development may be accomplished by proceeding through three steps in the analysis. First, the Ethiopian government's inducement of famine and its use of aid for its own purposes may be viewed in the context of the pattern of foreign dependency fostered by the alliance it formed with the Soviet Union, and with the role of food aid donated by the United States and the West. Secondly, the diplomatic role and formation of U.S. food aid policy during the famine and relief effort may be summarized to assess both the openness of Ethiopia to interdependencies and the ability of the United States to penetrate Ethiopian barriers. Finally, the strength of emerging principles of international relief operations in Ethiopia may be measured by noting their normative features and assessing the future of food shortages and food aid in Ethiopia.

Reluctant Aid or Aiding the Reluctant?

Dependency Theory and the Latest Stage of Ethiopian Development

Explaining the emergence of the People's Democratic Republic of Ethiopia (PDRE) in early 1987 out of a famine-plagued nation requires some historical perspective. No systematic application of the tenets of dependency theory to the patterns of Ethiopian development has yet been attempted,[1] but in terms of both famine inducement and national development, dependency (and world systems) theorists have been notably silent on the Ethiopian experience. Assertions of generalized dependency—especially of the Imperial government on the United States—have been equally balanced by denials that such a relationship existed. Because of the scarcity of previous attempts, and because of the actual progression in Ethiopian development, conceptualizing the relationship between the outbreak of famine and government approaches to national development throughout Ethiopian history in dependency terms is problematic.

State structure, foreign relations, policy rhetoric, and government programs during the famine period all suggest the possibility—if the general imagery of dependency theory is accepted, i.e., that more developed nations are responsible for the impoverishment of underdeveloped nations—that the Soviet Union fostered a dependency on the part of Ethiopia. While this may present a fairly straightforward policy explanation for inducement of famine during the current stage of Ethiopian development, and this explanation has points of comparison with other developmental experiences in recent history, it is not particularly viable in terms of dependency theory. There are three reasons for this: First, the fact that the West stepped in with massive amounts of aid and was a lucrative alternative to reliance on the Soviets for famine relief assistance is difficult to reconcile with dependency theory. Second, dependency theory generally does not admit Soviet relations with the third world into the realm of factors responsible for dependent development. Third, while the famine of 1983-86 had neo-Stalinist features at least partially attributable to Soviet influence, the inspiration for Mengistu's death policy must not be attributed to foreign ideology alone; frustrations with traditional obstacles to development, a willingness to sacrifice the peasantry, and fear of national disintegration were also at work.

The Spoils of Famine and Famine Relief

As a state of "socialist orientation," Ethiopia is outside the ranks of the communist nations proper. Perhaps for this reason, it is difficult to distinguish the spoils of Ethiopian famine during 1983-86 from the spoils of famine relief. Famine in the communist world is usually associated with policies designed to achieve rapid social change of a revolutionary character. Even with

The People's Democratic Republic of Ethiopia 171

Western aid, this was no exception in Ethiopia, as the authorities induced famine and were reluctant to obtain or use aid to provide effective relief until its contribution to the achievement of revolutionary goals could be assured.

In the midst of the famine, Ethiopian authorities were able to retain and expand their hold on peasant producers, implement a resettlement program contrary to the recommendations of most donors, villagize the bulk of the rural population, prolong military engagements with rebel forces, reconstitute themselves in a "democratic" guise, and pursue counterproductive economic policies. These achievements were largely possible because of large amounts of foreign aid intended for famine relief but having other consequences as well.

The influx of over $2 billion of aid during the famine period (compared to Ethiopia's annual GNP of about $5 billion) provided support for Ethiopia's communist development strategy, and U.S. food aid "probably, for the short term at least, strengthened the regime" (Henze 1985:84). While the WPE was formed during the early part of the famine, the formation of the People's Democratic Republic of Ethiopia must be counted as among the greatest spoils of the famine and relief effort. The PMGSE formally became the People's Democratic Republic of Ethiopia (PDRE) in February 1987: A new constitution was "approved" by referendum on 1 February and Mengistu was "unanimously elected" President by the *Shengo* (national assembly) on 10 September (*New York Times* 23 February 1987 and *Washington Post* 27 September 1987).

While U.S. aid may have intentionally contributed to noncommunist development in the countryside by making it possible for U.S.-based PVOs to support religious and voluntary organizations, it also strengthened socialist institutions by supporting the involvement of PAs in food distribution. As the major distributors of U.S. food, PVOs acted partly in the diplomatic manner assessed by some (e.g., Henze 1986), but were also victims of blackmail by the Ethiopian authorities (Niggli 1986:37).

The role of PVOs is most evident in their channelling of U.S. aid (indirectly to be sure, because the U.S. government prohibited direct support of resettlement) toward relief while Ethiopia and other donors channelled resources into the resettlement program. By virtue of donating over 800,000 MT of food aid for its distribution, and rehabilitation assistance, the United States subsidized the agricultural policies of the Ethiopian authorities by providing the resources for strengthening collective institutions. Of even greater consequence for socialist agricultural development, the United States provided direct support to PVO-operated programs that were reorganizing peasants in controlled villages throughout the country.

Yet another unintended effect of Western aid was the prolonging of the civil wars. Without Western aid to both sides, it is likely that either the

Ethiopian military would have crushed the insurgents or the rebels in Eritrea and Tigray would have been able to free themselves of Ethiopian sovereignty.[2] Instead, by providing aid to the Ethiopian government, resources were not distracted from the military fronts. Similarly, U.S. aid to support rebel organizations, their relief organizations, and the farmers living within their territory allowed the insurgents to continue the struggle. Overall, the long Ethiopian tradition of resolving crises in nationalism through military means prevailed.

Finally, the prospect of returning power to civilians is unlikely during the near future in light of the military's masquerading in politics, a guise which would not have been possible without Western famine aid. As Mengistu assumes presidential powers after the recent "constitutional referendum" and apparent entrenchment of the military in so-called civilian politics, the ideological blur between dictatorial and democratic rule will probably grow. Central controls are unlikely to be diminished by either the Politburo or the "parliamentary" Shengo. Displacement of Mengistu from his ruling position likewise seems to have been sealed off. The coup attempt in May 1989 shows the ineffectiveness of the opposition, and it may be some time before a major political change occurs.[3]

Ethiopia has a long tradition of turning external aid to internal advantage. This is, in itself, contrary to the general presumptions of dependency theory. Although the depth of the communist impulse must not be exaggerated, neither should the hold of Mengistu over the polity on distinctly Ethiopian grounds be underestimated. Traditional Ethiopian authoritarianism supports dictatorial powers to be sure, but many Ethiopian institutions cringe at the total control the regime attempts to exercise. Mengistu has also turned foreign aid to his personal advantage, effectively cleaning up his image by adopting civilian dress. In this sense, openness to the outside world is as much a part of Ethiopia's heritage as are national autonomy and circumspection. Ethiopians have drawn freely on external practices since their so-called 1,000-year sleep beginning around the middle of the first millenium. Normative patterns do not simply constrain external influences—itself a process not easily conceptualized by dependency theory. They also effectively coopt external factors and influences to the advancement of Ethiopian leaders' objectives for development. While Western efforts to influence Ethiopian social development after the resolution of the post-World War II situation generally took traditions into account (Korten 1972), it appears that the Ethiopian military leaders took the flexibility of Soviet developmental rhetoric into account in consolidating their power. Meanwhile, the West was soaked with a huge aid bill and the Ethiopian government made few policy concessions to Western recommendations, or to the economic and political interests of Western donors.

The People's Democratic Republic of Ethiopia 173

Foreign Dependence and Ethiopian Development

Despite the extension of the Soviet Union into the third world, dependency theory has generally been reluctant to recognize Soviet-inspired dependency. It has been observed, for example, that "it is not at all obvious that the powerful 'socialist' countries have exploited their less developed aid partners" (Chase-Dunn 1982:45). It has been perfectly obvious to dependency theorists, however, that the West has exploited *its* aid partners. Moreover, in pinpointing external sources of responsibility for underdevelopment in the West, dependency theory has rejected indigenous patterns as primary determinants of national development, which may be due to the paradigm's ethnocentrism, reluctance to engage in the historical and cultural inquiries necessary to understand them, and impatience with the slow pace of moderate social change (cf. Wiarda 1987).

Conceptualizing Ethiopian dependence and interdependence during the famine period of 1983-86 is facilitated by a clear sense of the stages of Ethiopia's national contacts with the external world. Capturing Ethiopian development in stages provides the necessary traditional background for analyzing social development and the exercise of national autonomy. It also serves as a framework for assessing the recent interventions of foreign countries, especially those of the Soviet Union since the late 1970s.

National autonomy. External interference with the autonomy of undeveloped nations is a core proposition of the dependency paradigm. Western interference with Ethiopian development, or even with the blossoming of the revolution (Bush 1985), would be posited by such theorists to explain the emergence of the famine. In many ways this premise posits external responsibility for all the ills of underdevelopment, but greatly underestimates the level of autonomy that Ethiopia has had as a nation.

Prior to the twentieth century, Ethiopia enjoyed an independence unrivalled by any other uncolonized empire (except perhaps for Thailand). Even though Ethiopia suffered a decline as a world power after the fall of Axum around the end of the first millennium, it experienced a renaissance after the empire was reintegrated by Emperor Menelik II in the 1890s, reflected by the new respect it was shown by Europe after it defeated Italy's bid for further penetration from the Red Sea coast during the battle at Adua in 1896.

During the second stage of modern Ethiopian development under the leadership of Emperor Haile Selassie I, autonomy was greatly reduced for a period. This stage stems from the Italian invasion and occupation of 1936-41 that was followed by a period of British administration and a fairly close association with the West and the United States. Clearly, the Ethiopian state

174 Reluctant Aid or Aiding the Reluctant?

was threatened. if not temporarily dissolved, by the Italian occupation. Even though Selassie established a government-in-exile, the British role in restoring the emperor to power by expelling the Italians from their five-year occupation guaranteed them a form of protectorate over Ethiopian territory, followed by a close alliance with the United States.

It is during this stage of Ethiopian development that the expectations of dependency theory are most easily operationalized, even if those expectations are not firmly supported. As will be seen, several bases of dependence might be invoked to show that Ethiopia was in fact experiencing dependent development after World War II and, during the time of its association with the United States, experienced regular famine. But the fact that famine was induced by laissez faire economic policies, and that relief was delayed by Imperial government indifference rather than political purpose or by any external drain on Ethiopian resources, suggests that Ethiopian famine had normative roots.

In contrast, the adoption of foreign ideology for political and economic development, and the conversion of domestic resources for massive military expenditures to pursue an unpopular struggle against secessionists so evident during the 1983-86 famine, suggests a much stronger external dynamic. Ties with the West were largely severed during the early years of the Ethiopian revolution, and a treaty of friendship and cooperation with the Soviets was signed in November 1978. With the Soviet alliance, Ethiopia was much less diversified in its domestic affairs and in foreign relations, perhaps indicative of a substantial sacrifice of national autonomy. But even if dependency theory were to recognize dependence on the Soviets, the extent of such dependence would not yield a satisfactory explanation of the Mengistu regime's position and performance.

While the Soviets had the greatest external influence on Ethiopian development prior to the famine period, they were not in command. Even with respect to the West, Ethiopia remained in control during the famine period despite the increased level of foreign activity within its borders, including foreign government missions and private agencies involved in relief and development. There was no twisting of arms from without either to induce the famine or to control or postpone relief operations. However, it may be that broader constraints on the exercise of national autonomy—such as the threat and reality of foreign intervention, foreign aid dependence, dependence of policy agendas and political institutions, or dependent patterns of economic development and trade—placed Ethiopia in a dependent position during the famine period.

The People's Democratic Republic of Ethiopia 175

Foreign intervention. Ethiopia has survived as a nation despite frequent threats of foreign invasion and intervention. Whether U.S. policy in Ethiopia during the famine years may be termed a form of nonmilitary humanitarian intervention (or "interference" in Ethiopian internal affairs, as claimed by Mengistu at a 1985 May Day rally [Wolde Giorgis 1989:201]), as opposed to a bid for influence in response to solicited aid, is an important question. Efforts to undermine specific regimes from without provide some evidence of dependence on external sponsors, and defensive measures may sometimes provide the rationale for abusing national minority groups. The Ethiopian experience during the past 15 years provides examples of the inner and outer limits of foreign intervention as a determinant of national policy. While dependency theory uniformly identifies the United States as the author of such exercises, there is much more evidence of Soviet-inspired intervention in the region, including Somalia.

The largely successful, although short-lived, foreign intervention illustrated by Italian colonization of the coast and occupation of the center has already been mentioned. Characterizing the intervention of the Soviets during the late 1970s is more complicated. Soviet support of insurgents during the Selassie regime led to the eventual embrace of Lt. Colonel Mengistu. The presence of insurgent groups, the ripeness of the opportunity for revolt, the Soviet Union's hopes to move up in the region from its impoverished Somalian client to the more populous and resourceful Ethiopian plateau, and the emergence of radical leadership in the PMAC, all inspired Soviet intervention (see Porter 1984:191-200). Whether the regime could have survived the Somali offensive without the outside assistance provided by the Soviets is unclear.

Because the Soviets were firmly entrenched by the time of the famine, responsibility on their part can not be posited on interventionist grounds. However, their intervention during the late 1970s may be indirectly tied to the famine of the 1980s. One explanation for the radicalization of the Ethiopian government after 1977 is that its very survival, and that of the Ethiopian nation, was guaranteed only after Soviet and Cuban aid came to its defense against the Somali invasion of the Ogaden. But if Ethiopia's national existence had come to depend upon its relationship with the United States, its nationhood would not have survived the severance of U.S. aid after the military revolution. The fact that it did is an important indicator of the independence of Ethiopian development. Ethiopia is almost routinely described as having switched from the United States to the Soviet Union for support. Dependency theory has never granted to fourth-world nations the autonomy to switch donors and sponsors. Explaining switching *outside of a domestic political economy* becomes necessary. In the Ethiopian case, dependency theorists have been reluctant to find Soviet heads at work. While it is true that the Soviets provided aid to revolutionary movements in the north, and supported revolutionary groupings in Addis Ababa, they did not embrace Mengistu's group until his power was secured after 1977 (Henze 1983). Instead, theorists have worked out a series of abandonment theses to show that the United States somehow forced the PMAC into the Soviet embrace (Marcus 1983; Spencer 1984).

To claim that the United States made efforts to "intervene" in Ethiopia during the famine period can hardly be taken seriously. Military support of insurgents under the Reagan Doctrine was minuscule. The lack of any viable domestic opposition to the Mengistu regime (thanks in large part to the purges of the Red Terror) demonstrated the inner limits on foreign intervention through the support of insurgency. Supporting insurgency through food aid would have been more properly characterized as humanitarian aid for the civilian populations than as military aid to support an opposition movement. Finally, the massive influx of food aid for distribution in regions under Ethiopian government control could hardly be viewed as interventionist, especially given its supportive effects. The impotence of the economic sanctions proposed by the sanctions movement in Congress demonstrated the outer limits on foreign intervention in Ethiopia, due to the weakness of U.S. economic ties to Ethiopia and its relative economic freedom vis-a-vis the West. In short, the configuration of Ethiopian society rather than foreign intervention from the East or West must be held responsible for the famine, even though Soviet policy agendas and political institutions were substantially adopted by the Mengistu regime.

Policy agendas and political institutions. Overreliance on the ideology or resources of external sponsors for pursuing specific programs and policies is another potential basis for dependency. Prior to and during the famine, the Soviet model of political and agricultural development certainly appears to have contributed to Ethiopian policies leading to famine inducement. Material support was provided to pursue a military settlement of internal opposition movements. Ideological support, at the very least, was provided for policies of collectivization, resettlement, villagization, and economic centralization. Whether this was solicited by pro-Moscow elements in the Ethiopian government or compelled from without remains to be settled. There is some Western precedent for such broad influence. The Italian occupation, British administration after the restoration of Selassie, and U.S. support in the fields of education, health development, military administration, agriculture, and many others, all served to mobilize Ethiopian policies in a foreign mold.

However, two factors diminish the influence of external sponsors—from the East or West—on policy agendas. First, externally-supported policies have often failed in their purpose. U.S. support of land reform under Selassie was undermined by domestic opposition from provincial authorities (Schwab 1972). Other policies desired and promoted by U.S. advisers did not materialize. Similarly, Soviet encouragement of the formation of the Workers' Party of Ethiopia was long delayed by Ethiopian resistance, and while originally supporting resettlement and collectivization policies, recent Soviet suggestions that collectivization be moderated have fallen on deaf ears. Despite massive Soviet military aid and advice for crushing the insurgents, the Eritrean and Tigrayan rebels have taken the upper hand in their administrative regions. In terms of foreign policy also, the Ethiopian government spurned the Soviets in rejecting Castro's plan for a federation among the then "socialist" states (of Ethiopia, Somalia, and the People's Democratic Republic of Yemen) in the Horn of Africa (Selassie 1980:111), even while it went decidedly pro-Soviet in the diplomatic arena.

A second, related factor diminishing external determinants of national development is the strong influence of Ethiopian traditions that may incorporate rather than be subordinated to the process of external influence. Political systems remain rooted in old Ethiopian patterns. Continuities in development are at least as important as are the contrasts supported by alliances with the developed world. Efforts to modernize political institutions on the model of the British political system achieved only limited success, largely because Ethiopian monarchism undercut these Western influences. Constitution making in Ethiopia under Selassie was partly based on the British Westminster model (although not as it was exported to Commonwealth countries in Africa) but also on the Washington model (Brietzke 1982). Monarchism, while not absolute, precluded the formation of political parties or other representative institutions (Clapham 1970). Ethnic conflict was only partly assuaged through mediation of monarchical institutions. Most often they were suppressed by peripheral elites.

Recently, greater penetration of the Soviet model of political organization has been accomplished. Central Committee control, the establishment of the Workers' Party of Ethiopia as the political vanguard, and "demilitarizing" military leaders followed in the footsteps of the Soviet program. Ethiopia's experience with near dictatorship from the center over regions in the periphery has been developing gradually long before the abrupt transition occasioned by Mengistu's rule. In the urban political sectors, Selassie's repression of only the most vocal of internal opponents has given way; stifling even the most modest of expressions of dissent by harsh measures has become the norm following the Red Terror. Domestic institutions for maintaining military prominence and for stifling internal dissent have indigenous origins, but have recently been buttressed by East German internal security advisors. Whether Moscow's approach to managing the nationalities problem will be successfully implemented during the short term, or a military solution will be further pursued, remains one of the most pressing issues of the day.

Just as Soviet influence is apparent in the modernization of Ethiopian political institutions, there is considerably more evidence from the foreign aid context that the Soviets have established some form of dependency, both by achieving communist policy goals and by coming closer to overcoming the obstacles to external penetration posed by Ethiopian traditions.

Foreign aid. Dependence on particular sources of outside aid and support has been a strong basis for dependency arguments. To apply such arguments to Ethiopia—based far more on rhetorical notions than the facts of development and the donor-recipient relationship—Ethiopia must be determined to have been dependent on U.S. and Western aid during the period of the famine. Dependency would be predicated on the prerevolutionary relationships between Ethiopia and the West, which would be presumed to have placed Ethiopia in a position of needing Western aid to prevent the famine prior to its outbreak in 1983. The inevitability implied by this would also mean that Ethiopian policies were largely irrelevant.

Over the years prior to the revolution, Ethiopians had come to look first to the United States as a high-rank source of foreign support, although they obtained aid from many other countries as well, including the Soviet Union. The thesis that U.S. aid created an Ethiopian dependency may be based on economic as well as military forms of aid. Economically, the United States provided substantial aid to Ethiopia, was the largest single importer of Ethiopian produce, was a modest source of capital investment, and exported manufactured goods to Ethiopia during the Selassie era. But there is no evidence that the United States so dominated the scene that the hands of Ethiopian entrepreneurs or the economic policy of the Ethiopian government were tied by economic relationships with the United States.

Similarly, the United States provided substantial military aid to Selassie's government (Mariam 1987). Much has been made of the Kagnew communications facility in Eritrea as a source of "dependency." This quid for supposedly important Ethiopian quos has been argued to have been a source of U.S. control over the domestic policy of Ethiopia. While representing a U.S. presence and strong ties with Ethiopia, it is not clear how the base could have contributed to the process of Ethiopian "underdevelopment." Because it came with perquisites vis-a-vis the United States, it may have had precisely the opposite effect. More generally, there is no evidence that Selassie's government was ever constrained by its military relationship with the United States. In fact, Selassie's military was never tested in a border contest, suggesting that military aid was a benefit rather than a burden.[4] The fact that the emperor passionately sought such assistance also suggests that aid was beneficial rather than burdensome (Spencer 1984). Some measure of the lack of dependency is provided by the coup attempt of 1960. Selassie survived this domestically-inspired threat to his rule without a loud call for U.S. support. Equally telling is the fact that the United States basically stood by during the events without any effort to intervene or to protect the Selassie regime (Marcus 1983:116-149).

Further evidence of independence—during the Western alliance as well as in the current period—is the diversity of Ethiopia's sources of aid. Under Selassie's governance, it would have been very difficult to maintain that an aid dependency on the United States had developed. Ethiopia was involved in too many external aid relationships and the emperor was too adept at managing them so as to avoid becoming overly reliant on any one. While the Soviets had until recently been lavish with military aid for pursuing engagements with northern insurgents as well as to maintain military hegemony, they continue to be relatively cheap with development assistance and capital investment, as are their Eastern European associates. Since military hardware support has not been accompanied by financial aid for supporting the day-to-day needs of military personnel, Ethiopia has had to broaden its aid sources and only some aspects of the internal dynamics of the classical dependency situation have developed. While Mengistu renewed some amount of Israeli military assistance—a source of consternation to several of the surrounding Arab nations—the regime's largest source of developmental assistance continues to be the West.

Aid donated during the famine period has generally been a boon to Ethiopian development, despite restrictions on developmental assistance imposed by some donors. International organizations also have large development programs in many regions of the country. As will be discussed below, because of the prospects of large food deficits far into Ethiopia's future, the possibility of dependence on foreign food aid to feed the rural populations is very great. Once again, this is much more the result of Ethiopian policy choices than the impact of Western aid itself. Moreover, there is little evidence that food aid will lead to Western food trade or changes in Ethiopian economic development, the presumed motivation for the fomentation of dependence.

Economic development and foreign trade. Neither patterns of economic development nor foreign trade provide evidence of Ethiopian dependence. International trade under Selassie was diversified and encouraged (Reimer 1975). A variety of investors from abroad stimulated production for internal consumption as well as for export. It is true that returns on investment contributed to the formation or consolidation of economic elites. But whether they produced new patterns of stratification or further impoverished an already destitute peasantry is not as clear as dependency theorists would have it. Diversity in Ethiopian trade partners, restrictions on diverse foreign investors, and concentrated wealth in the hands of Ethiopian elites diminish the credibility of explanations positing dependence on a single foreign country. On the contrary, Ethiopia's position in the world economy appears to have been buttressed by U.S. and other Western nations' support.

Parallels in the current context of foreign trade support this proposition. Even if presumed to operate under the Soviet grip, the Ethiopian government continues to have some autonomy in its economic and political relations with the outside world. Diversification of trading partners is discouraged by the Soviet Union. Agricultural commodities may be transported to the Soviet Union in a form of barter for military equipment and consumer goods that Ethiopians regard as inferior. The Soviets took the position of middleman with respect to Ethiopian petroleum imports after the oil crisis and there is some evidence that Moscow subsequently took advantage of this to exert leverage on the PMGSE by controlling its oil imports (cf. Henze 1981:69-70).

Even as the PMGSE is open to aid from the West, its restrictions on domestic market activity and the importation of Western goods are severe. Duties make imports very expensive, and taxes on income make entrepreneurial activity a burden. Nonetheless, Western goods continue to be a source of satisfaction and status, partly because of the vitality of the "free trade zone" in eastern Hararghe and partly because of the wide variety of the modern Western goods that had been available through the Afetieissa market of Dire Dawa (Hancock, Pankhurst, and Willets 1983:176) until the late 1980s.

Despite the tight reigns the Soviets would hold over the trade of Ethiopian commodities, Ethiopia continues to maintain currency ties with the West and retains its longstanding pattern of circulating hard currency. Addis is able to obtain hard currency through coffee and a few other exports to the West. The United States continues to be the largest importer of Ethiopian coffee, but it is widely recognized that this does not give significant leverage to the United States. An unsuccessful effort to impose a trade embargo on Ethiopian coffee imports showed that this leverage, weak as it is, was not used. Export earnings from the narcotic *chat* plant to countries around the Horn of Africa are another source of foreign exchange.

The People's Democratic Republic of Ethiopia 181

A Soviet Dependency?

In light of the foregoing, whether it is analytically useful to view Ethiopia's current relationship with the Soviet Union as a "dependent" one is subject to some doubt. Several Ethiopianists have proposed such a characterization, but it is unlikely to be acceptable to the dependency paradigm in the sociology of development. For example, Keller (1988:268) has asserted that Ethiopia's military and economic dependence increased during the first decade of the revolution.

However, ideology and theoretical structure would preclude the dependence paradigm from acknowledging any form of dependence on the Soviet Union, particularly in the case of Ethiopia. Not only would such recognition conflict with the premise of anti-imperialist movements and the world socialist revolution, it would require a re-visioning of the Ethiopian revolution. Unless the Soviet alliance is viewed as a liberation, dependency theory would most likely invoke a "dependency substitution" from West to East, or the thesis that dependence on the Soviet Union is in fact a disguised form of dependence on the West "in the last instance."

Key props for the "dependency in the last instance upon the West" thesis are Ethiopia's continuing currency ties with the West and the peculiar circulation patterns of its hard currency. This line of speculation proceeds at a very abstract level, but the key point is that Ethiopian economic relations with the Soviets only disguise the ultimate dependence of the Ethiopians (and the Soviets) on the capitalist world economy.[5] Trade and aid relationships are suspected of exploiting the Ethiopian economy through poor export prices, which but for Soviet protection would devastate the nation.

This argument is specious for at least two reasons. First, the vagaries of the international marketplace, far from conspiring against Ethiopian development, have often been quite favorable. This was especially true during the early years of Derg rule when world coffee prices soared. Domestic crises, not beatings delivered by the world economy, were responsible for the economy's faltering and the Derg's turn toward the Soviets.

Second, the Soviets reap short- and long-term rewards from Ethiopia's clientelistic position. A tightly controlled market for disposal of military and consumer items is most likely a bane to the Soviet domestic economy. On the other hand, it is hard to see how the West could gain from Ethiopian economic ills, which are more of a burden than a benefit. Policy efficacy (above and beyond the domestic politics of efficiency) was an issue from the beginning of the U.S. aid program in Ethiopia (see Marcus 1983), and the U.S. government's assessments of the benefits and burdens of donor status in the Ethiopian context weighed heavily on the burden side when the Soviets invested militarily in Ethiopia during the late 1970s. But since that time, the aid program of the United States has not been totally freed of Ethiopia's drain on developmental resources or been relieved of onerous responsibilities (cf. Farer 1980). This is made clear from the United States's involvement in the famine relief operation of 1983-86.

Humanitarianism and Developmentalism in Food Policy

In geopolitical terms, the U.S. response to the Ethiopian famine cuts against the clientelistic predictions of the dependency paradigm, highlighting humanitarianism as a vital force. The United States made no serious effort to intervene militarily, even though the ideological prime of the Reagan Doctrine was available for the purpose. Nor did the U.S. government make a substantial effort through diplomacy to influence Ethiopian policy or social organization. This may be partly explained by the fact that the United States had no economic interest in Ethiopia, and even the proposal of the sanctions movement to sever the most significant trade relations between the two countries did not mature into official policy.

If humanitarianism is to be viewed as the primary motivation for the aid program in rebel- and government-controlled areas, then the mobilization and distribution of donor resources must be viewed in this context, which in turn raises questions about why military and political objectives were not pursued or achieved. Humanitarian objectives were in the ascendancy largely as the result of USAID's relative autonomy from the foreign policy establishment and the constraints of democratic decision making on foreign policy objectives. Most importantly, the norms of developmentalism in foreign food aid policy, also substantially shared by USAID, displaced foreign policy restrictions on the relief effort stemming from the developmental prohibitions of the Hickenlooper and Brooke Amendments to U.S. foreign assistance legislation.

Achievement of Donor Objectives

There is little doubt that without U.S. and Western food aid, the Ethiopian famine would have raged to much larger peaks. It is generally recognized that one achievement of U.S. food aid was the saving of the lives of hundreds of thousands, perhaps even millions, of Ethiopians.[6] In this sense, there is no doubt that U.S. policy did not fail its humanitarian purpose.

But whether the United States gained anything from the famine relief program, in terms of improved relationships with the Ethiopian government,

The People's Democratic Republic of Ethiopia 183

is far from clear. Even though some observers have noted that Ethiopians perceived a need for Western capital (Marcus 1985) and identified social forces in the Ethiopian government favoring reassociation with the United States (Selassie 1984:270), little progress has been made in these directions. On the other hand, the consolidation and strengthening of the Ethiopian state and its ties to Moscow have been observed (Pascoe 1987), apparently made possible partly by Western aid. Moderates have suggested that a "waiting game" be continued, with nothing having been gained by the relief effort other than keeping a foot in the door (Korn 1986a:182-183).

From the standpoint of the U.S. foreign policy establishment, future prospects for relations between the United States and Ethiopia are poor. For the United States to engage Ethiopia in "dialogue through normal channels" (Crocker 1986), some policy reform by the Ethiopian government seems necessary. Providing food aid apparently had some impact on the settlement of U.S. claims stemming from Ethiopia's nationalization of assets,[7] but U.S. Department of Commerce (1986) predictions for economic relations remain bleak. The fact that no sanctions have yet been imposed by the United States in terms of trade embargoes is significant; however, even though it now seems to have run out of steam, the fact that the sanctions movement was still alive in 1987 (see Roth 1987) precluded stronger ties at that important point in time. It is unlikely that U.S. opposition will go any further, and appeals for U.S. military aid to insurgents (e.g., Deressa 1987) are unrealistic.

Explaining the inconclusiveness of U.S. government achievements in other than humanitarian terms is far from easy. Criticisms of U.S. policy toward the Ethiopian government ranged from disappointment over the failure to support the insurgents to frustration over the unwillingness of the U.S. government to brush aside legislative restrictions in order to explicitly support the Ethiopian regime with developmental assistance. In one view, the United States should first have required positive change from the regime before providing aid (Clay and Holcomb 1985). Indeed, termination of humanitarian assistance had been recommended (Pascoe 1987:9-10). The limitation of this view is that its failure to realistically assess the prospects of the Ethiopian government's compliance would have prohibited aid absolutely: The government was unlikely to have altered its policies in order to protect peasants from death by famine.

A contrasting view was that the United States should have provided developmental aid to the PDRE, largely to show pro-Western elements in the government the United States's willingness to support moderation. The principal shortcoming of this view is that it is too optimistic and would not have required enough or carried any assurances that reforms would have followed. Moreover, there was a tendency among Ethiopian moderates (including the RRC commissioner and deputy commissioner and Ethiopia's foreign minister) to defect and to seek asylum in the West rather than to promote reform in the Ethiopian government. In addition, by law the United States was prohibited from providing developmental assistance to Ethiopia.

Overall, the United States appears to have adopted a bifurcated approach of providing humanitarian support while applying pressure for moderation and reform. Why this was the case and why foreign policy objectives failed may be attributed to three factors. First, USAID had considerable autonomy from the State Department, the Pentagon, and the foreign policy establishment in general. Second, democratic constraints on U.S. policy, including the food lobby, mass organizations, and the left wing in Congress, prevented the formation of a foreign policy response. Third, the norms of developmentalism diluted the effects of external influences on Ethiopian policies and programs.

Relative Autonomy of USAID

Although Washington controlled appropriations and commitments, at the outset of the Ethiopian relief effort the details of program operation were largely controlled by officials working in the field. In this sense, assertions that the National Security Council made all "major decisions regarding aid to Ethiopia" (Smith 1987:6) are meaningless beyond the commitment of overall aid levels. Overseas missions tend to regulate their own affairs despite attempts by executive and congressional authorities to curb their discretion (Hoben 1980). For the most part, USAID's locus of decision making was in the U.S. Embassy in Addis Ababa rather than in Washington. This resulted in a number of autonomous characteristics in USAID's Ethiopian famine relief operations, and the relative absence or ineffectiveness of power plays in Washington maximized USAID flexibility in the field.

In famine situations, autonomy may be heightened by administrative necessity (cf. Green 1977). Effective operation of aid programs requires the concentration of decision-making authority in the hands of a relatively small group of officials. The administration and implementation of the U.S. food aid program in Ethiopia was controlled by a small number of regular officials assisted by a larger number of temporary employees. This facilitated the control of information no less than decisions about the allocation of aid resources to agencies involved in distribution. Strategies in the field were often based on the loose delegation of authority to U.S.-based PVOs, which further heightened the autonomy of the emergency food aid program vis-à-vis the foreign policy establishment. Delegation of distributional responsibilities to U.S.-based PVOs and other agencies further diluted controls from Washington.

Autonomy in the field was certainly not absolute. In famine relief situations, the elements of chaos and operational confusion may diminish the ability of the aid agency to fashion well-planned operational programs. Moreover, power factors involving the national policies of the recipient government may strictly control the micropolicies of donors. As a result of these factors, the Ethiopian government's policies largely controlled PVO operations and USAID strategy. Normative features of famine relief efforts may likewise limit autonomy by fostering a reliance on traditional patterns of response rather than on newly planned initiatives by the aid agency. PVOs unprepared for resettlement and villagization programs had little recourse outside of their ordinary distributional strategies.

With the exception of a few policy decisions—i.e., regarding cross-border operations, the Food for the North initiative, and the prohibition of assistance to resettlement—USAID's Addis Ababa staff appeared to be directed by a long-standing regulatory system rather than being responsive to the geopolitical concerns of Washington. But relative autonomy in the policy for Ethiopian famine relief should not be taken too far. Politics of larger consequence than in-country distribution of food aid commodities became involved as the levels of aid were heightened and substantive restrictions on aid were imposed. The locus of decision making gradually shifted toward Washington as the macropolitics of the policy formation process gained momentum between 1984 and 1986. But rather than losing control in favor of the foreign policy establishment, democratic decision making largely supported USAID's humanitarian and developmentalist program in Ethiopia.

Democratic Constraints on U.S. Food Aid Policy.

A more inclusive explanation for the failure of U.S. foreign policy objectives—beyond the autonomy of USAID and the goals of the PL-480—is that the very process of food aid policy formation was subject to democratic constraints and multiple constituencies, which are unlikely to produce the level of consensus required to formulate foreign policy objectives. No coherent ideology of food aid for Ethiopian famine relief emerged; there developed instead one of the most divisive factors in the politics of U.S. policy making. Divisiveness in ideology may affect policy for famine relief with particular vigor when the government of the recipient country is Marxist. Left and right divisions naturally arose over aiding the Ethiopian regime, which was seen by many to be folded under the wing of the Soviet Union. Contentions over the reasons for famine and the need for aid, whether and to what extent aid should be provided, and under what conditions if any it should be delivered, had an ideological base to be sure.

While divisions between the Left and Right fueled the ideological debate, they also had a modest effect on program administration. Party politics revealed ideological schisms between Democrats and Republicans, even though they were not hard and fast. Certainly Democrats had a political stake in attacking the administration's Ethiopian famine relief policy. But it was within the government itself, perhaps mirroring the cleavage in party politics, that the divisions in national ideology were most relevant to food aid policy. Congressional and administration proposals incorporated such outlooks, and adherents may have attempted to push them down the pipeline to USAID officials in the field and to PVO officers in Ethiopia.

Public opinion also functioned as a "principle of balance" (Lasswell 1941:141) to neutralize extremist ideologues of Right and Left. Mass and elite outlooks followed the expected pattern (cf. Geiger and Hansen 1968:340), as the ideology of pure need was pitted against the cost-effectiveness of aid. Mass opinion is usually shallower, based on less complete information, and carefully molded by its sponsors to elicit a charitable response, while elites are generally more responsive to the political and economic principles at stake.

To the extent that a coherent ideological position was formulated in terms of the Reagan Doctrine, there is little evidence of presidential leadership during the Ethiopian famine relief effort or in Ethiopian policy generally outside of President Reagan's occasional addresses to the UN General Assembly and other bodies. A slightly larger vice-presidential role was evident in negotiating the Food for the North initiative. Presidential politics did not fulfil its executive mandate; nor did it fully extend to U.S. policy for famine relief. The Reagan Doctrine for combatting Marxist regimes did not have the effect in Ethiopia that would be predicted by strong presidential leadership. Instead, presidential politics was enveloped in the broader context of democratic decision making.

Interagency struggles at intermediate levels of the administration further eclipsed any presidential mandate. There was a buildup of momentum for executive initiative from below, both from within the administration and from without through Congress. This was due in part to the fact that there was no high-level administrative presence in Ethiopia and the Embassy staff was minuscule. Even without this limitation, there is precedent for presidential opposition to the aid agency because of its connections and sympathy with the recipient country and its overvaluation of aid (cf. Lindblom 1968:15). National Security Council opposition to aid at an early point in the Ethiopian famine revealed conflicts within the administration. In Washington, anti-communist ideology and operational philosophy reached an uncomfortable compromise for Ethiopian policy that extended from the Pentagon and the State Department to the Food for Peace bureau of USAID. Neither of these sources of foreign policy leadership attained hegemony over USAID operations or ideology, however. Field-level precision in decision making remained

The People's Democratic Republic of Ethiopia 187

beyond the competence of high level officials, and minor officials in the field exercised considerable discretion over program management.

Dialectical relationships between congressional appropriations and administration allocations represented the tightest convergence of institutional structure and policy process for Ethiopian famine relief. Whether policy programs are viewed as presidential initiatives or as congressional packages, the compromise between authorities also reflects administrative power-sharing with Congress, while deference to congressional budgetary processes represents accommodation to the interests of foreign policy establishmentarians, humanitarian lobbyists, and the domestic farm economy.

Hearings held by congressional panels served as fact-finding sessions and as methods for filtering national ideology into the policy formation process, resulting in a partial fusion of national ideology and presidential politics. Congressional participation in policy formation was affected indirectly by electoral politics, but more directly by its role as a broker of macropolitical constituencies and as a quasi-decision-making body. Policy proposals of the administration and of Congress usually carried ideological baggage to be unpacked and moderated by conflicting proposals during negotiations. During the formation of U.S. policy for Ethiopian famine relief, congressional panels were largely springboards for sustaining the administration's course of action, inasmuch as witnesses from the executive side tended to predominate. But witnesses from outside the administration provided a counterpoint for ideological skirmishes as well as a rational basis for adjusting famine relief policy.

Segmentation of congressional power in functional terms served to diversify, then incorporate, macropolitical interests in the course of approving food aid funding. Congress's deference to executive decisions on the commitment of funds to particular countries did not preclude efforts of legislators to earmark aid. Authorizing and then appropriating funds for famine relief activities cut across a committee structure which bifurcated the procedural from the substantive domains of policy making, but specialized committees—such as the House Select Committee on Hunger and powerful substantive committees on foreign affairs in the House and Senate—were active in both domains.

Limited interest by voting publics in foreign policy rendered electoral politics a very tenuous base of support for an Ethiopian policy based on foreign policy concerns, especially given the strong countervailing humanitarian concerns involved. U.S.-based PVOs had domestic interests in and constituencies for the macropolitics of humanitarianism, and a large stake in the field setting of U.S. food aid policy for Ethiopian famine relief. PVOs with responsibilities for distributing relief commodities in Ethiopia had direct linkages with the humanitarian lobby, which provided a conduit for macropolitical involvement. U.S.-based PVOs tilted consistently toward the idealist, which is not to say utopian, position with respect to Ethiopian policy.

Developmentalism and Policy Continuity

Despite the divisiveness of ideological groupings and institutional morphology of democratic decision making, the famine relief operation in Ethiopia performed relatively free of ideology. The Ethiopian famine relief program did not represent a substantial shift in U.S. policy attributable to the Republican administration. In fact, continuity with Kennedy's Food for Peace policy and Carter's New Directions policy is evident in the Reagan administration's policy initiatives in Ethiopia. Relief operations were shaped partly by normative considerations, supporting assessments of an *emerging* normative order in food aid for famine relief (Puchala and Hopkins 1982). Moreover, there is evidence that this normative order carried with it the specific norms of "developmentalism," which helps to explain the inefficacy of U.S. prohibitions on developmental aid to Ethiopia.

Two structural developments in famine relief programs contributed to these consequences. First, the administrative framework for famine aid must be taken by each administration largely as it is inherited. Somewhat like the bureaucracies that are involved in famine relief, policies may come to take on a life of their own, resisting particular presidential and congressional controls. At this level, the Ethiopian operation demonstrated several administrative principles in the development of normative order in famine relief operations. Improvements in USAID's technical expertise and operational procedures, as reflected in its regulatory system for administering the distribution of food aid, and its closer relationships with PVOs, designed to tap the expertise of the latter, as well as its collaboration with international organizations having famine relief responsibilities (including WFP and UNDRO), are all a part of this administrative regime.

Second, regulating beneficiary status under U.S. food aid policy for famine relief and other purposes has progressed from the jurisdiction of administrative decisions to the target of macropolitics. The Food for Peace program had originally permitted a great deal of reliance on recipient governments to distribute food commodities. Successes as well as failures in relieving famine were made a part of the historical record of this approach. Under the New Directions policy of Carter, greater attentiveness to individual beneficiaries was required. Basic needs of individuals, and the responsibility of governments to respect the human rights of their subjects, defined the macropolitical environment for regulating beneficiary status (Walczak 1981). A persistent, if not defining, issue throughout the formation of U.S. policy for Ethiopian famine relief during 1983-86 concerned assurances that intended need-based beneficiaries would be reached. The Reagan administration's policy in this context attempted to circumvent the state distribution system in Ethiopia—largely by building its own through PVOs. The greater involvement of PVOs and international agencies in emergency food distribution, as well as macropolitical objectives for reaching intended beneficiaries, effectively transformed operations into developmental programs. For the U.S. relief operations, this resulted in the development of infrastructure that was then subordinated to Ethiopian authorities to be exploited in socialist development programs. And while U.S. policy specifically prohibited developmental assistance throughout the major part of the relief effort, U.S. aid had a definite developmental impact.

Food Deficits and Food Aid in Ethiopia's Future

If the transformation of humanitarian values—evident in distributing food to people in need regardless of the political realities of the situation (Pezzullo 1989)—led to a strengthening of Ethiopia's socialist development orientation, did the relief operation contribute to the prevention of future famines in Ethiopia? It is perhaps ironic, if not surprising, that Ethiopia, a client of the Soviet Union if not an actual dependent, faces a future of heavy reliance on the West for food aid. Ethiopia is almost certain to experience structural food deficits until the turn of the century (FAO 1988:4) and there is little that can be done outside the macropolitical context to eliminate short-term deficits.

All things considered, however, the probability that famine in Ethiopia will resurge to the 1983-86 level is relatively small. Prospects for famine resistance in Ethiopia during the short term have little to do with attaining a self-sufficient food status. Food security is likely to be achieved only at the price of some kind of food aid dependency in the future. Food aid is likely to be a regular need in Ethiopia—exceeding 1 million MT in 1988—especially if the PDRE continues to pursue its current course of agricultural development. There are most likely enough agencies entrenched in Ethiopia to mobilize and distribute Western food to avert famine in the event of another major food shortage. USAID received requests for over 34,000 MT of food for FY1989, and even the Soviets made an almost unheard of donation of 250,000 MT of grain to Ethiopia (see *Christian Science Monitor* 18 February 1988).

Without changes in PDRE policy, the programs responsible for inducing famine will continue to produce food deficits. However, changes in either food policy or in political structure are unlikely. The Ethiopian government made few concessions to the policy recommendations of the Western donors, multilateral institutions, or even moderate advisers of the Soviet Union.

Continued movement toward collectivization is likely. Government policy in this direction has persisted despite European Economic Community (EEC), World Bank, U.S. government, and independent recommendations against it. An evaluation of agricultural policies commissioned to the International Labor Organization by the PMGSE was effectively quashed. The World Bank and EEC had conditioned further aid on the reform of Ethiopian agricultural policies. The Ethiopian government had made few concessions until late December 1987, and observers have disagreed both on the significance of the Ethiopian government's agreement and on whether the agreement called for enough in substantive terms (see, e.g., *Washington Post* 7 February 1988.)

Internal political settlements are necessary, as are governmental concessions to the private sector and the emigrant populations, if prospects for Ethiopian development are to improve. The Ethiopian future does not appear to include nontotalitarian political structures. Even if restoration of monarchism were desirable, the cultural and institutional bases for monarchism were all but destroyed as members of previously royal families languished in political prisons until as late as 1989. The sole surviving son of the late emperor announced in London on 6 April 1989 that he was acceding to the throne. While a restorationist movement has formed in the United States (see ENATAD 1987), it has little support. No real prospects of a settlement of the Eritrean and Tigrayan insurgencies are in sight. Former President Jimmy Carter's recent mediation efforts come in a long line of such attempts to resolve the Eritrean conflict and there is little room for optimism that the continuation of talks will soon have an effect on the conduct of combatants in the field.

Prospects for Ethiopia's bootstrapping itself out of fourth-world status via the communist alliance are dismal. Mengistu is less willing than Castro to serve as an agent for Moscow, even though Ethiopian pilots have served in Angola. Whether the Soviet Union will give up on Ethiopia (and alleviate its arms pushing) is another important consideration (cf. Farer 1980). The displeasure expressed by Moscow over Mengistu's inability to resolve the civil wars in the north, and its asserted unwillingness to continue military aid, was apparently one factor behind Mengistu's trip to East Germany to solicit arms during the coup attempt in May 1989.

Expecting U.S. food aid policy to result in moderation or reversal of PDRE policies is not realistic, especially in light of the cancellation of recent high-level State Department visits (*New York Times* 13 January 1988). In such a context, food aid is unlikely to soon result in diminishing Ethiopia's structural food deficit.

Ethiopian independence of the West, rather than dependence, was largely responsible for the inducement of the 1983-86 famine. Whether food security, much less self-sufficiency, can be obtained through this orientation (as might

The People's Democratic Republic of Ethiopia 191

be expected from the utopian visions of dependency theorists) remains to be seen. In any event, Ethiopian development will continue to pose a vexing challenge to the explanatory and prescriptive dilemmas inherent in the strictures of the dependency paradigm.

Notes

1. See Lyons (1986:53), who characterizes the relationship between Ethiopia and the U.S. in "patron-client" terms and concludes that Ethiopia was never a "U.S. satellite or puppet." See also Lefebvre (1987) on *donor* dependency in the relationship.
2. Recent events in northern Ethiopia suggest that the latter would have occurred, i.e., that the rebel forces would have fared better without Western aid to both sides.
3. One may only speculate that the delay between the coup attempt in 1960 and the overthrow of the Imperial regime in 1974 may be replicated by a long delay between the coup attempt in 1989 and an overthrow of the communist regime in the twenty-first century.
4. The Ethiopian military's participation in the UN forces in the Congo and troops who fought in Korea added prestige no less than experience.
5. The relationships between the Soviet world and the capitalist world economy from the point of view of dependency theory are discussed by Szymanski (1982).
6. Seven million, according to a recent Senate Judiciary Committee Subcommittee on Immigration and Refugee Policy report (U.S. Senate 1986:5).
7. The terms of the $7 million settlement agreement are described by Leich (1986).

References

Official Documents, Reports, and Unpublished Materials

Abate, Yohannis
1984 Civil Military Relations in Ethiopia. *Armed Forces and Society*, 10(3), 380-400.
Abegaz, Berhanu
1988 Economics of Surplus Squeeze Under Peripheral Socialism: An Ethiopian Illustration. *Studies in Comparative International Development*, 23 (Fall), 51-77.
Aboucher, Alan
1984 The Firm in Abyssinia: Capitalism, Socialism, and Economic Development in Ethiopia. *The ACES Bulletin*, 26(4), 25-42.
ADAB See Australian Development Assistance Bureau
Agyeman-Duah, Baffour
1986 The U.S. and Ethiopia: The Politics of Military Assistance. *Armed Forces and Society*, 12(2), 287-307.
Amin, Samir
1972 Underdevelopment and Dependence in Black Africa: Origins and Contemporary Forms. *Journal of Modern African Studies*, 10(4), 503-524.
Amnesty International
1978 *Human Rights Violations in Ethiopia* (AFR/25/10/87). London: Amnesty International, November.
Appleby, Andrew B.
1978 *Famine in Tudor and Stuart England*. Palo Alto, CA: Stanford University Press.
Atwood, David
1987 1987 Food Need Assessment for Ethiopia. USAID: ST/RD, 28 May.

Australian Development Assistance Bureau (ADAB)
1984   *Food Aid to Ethiopia: A Review of the Australian Program.* Smithfield, Australia: Alken Press.
Balsvik, Randi Ronning
1985   *Haile Selassie's Students: The Intellectual and Social Background to Revolution 1952-1977.* E. Lansing, MI: MSU African Studies Center Monograph No. 16.
Barnes, LaFayette A.
1985   Ethiopian Famine: International Response. *Congressional Research Service,* May, 5-9.
Bates, Robert H.
1981   *Markets and States in Tropical Africa: The Political Basis of Agricultural Policies.* Berkeley: University of California Press.
Bazyler, Michael J.
1987   Reexamining the Doctrine of Humanitarian Intervention in Light of the Atrocities in Kampuchea and Ethiopia. *Stanford Journal of International Law,* 23(2), 547-620.
Bernstein, Thomas P.
1984   Stalinism, Famine, and Chinese Peasants: Grain Procurements During the Great Leap Forward. *Theory and Society,* 13(3), 339-378.
Bezabih, Alemayehu
1981   *Agrarian Structure and Social Classes in Ethiopia: An Historical Perspective.* United Nations Research Institute for Social Development Working Paper, Food Systems and Society. Geneva: UNRISD.
Bienen, Henry
1987   Domestic Political Considerations for Food Policy. In, John W. Mellor, C.L. Delgado and M. J. Blackie (eds.), *Accelerating Food Production in Sub-Saharan Africa.* Baltimore: Johns Hopkins University Press.
Bole, Janice J.
1986   Feast or Famine: Do Ethiopians Have a Choice? *Dickensen Journal of International Law,* 5(1), 103-131.
Bolling, Landrum R.
1982   *Private Foreign Aid: US Philanthropy for Relief and Development.* Boulder, CO: Westview.
Bondestam, Lars
1981   Understanding Hunger and Predicting Starvation. *UN Food and Nutrition Bulletin,* 3(4), 1-4.
Borton, Nan
1986   *The UN and the US Private Sector in African Famine Response (1984-1986).* Washington, D.C.
Borton, John
1989   UK Food Aid and the African Emergency 1983-86. *Food Policy,* August, 232-240.

Boserup, Ester
1981   *Population and Technological Change: A Study of Long-Term Trends.* Chicago: University of Chicago Press.
Boyer, Peter J.
1985   Famine in Ethiopia: The TV Accident That Exploded. *Washington Journalism Review,* January, 19-21.
Brandenburg, P.F., S.N. Burgess, et al.
1986   Feast or Famine: Issues, Problems, and Procedures Relating to Massive Relief Efforts with a Focus on the African Crisis. *Vanderbilt Journal of Transnational Law,* 19, 333-464.
Brauman, Romy
1986a   Famine Aid: Were We Duped? *Reader's Digest,* October, 65-72.
1986b   Not *If* the Aid Got Through, But *How* the Aid Was Used. *Washington Post,* 1 November.
Bread for the World
1983   *Chronology of Responses to Ethiopian Famine, 1982-1983.* Washington, D.C., 6 October.
Brietzke, Paul H.
1982   *Law, Development, and the Ethiopian Revolution.* E. Brunswick, NJ: Associated University Presses.
Bush, Rod
1985   A Report From Ethiopia: Famine and Revolution in Africa. *Contemporary Marxism,* 11, 113-125.
CARE
1986a   *Report on Inventory Procedures: Save the Children Federation (USA) in Ethiopia-Drought Relief Program.*
1986b   *Program Profile.* Dire Dawa.
1986c   *Distribution Details, 1985-1986.* Dire Dawa.
Cartwright, J.
1983   *Political Leadership in Africa.* New York, NY: St. Martins.
Catholic Relief Services (CRS)
1986   *Ethiopia 1986 Emergency Relief Program for JRP.* March.
CDAA/JRP   See Church Drought Action Africa/Joint Relief Partners
Chase-Dunn, Christopher
1989   Politics and Famine Relief. In, Bruce Nichols and Gil Loescher (eds.), *The Moral Nation: Humanitarianism and U.S. Foreign Policy Today.* Notre Dame, IN: Notre Dame University Press.
1982   Socialist States in the Capitalist World Economy. In, Chase-Dunn (ed.), *Socialist States in the World System.* Beverly Hills, CA: Sage. Cuny, Frederick C.
Church Drought Action Africa/Joint Relief Partners (CDAA/JRP)
1986   *Distribution Details,* 1985-1986. Addis Ababa.

Clapham, Christopher
1988   Transformation and Continuity in Revolutionary Ethiopia. Cambridge: Cambridge University Press.
1987   Revolutionary Socialist Development in Ethiopia. *African Affairs*, 86(343), 151-165.
1985   Ethiopia: The Institutionalization of a Marxist Military Regime. In, Christopher Clapham and George Phillip (eds.), *The Political Dilemmas of Military Regimes*. New Jersey: Barnes & Noble.
1970   The Functions and Development of Parliament in Ethiopia. *Proceedings of the Third International Conference of Ethiopian Studies, 1966*. Addis Ababa: Institute for Ethiopian Studies.

Clark, Lance
1986   *Early Warning Case Study: The 1984-85 Influx of Tigrayans into Eastern Sudan*. Washington, D.C.: Refugee Policy Group Working Paper No. 2, March.

Clarke, John
1987   *Ethiopia's Campaign Against Famine: Resettlement and Rehabilitation*. London: Harney and Jones, Ltd.

Clay, Jason W.
1989   Ethiopian Famine and the Relief Agencies. In, Bruce Nichols and Gil Loescher (eds.), *The Moral Nation: Humanitarianism and U.S. Foreign Policy Today*. Notre Dame, IN: Notre Dame University Press.
1988   Villagization in Ethiopia. In, Jason W. Clay, Sandra Steingraber and Peter Niggli, *The Spoils of Famine: Ethiopian Famine Policy and Peasant Agriculture*. Cambridge, MA: Cultural Survival Report No. 25.
1986   Research Report: Refugees Flee Ethiopian Collectivization. *Cultural Survival Quarterly*, 10(2), 80-85.

Clay, Jason W. and Bonnie Holcomb
1985   *Politics and the Ethiopian Famine, 1984-1985*. Cambridge, MA: Cultural Survival.

Cohen, John M.
1984   Agrarian Reform in Ethiopia: The Situation on the Eve of the Revolution's 10th Anniversary. Cambridge, MA: Harvard Institute for International Development, *Development Discussion Paper No. 164*, April.

Cohen, John M., and N. Isaksson
1987   Villagization in Ethiopia's Arsi Region. *Journal of Modern African Studies*, 25(3), 435-464.

Conquest, Robert
1986   *The Harvest of Sorrow*. New York: Oxford University Press.

Crocker, Chester A. (U.S. Department of State).
1986 U.S. and Soviet Interests in the Horn of Africa. Address before the World Affairs Council, 13 November 1985. Printed in *Department of State Bulletin*, January.
CRS See Catholic Relief Services
Cuny, Frederick C.
1989 Politics and Famine Relief. In, Bruce Nichols and Gil Loescher (eds.), *The Moral Nation: Humanitarianism and U.S. Foreign Policy Today*. Notre Dame, IN: Notre Dame University Press.
Cutler, Peter
1984 Famine Forecasting: Prices and Peasant Behavior in Northern Ethiopia. *Disasters*, 8(1), 48-56.
Dalrymple, Dana G.
1964 The Soviet Famine of 1932-1934. *Soviet Studies*, 15(3), 250-284.
de Castro, Josue
1977 *The Geopolitics of Hunger*. New York: Monthly Review.
Degefu, Workineh
1987 Some Aspects of Meteorological Drought in Ethiopia. In, Michael Glantz (ed.), *Drought and Hunger in Africa*. Cambridge: Cambridge University Press.
Dejene, Alemneh
1987 *Peasants, Agrarian Socialism, and Rural Development in Ethiopia*. Boulder, CO: Westview.
1985 Smallholder Perceptions of Rural Development and Emerging Institutions in Arsi Region Since the Ethiopian Revolution. Cambridge, MA: Harvard Institute for International Development, *Development Discussion Paper No. 192*.
Deressa, Jonas
1987 Rebel Aid. *The New Republic*, 24 April, 36-39.
Dines, Mary
1988 Ethiopian Violations of Human Rights in Eritrea. In Lionel Cliffe and Basil Davidson (eds.), *The Long Struggle of Eritrea for Independence and Constructive Peace*. Trenton, NJ: Red Sea Press.
Doulos, Mikael
1986 Christians in Marxist Ethiopia. *Religion in Communist Lands*, 14(2), 134-147.
Eicher, Carl
1982 Facing Up to Africa's Food Crisis. *Foreign Affairs*, (Fall), 151-174.
ENATAD See Ethiopian National Alliance to Advance Democracy
ERCS See Ethiopian Red Cross Society

Erlich, Haggai
1983a   The Ethiopian Army and the 1974 Revolution. *Armed Forces and Society*, 9(3), 455-481.
1983b   *The Struggle over Eritrea, 1962-1978; War and Revolution in the Horn of Africa*. Stanford: Hoover Institution.
Eshete, Aleme
1982   *The Cultural Situation in Socialist Ethiopia*. Paris: UNESCO.
Ethiopian National Alliance to Advance Democracy (ENATAD)
1987   *Declaration*. Washington, D.C.: 1986.
Ethiopian Red Cross Society (ERCS)
1985   *Ethiopian Red Cross Society, 1935-1985*. Addis Ababa: ERCS.
1983   *ERCS Pointer*. Addis Ababa.
FAO   See United Nations Food and Agriculture Organization
Farer, Tom J.
1980   Lusting for Defeats: Masochistic Politics and the Horn of Africa. *Williamette Law Review*, 17, 203-219.
1979   *War Clouds Over the Horn of Africa: The Widening Storm* (2d ed.). Washington, D.C.: Carnegie Endowment for International Peace.
Faught, William A.
1987   *An Appraisal of Ethiopia's Agricultural Prospects*. Addis Ababa: USAID/E, 23 April.
Finney, Lynne Dratler
1983   Development Assistance—A Tool of Foreign Policy. *Case Western Reserve Journal of International Law*, 15, 213-252.
Firebrace, James with Stuart Holland
1985   *Never Kneel Down: Drought, Development, and Liberation in Eritrea*. Trenton, NJ: Red Sea Press.
GAO   See U.S. General Accounting Office
Geiger, Theodore and Roger D. Hansen
1968   The Role of Information in Decision Making on Foreign Aid. In, Raymond A. Bauer and Kenneth J. Gergen (eds.), *The Study of Policy Formation*. NY: The Free Press.
George, Susan
1977   *How the Other Half Dies: The Real Reason for World Hunger*. Montclair, NJ: Allenheld, Osmun.
Gilkes, Patrick
1982   Building Ethiopia's Revolutionary Party. *MERIP Reports*, 12(5), 22-26.
Gill, Peter
1986   *A Year in the Death of Africa: Politics, Bureaucracy, and the Famine*. London: Paladin.

Goyder, Hugh and Catherine
1988   Case Studies of Famine: Ethiopia. In, Donald Curtis, Michael Hubbard, and Andrew Shepherd (eds.), *Preventing Famine: Policies and Prospects for Africa*. London and New York: Rutledge.
Green, Stephen
1977   *International Disaster Relief: Toward a Responsive System*. New York: McGraw-Hill.
Griffin, Keith and Roger Hay
1985   Problems of Agricultural Development in Socialist Ethiopia: An Overview and a Suggested Strategy. *The Journal of Peasant Studies*, 13(1), 37-66.
Hadwiger, Don
1970   *Federal Wheat Commodity Programs*. Ames, IA: Iowa State University Press.
Hancock, Graham
1985   *Ethiopia: The Challenge of Hunger*. London: V. Gollancz.
Hancock, Graham, Richard Pankhurst, and Duncan Willets
1983   *Under Ethiopian Skies*. London: editions HL.
Hansen, Art and A. Oliver-Smith (eds.)
1982   *Involuntary Migration and Resettlement*. Boulder, CO: Westview.
Harbeson, John W.
1979   Socialist Politics in Revolutionary Ethiopia. In C. Rosberg and T. Callaghy (eds.), *Socialism in Sub-Saharan Africa: A New Assessment*. Berkelcy: University of California.
Harff, Barbara and Ted Robert Gurr
1988   Toward Empirical Theory of Genocides and Politicides: Identification and Measurement of Cases since 1945. *International Studies Quarterly*, 32, 359-71.
Harris, Myles F.
1987   *Breakfast in Hell: A Doctor's Eyewitness Account of the Politics of Hunger in Ethiopia*. NY: Poseidon Press.
Harrison, Paul
1987   *The Greening of Africa: Breaking Through in the Battle for Land and Food*. New York: Penguin.
Henze, Paul B.
1986   Exploiting Famine—And Capitalizing on Western Generosity. *Global Affairs*, 1(2), 87-99.
1985   *Communist Ethiopia-Is It Succeeding*. Santa Monica, CA: RAND (P-7054).
1984   Arming the Horn 1960-1980: Military Expenditures, Arms Imports, and Military Aid in Ethiopia, Kenya, Somalia, and Sudan, with Statistics on Economic Growth and Governmental Expenditures. In, S. Rubensen (ed.), *Proceedings of the Seventh International Conference of Ethiopian Studies*. East

Lansing, MI: Michigan State University.
1983   Getting a Grip on the Horn: The Emergence of the Soviet Presence and Future Prospects. In, Walter Laqueur (ed.), *The Pattern of Soviet Conduct in the Third World*. New York: Praeger.
1981   Communism and Ethiopia. *Problems of Communism*, May-June, 55-74.

Hess, Robert L.
1970   *Ethiopia: Modernization of Autocracy*. Ithaca, NY: Cornell University Press.

Hoben, Allan
1980   Agricultural Decision Making in Foreign Assistance: An Anthropological Analysis. In, Peggy F. Bartlett (ed.), *Agricultural Decision Making: Anthropological Contributions to Rural Development*. New York: Academic Press.

Holt, J.F.J.
1983   Ethiopia: Food for Work or Food for Relief. *Food Policy*, August, 187-201.

Horowitz, Irving Louis
1982   *Beyond Empire and Revolution: Militarization and Consolidation in the Third World*. New York: Oxford University Press.

Hussein, A.M.
1976   The Political Economy of the Famine in Ethiopia. In, A.M. Hussein (ed.), *Rehab: Drought and Famine in Ethiopia*. London: International African Institute.

ICIHI   See Independent Commission on International Humanitarian Issues
ICRC   See International Committee of the Red Cross
IDI   See International Disaster Institute
IMF   See International Monetary Fund

Independent Commission on International Humanitarian Issues (ICIHI)
1985   *Famine: A Man-Made Disaster?* New York: Vintage.

Insel, Barbara
1985   A World Awash in Grain. *Foreign Affairs*, Spring, 892-911.

International Bank for Reconstruction and Development (World Bank)
1984   *World Development Report*. New York: Oxford University Press.
1983   *Ethiopia: The Agricultural Sector—An Interim Report* (2 vols.). Washington, D.C.: The World Bank, 26 January.

International Committee of the Red Cross (ICRC)
1987   *International Review of the Red Cross*, 258, 317.
1985   *Red Cross in Ethiopia*. Geneva: April.

International Disaster Institute (IDI)
1983   Drought and Famine Relief in Ethiopia. *Disasters*, 7(3), 164-168.

References 201

International Monetary Fund (IMF)
1987   *Government Finance Statistics Yearbook, 1987.* Volume XI. Washington, D.C.
INTERTECT
1986   *Executive Summary Assessment: Food Needs for the Consortium of CRS, ECS, EECMY, LWF Food Distribution Network in Ethiopia.* January.
Jacobs, Dan
1987   *The Brutality of Nations.* New York: Knopf.
Jansson, Kurt
1987   The Emergency Relief Operation: The Inside View. In, Jansson, K., M. Harris and A. Penrose, *The Ethiopian Famine.* London: Zed Books.
Kaplan, Robert D.
1988   *Surrender or Starve: The Wars Behind the Famine.* Boulder, CO: Westview.
Keating, Robert
1986   Live Aid: The Terrible Truth. *Spin,* 75-80.
Kelemen, Paul
1985   *The Politics of the Famine in Ethiopia and Eritrea.* Manchester: University of Manchester, Department of Sociology Occasional Paper No. 17.
Keller, Edmond J.
1988   *Revolutionary Ethiopia: From Empire to People's Republic.* Bloomington, IN: Indiana University Press.
1985   State, Party, and Revolution in Ethiopia. *African Studies Review,* 28(1), 1-17.
Kent, Randolph C.
1983   Reflecting upon a Decade of Disasters: The Evolving Response of the International Community. *International Affairs* (London), 693-711.
Kjekshus, Helge
1977   *Ecology Control and Economic Development in East African History.* London: Heinemann.
Korn, David A.
1986a   *Ethiopia, the United States, and the Soviet Union.* London: Croom-Helm.
1986b   Ethiopia: Dilemma for the West. *The World Today,* 4(1), 4-7.
Korten, David C.
1972   *Planned Change in a Tradition Society.* New York: Praeger.
Lasswell, Harold D.
1941   *Democracy Through Public Opinion.* George Bates Publishing Co.
League of Red Cross Societies (LICROSS)
1986   *Distribution Details, 1985-1986.* Addis Ababa.

Lefebvre, Jeffrey A.
1987   Donor Dependency an American Arms Transfers to the Horn of Africa: The F-5 Legacy. *Journal of Modern African Studies*, 25(3), 465-488.
Lefort, Rene
1983   *Ethiopia, an Heretical Revolution?* London: Zed Press.
Legum, Colin
1987   USSR Policy in Sub-Saharan Africa. In, Korbonsky and Fukuyama (eds.), *The Soviet Union in the Third World: The Last Three Decades*. Ithaca: Cornell University Press.
Leich, Marian Nash
1986   Claims Settlement Agreements: United States—Provisional Military Government of Socialist Ethiopia. *American Journal of International Law*, 80, 344-345.
Lewis, W. Arthur
1984   *The Evolution of the International Economic Order*. Princeton: Princeton University Press.
LICROSS   See League of Red Cross Societies
Lindblom, Charles B.
1968   *The Policy Making Process*. Englewood Cliffs, NJ: Prentice-Hall.
Lirenso, Alemayehu
1984   Some Effects of Grain Marketing Policy on the Production and Consumption of Food Grains in Ethiopia. Paper presented at the Meeting of Inter-African Research Working Groups on State Policies on Agriculture and Food Production in Africa. Addis Ababa: September.
Luckman, R., and D. Bekele
1984   Foreign Powers and Militarism in the Horn of Africa. *Review of African Political Economy*, 30, 9-20.
Lyons, Terrence
1986   The United States and Ethiopia: The Politics of a Patron-Client Relationship. *Northeast Africa Studies*, 8(2-3), 53-75.
Magistad, Mary Kay
1987   On the Razor's Edge. *Africa Report*, May-June, 61-64.
Malhuret, Claude
1985   *Mass Deportations in Ethiopia*. Paris: Medecins Sans Frontieres.
Marcus, Harold G.
1985   Africa's Poverty Squeeze: Poverty, Hunger, and Refugees. Reprinted in U.S. House, Committee on Foreign Affairs, Hearings on *"Human Rights and Food Aid in Ethiopia"*, 16 October, pp. 192-193.
1983   *Ethiopia, Great Britain, and the United States*. Berkeley: University of California Press.

Mariam, Alemayehu Gebre
1987   U.S. Military Aid to Ethiopia, 1942-1977. *Towson State Journal of International Affairs*, 21(2), 93-112.
Markakis, John and Nega Ayele
1986   *Class and Revolution in Ethiopia*. Trenton, NJ: Red Sea Press.
Mazrui, Ali A., and Michael Tidy
1984   *Nationalism and New States in Africa*. London: Heinemann.
McCann, James
1987   The Social Impact of Drought in Ethiopia: Oxen, Households and Some Implications for Rehabilitation. In, M. Glantz (ed.), *Drought and Famine in Africa: Denying Famine a Future*. Cambridge: Cambridge University Press.
McClellan, Charles W.
1984   State Transformation and Social Reconstruction in Ethiopia: The Allure of the South. *International Journal of African Historical Studies*, 17(4), 657-675.
Medhanie, Tesfatsion
1986   *Eritrea: Dynamics of a National Question*. Amsterdam: B.R. Gruner.
Meillassoux, Claude
1974   Development or Exploitation: Is the Sahel Famine Good Business. *Review of African Political Economy*, 1(1), 27-33.
Mengisteab, Kidane
1989   The Nature of the State and Agricultural Crisis in Post-1975 Ethiopia. *Studies in Comparative International Development*, 24(1), 20 38.
Mudge, George Alfred
1970   Starvation As a Means of Warfare. *International Lawyer*, 4(2), 228-68.
Nelson, Harold D., and Irving Kaplan (eds.)
1981   *Ethiopia: A Country Study*. Washington, D.C.: Government Printing Office.
Nichols, Bruce and Gil Loescher (eds.)
1989   *The Moral Nation: Humanitarianism and U.S. Foreign Policy Today*. Notre Dame, IN: Notre Dame University Press.
Niggli, Peter
1986   *Ethiopia, Deportations and Forced-Labour Camps: A Study*. Berlin: Berliner Missionswerk.
Novicki, Margaret A.
1984   Ethiopia's Drought and Famine Crisis. *Africa Report*, Jan-Feb, 47-49.
OFDA   See USAID Office of Foreign Disaster Assistance
OLF   See Oromo Liberation Front
Oromo Liberation Front (OLF)
1986   *Oromia Speaks*. September.

Ostefeld, David
1986   Famine in Africa. *Journal of Social, Political and Economic Studies*, 10(3), 259-274.
Pankhurst, Richard
1968   *Economic History of Ethiopia*. Addis Ababa: Haile Selassie I University Press.
Pascoe, William
1987   *Time for Action Against Mengistu's Ethiopia*. Heritage Foundation Backgrounder No. 568. Washington, D.C.: Heritage Foundation, 11 March 1988.
Pateman, Roy
1988   Drought, Famine, and Development. In, Lionel Cliffe and Basil Davidson (eds.), *The Long Struggle of Eritrea for Independence and Constructive Peace*. Trenton, NJ: Red Sea Press.
Patinkin, Mark
1985   *An African Journey*. Grand Rapids, MI: Eerdmans Publishing.
Perham, Marjorie
1969   *The Government of Ethiopia*. Evanston, IL: Northwestern.
Peterson, Donald
1986   Ethiopia Abandoned? An American Perspective. *International Affairs*, 62(4), 627-645.
Pezzullo, Lawrence A.
1989   Catholic Relief Services in Ethiopia: A Case Study. In, Bruce Nichols and Gil Loescher (eds.), *The Moral Nation: Humanitarianism and U.S. Foreign Policy Today*. Notre Dame, IN: Notre Dame University Press.
Phillips, James A., and Richard D. Fisher, Jr.
1984   *A Plan for Rescuing Starving Ethiopians*. Heritage Foundation Backgrounder No. 400. Washington, D.C.: Heritage Foundation.
Porter, Bruce D.
1984   *The USSR in Third World Conflicts: Soviet Arms and Diplomacy in Local Wars, 1945-1980*. Cambridge: Cambridge University Press.
Puchala, Donald J., and Raymond F. Hopkins
1982   International Regimes: Lessons from Inductive Analysis. *International Organization*, 36(2), 61-91.
Rahman, Md. Ansur
1979   Transition to Collective Agriculture and Peasant Participation—North VietNam, Tanzania and Ethiopia. *The Bangladesh Development Studies*, 7(3), 1-22.
Rahmato, Dessalegn
1985   *Agrarian Reform in Ethiopia*. Trenton, NJ: Red Sea Press.

Reimer, Richard
1975　　　Ethiopian Agricultural Exports: A Brief Survey. *Rural Africana*, 28(Fall), 119-137.
Relief and Rehabilitation Commission (RRC)
1986　　　Early Warning System Monthly Report for July. Addis Ababa: RRC/Early Warning and Planning Services, 16 August.
1985a　　*Mode of Operation and Staffing of the Non-Governmental Organizations Operating in Ethiopia under the Auspices of the RRC.* Addis Ababa.
1985b　　*Distribution Plan for Bilateral Commodities.* Addis Ababa.
1985c　　*The Challenges of Drought.* Addis Ababa: RRC.
1985d　　*Food Situation in Ethiopia, 1981-1985: Trend Analysis Report.* Addis Ababa: October.
1985e　　In Cooperation with "Sertoder," Organ of the Central Committee of the Worker's Party of Ethiopia. Addis Ababa: August.
1984a　　*Assistance Requirements 1984.* Addis Ababa.
1984b　　*Joint RRC-UNICEF Workshop on Technical and Institutional Improvements in the Early Warning System.* Nazareth: October.
1975　　　*Pre-Disaster Planning Program.* Addis Ababa: RRC, 22 May.
Rogge, John R.
1985　　　*Too Many, Too Long: Sudan's Twenty Year Refugee Dilemma.* Totowa, New Jersey: Rowman & Allanheld.
Roth, Toby
1987　　　Time to Act Against Ethiopian Holocaust. *Conservative Digest*, April, 85-88.
RRC　　　See Relief and Rehabilitation Commission
Rubensen, Sven
1976　　　*The Survival of Ethiopian Independence.* London: Heinemann.
Samuels, J.W.
1979　　　The Relevance of International Law in the Prevention and Mitigation of Natural Disasters. In, L. Stephens and S. Green (eds.), *Disaster Assistance: Appraisal, Reform and New Approaches.* New York: New York University Press.
Sauldie, Madan M.
1982　　　*Ethiopia: Dawn of the Red Star.* Bombay: Asia.
Save the Children Federation (SCF)
1986　　　*RRC Evaluation of SCF.* March.
1985a　　*Training Report: Relief and Rehabilitation Project-Yifat na Timuga, Ethiopia.*
1985b　　*Summary Report of US AID Food.* Westport, CT.
1985c　　*Supporting Document to SCF's Request for Grain from USAID.*
SCF　　　See Save the Children Federation

Schellinski, Kristina
1986   The Cave Children of Sekota. *Action for Children*, 1, 4-5.
Schraeder, Peter J.
1986   Involuntary Migration in Somalia: The Politics of Resettlement. *Journal of Modern African Studies*, 24(4), 641-662.
Schwab, Peter
1985   *Ethiopia: Politics, Economics and Society*. Boulder, CO: Lynne Reinner.
1972   *Decision-Making in Ethiopia: A Study of the Political Process*. Rutherford, NJ: Fairleigh Dickensen University Press.
Scoville, Orlin J.
1985   Relief and Rehabilitation in Kampuchea. *The Journal of Developing Areas*, 20, 23-36.
Selassie, Bereket Habte
1984   The American Dilemma on the Horn. *Journal of Modern African Studies*, 22(2), 249-272.
1980   *Conflict and Intervention in the Horn of Africa*. NY: Monthly Review.
Shawcross, William
1984   *The Quality of Mercy*. NY: Simon & Schuster.
Shehim, Kassim
1985   Ethiopia, Revolution and the Question of Nationalities: The Case of the Afar. *Journal of Modern African Studies*, 23(2), 331-348.
Shepherd, Jack
1985a   Ethiopia: The Use of Food As an Instrument of U.S. Foreign Policy, *Issue: A Journal of Africanist Opinion*, 14, 4-9.
1985b   The Politics of Food Aid. *Africa Report*, March-April, 51-54.
1985c   Congress and the White House at Odds. *Africa Report*, May-June, 25-29.
1975   *The Politics of Starvation*. New York: Carnegie Endowment for International Peace.
SIM, International
1986   Letter to the author dated 7 March (from Don Stilwell).
Sivini, Giordano
1986   Famine and the Resettlement Program in Ethiopia. *Africa* (Rome), 41(2), 211-242.
Smith, Gayle
1987   Ethiopia and the Politics of Famine Relief. *Middle East Report*, March-April, 31-37.
Snyder, Charles P.
1986   African Ground Forces. In, B. Arlinghaus and P. Baker (eds.), *African Armies: Evaluation and Capabilities*. Boulder, Co: Westview.

Spencer, John H.
1984   *Ethiopia At Bay: A Personal Account of the Haile Selassie Years*. Algonac, MI: Reference Publications.
1976   Statement. In U.S. Senate, *Hearings on "Ethiopia and the Horn of Africa."* Subcommittee on Africa, Committee on Foreign Relations, 94th Cong., 2d Sess., 4-6 August.

Survival International
1988   *For Their Own Good . . . Ethiopia's Villagization Program*. London: Survival International.
1986   *Ethiopia's Bitter Medicine: Settling for Disaster*. London: Survival International.

Swenson, John (CRS)
1986   Food Aid Distribution in Ethiopia. Presentation at the Food and Law Conference: "The Legal Faces of the Hunger Problem." Howard University School of Law, Washington, D.C., 17 October.

Szymanski, Albert
1982   The Socialist World System. In Chase-Dunn (ed.), *Socialist States in the World System*. Beverly Hills, CA: Sage.

Teferi, Abebe
1984   State Policies, Agricultural Development and Food Production in Ethiopia. Paper presented at the Meeting of Inter-African Research Working Groups on State Policies on Agriculture and Food Production in Africa. Addis Ababa: September.

The White House
1986   White House Statement, 30 October.
1984   White House Statement: Food Assistance to Ethiopia. Printed in *State Department Bulletin*, 7 January 1985.

Thomas, Maria
1987   A State of Permanent Revolution: Ethiopia Bleeds Red. *Harpers*, 274, January, 53-60.

Torry, William
1984   Social Science Research on Famine: A Critical Evaluation. *Human Ecology*, 12(3), 227-252.

Turton, David
1985   Mursi Response to Drought: Some Lessons for Relief and Rehabilitation. *African Affairs*, 84(336), 331-346.

UNDP/ILO   See UN Development Programme/International Labor Organization
UNITAR   See United Nations Institute for Training and Research
United Nations Development Programme/International Labor Organization (UNDP/ILO)
1982   *Logistical and Technical Support for Food Aid Transport—Ethiopia: Project Findings and Recommendations*. Geneva: UNDP/ILO.

United Nations Food and Agriculture Organization (FAO)
1988 *Trends in Agricultural Development in Ethiopia.* Addis Ababa.
1983 *Approaches to World Food Security.* FAO Economic and Social Development Paper No. 32. Rome: FAO.
1982 *Agrarian Reform and Rural Development in Ethiopia.* Report of the High-Level WCARRO Follow-Up Mission to Ethiopia, 3-9 May 1982. WCARRO Mission No. 7. Rome: FAO.
United Nations Institute for Training and Research (UNITAR)
1982 *Model Rules for Disaster Relief Operations.* UNITAR Policy and Efficacy Studies, No. 8. NY.
United Nations Research Institute for Social Development (UNRISD)
1976 *Famine Risk and Famine Prevention in the Modern World: Studies in Food Systems Under Conditions of Recurrent Scarcity.* Geneva.
UNRISD See United Nations Research Institute for Social Development
UN World Food Programme/E (WFP)
1986 *USA Food Aid Deliveries to Ethiopia.* Addis Ababa, 21 August.
1985 *Ethiopia 2488 Expansion.* Addis Ababa, 1985.
USAID/E
1987a *Ethiopia Drought/Famine: Final Disaster Report.* Addis Ababa: May.
1987b *1987 Food Need Assessment for Ethiopia.* Addis Ababa: 28 May.
1986 *Briefing Book.* Addis Ababa: USAID.
USAID Office of Foreign Disaster Assistance (OFDA)
1985 *Annual Report FY1985.* Washington, D.C.: USAID.
USAID/W
1987 Memo on Crossborder Feeding Programs. USAID/AFR/EA (prepared by Steven Mintz). Washington, D.C.: USAID.
1986a *AID Handbook 9.* Washington, D.C.: USAID.
1986b Letter from Office of Food for Peace to SCF. 5 March.
1985 *Advisory Committee on Voluntary Foreign Aid.* Washington, D.C.: USAID.
1984a *Record of Negotiations: Emergency Relief Assistance to Ethiopia.* Washington, D.C.: 2 November.
1984b *The AID-PVO Partnership: Sharing Goals and Resources In the Work of Development.* Office of Private and Voluntary Cooperation, Bureau for Food for Peace & Voluntary Assistance. Washington, D.C.: April.
U.S. Department of Agriculture
1985 *World Food Needs and Availability.* Washington, D.C.
U.S. Department of Commerce
1986 *Foreign Economic Trends and Their Implications for the United States: Ethiopia.* Washington, D.C.: International Trade Administration, January.

References 209

U.S. Department of State
1986   Telegram R-172203Z, March.
1985a   14 June Statement.
1985b   Telegram R-030539Z, April.
1985c   Telegram 1411Z3Z, February.
1984a   *Country Reports on Human Rights Practices, 1983.* Washington, D.C.: Government Printing Office.
1984b   Telegram R-120733Z, 7 December.
1984c   Press Briefing on "Opposition to Resettlement of the Ethiopian Population and Support for a Food Truce." Washington, D.C. 12 December.
U.S. G.A.O.   See U.S. General Accounting Office
U.S. General Accounting Office (GAO)
1986   *Famine in Africa: Improving U.S. Response Time for Emergency Relief.* NSIAD-86-56. Washington, D.C.: April.
1985a   *The United States' Response to the Ethiopian Food Crisis.* GAO/NSIAD-85-65. Washington, D.C.: 8 April.
1985b   *Transportation of Public Law 480 Commodities—Efforts Needed to Eliminate Unnecessary Costs.* GAO/NSIAD-85-74. Washington, D.C.: 18 June.
1985c   *An Overview of the Emergency Situation in Ethiopia.* GAO/NSIAD-85-70. Washington, D.C.: 12 April.
U.S. General Accounting Office (GAO)—Comptroller General
1976   *Need for an International Disaster Relief Agency.* Washington, D.C.: 5 May.
U.S. House
1986   *Hearing on "Economic Sanctions Against Ethiopia."* Subcommittee on International Economic Policy and Trade, Committee on Foreign Affairs, 99th Congress, 2d Sess., 25 September.
1985a   *Briefing and Markup on "African Famine Situation"* (H.R. 1096). Committee on Foreign Affairs, 99th Cong., 1st Sess., 30 January and 19 February.
1985b   *Hearing on "Food Aid and the Role of the Private Voluntary Organizations."* Select Committee on Hunger, 99th Cong., 1st Sess., 18 April.
1985c   *Hearing on "African Famine Relief and Rehabilitation."* Select Committee on Hunger, 99th Cong., 1st Sess., 25 July.
1985d   *Hearing on "Human Rights and Food Aid in Ethiopia."* Subcommittee on Human Rights and International Organizations and Subcommittee on Africa, Committee on Foreign Affairs, 99th Cong., 1st Sess., 16 October.
1985e   *Hearing on "Famine and Recovery in Africa: The US Response."* Select Committee on Hunger, 99th Cong., 1st Sess., 5 December.

1985f	*Hearing on "Emergency Famine Relief Needs in Ethiopia and Sudan."* Subcommittee on Africa, Committee on Foreign Affairs, 99th Congress, 1st Session, 19 September.
1984a	*"The Impact of U.S. Foreign Policy on Seven African Countries*, Report of a Congressional Study Mission to Ethiopia. . . . 6-25 August 1983."* Committee on Foreign Affairs, 9 March.
1984b	*Hearing on "The Human Rights Situation in South Africa, Zaire, The Horn of Africa, and Uganda."* Subcommittee on Human Rights and International Organizations, Committee on Foreign Affairs, 98th Cong., 2d Sess., 21 June and 9 August.
1984c	*Joint Hearings on "World Food and Population Issues—Emergency Assistance to Africa."* Committee on Foreign Affairs and Select Committee on Hunger, 98th Cong, 2d Sess., 2 August and 13 September.
1983a	*Hearings on "The World Food Situation."* Committee on Foreign Affairs, 98th Cong., 1st Sess., 26 and 27 July.
1983b	*Hearing on "Food Crisis in Africa."* Subcommittee on African Affairs, Committee on Foreign Affairs, 98th Cong., 1st Sess., 1 November.
1980	*Hearing on "Food Needs in East Africa."* Subcommittee on Africa, Committee on Foreign Affairs, 96th Cong., 2d Sess., 19 June.
1975	*Hearing on "US Policy and Request for Sale of Arms to Ethiopia."* Subcommittee on International Political and Military Affairs, Committee on Foreign Affairs, 94th Cong., 1st Sess., 5 March.

U.S. Senate

1986a	*Hearing on "Ethiopia Update: Forced Population Removal and Human Rights."* Committee on Foreign Relations, 99th Cong., 2d Sess., 6 March.
1986b	*Minority Staff Report on "Ethiopia and Sudan One Year Later: Refugee and Famine Recovery Needs."* Subcommittee on Immigration and Refugee Policy, Committee on the Judiciary, May.
1985a	*Hearing on "The Famine Effects on African Refugees"* (Oversight on the Issue of Emergency Food Aid and Famine Relief to Refugees in Sub-Saharan Africa). Subcommittee on Immigration and Refugee Policy, Committee on the Judiciary, 99th Cong., 1st Sess., 7 February.
1985b	*Senate Report 99-4 to Accompany S. 457: African Famine Relief and Recovery Act of 1985.* Committee on Foreign Relations, 99th Cong., 1st Sess., 23 February.
1984a	*Hearing on "Hunger in Africa."* Subcommittee on African Affairs, Committee on Foreign Relations, 98th Cong., 2d Sess., 1 March.

1984b	*Joint Hearings on "Food Aid in Africa: Lessons of 1984, Prospects for 1985."* Subcommittee for African Affairs, Committee on Foreign Relations, and Subcommittee on Foreign Agricultural Policy, Committee on Agriculture, Nutrition and Forestry, 98th Cong., 2d Sess., 19 September.
1976	*Hearings on "U.S. Relations with Ethiopia and the Horn of Africa."* Subcommittee on African Affairs, Committee on Foreign Relations, 94th Cong., 2d Sess., 4-6 August.

Vandevelde, Kenneth J.
1989   Reassessing the Hickenlooper Amendment. *Virginia Journal of International Law,* 29, 115-167.

Vestal, Theodore M.
1986   Famine in Ethiopia: Crisis of Many Dimensions. *Africa Today,* 32(4), 7-28.

Walczak, James R.
1981   New Directions in U.S. Food Aid: Human Rights and Economic Development. In, Ved P. Nanda, James R. Scarret, and George W. Shepherd (eds.), *Global Human Rights: Public Policies, Comparative Measures, and NGO Strategies.* Boulder, Co: Westview.

WFP   See UN World Food Programme/E

Wiarda, Howard J.
1987   Ethnocentrism and Third World Development. *Social Science and Modern Society,* 24(6), 55-64.

Wolde Giorgis, Dawit
1989   *Red Tears: War, Famine, and Revolution in Ethiopia.* Trenton, NJ: Red Sea Press.
1987   Speech Presented to the Royal Institute of International Affairs, London, July 1987. Printed in *Africa Events,* 3(8), 16-22.
1984   Introductory Statement by Dawit Wolde Giorgis, Chief Commissioner. Addis Ababa: RRC, October.

Wolde-Mariam, Mesfin
1984   *Rural Vulnerability to Famine in Ethiopia: 1958-1977.* New Delhi: Viskos Publishing House.

Wood, Adrian P.
1976   Farmers' Response to Drought in Ethiopia. In, A.M. Hussein (ed.), *Rehab: Drought and Famine in Ethiopia.* London: International African Institute.

Wood, Robert and Tom Mmuya
1986   The Debt Crisis in the Fourth World: Implications for North-South Relations. *Alternatives,* 11, 107-131.

World Affairs Report
1985   Ethiopia. *World Affairs Report,* 5(2), 550-555.

World Bank   See International Bank for Reconstruction and Development

World Vision Relief Organization (WVRO)
1986   *World Vision Relief Organization's FY1986 Emergency Relief Proposal for Ethiopia including PL-480 and Section 416 Commodities.*
1985a   World Vision Relief Organization PL 480 Title II Proposal to Office of Food for Peace.
1985b   *Monthly Project Report-November, 1985.* Addis Ababa: 3 December 1988.
n.d.   *People & Projects.* Monrovia, CA: WVRO.
Worrick, Thomas
1986   *1986 Emergency Food Need Assessment For Ethiopia.* USAID; AFR/TR/ARD, 21 February.
Wubneh, Mulatu and Yohannis Abate
1988   *Ethiopia: Transition and Development in the Horn of Africa.* Boulder, CO: Westview Press.
WVRO   See World Vision Relief Organization
Zartman, I. William
1985   *Ripe for Resolution.* New York: Oxford University Press.
Zewde, Bahru
1976   An Historical Outline of Famine in Ethiopia. In, A.M. Hussein (ed.), *Rehab: Drought and Famine in Ethiopia.* London: International African Institute.

Miscellaneous

Africa Confidential
    7 May 1986
Africa Report
    July-August 1986
    March-April 1985
    January-February 1985
Christian Science Monitor
    18 February 1985
    5 October 1985
    29 October 1986
Congressional Record
    28 February 1985
Ethiopian Herald
    6 August 1986
    12 April 1987
Jeune Afrique
    9 February 1984
    25 February 1987
Manchester Guardian
    4 January 1985

Newsweek
    4 October 1983
New York Times
    1 May 1977
    9 November 1984
    26 November 1984
    14 March 1985
    23 February 1987
UN Chronicle
    Volume 22, No. 1, 1985
Wall Street Journal
    4 April 1986
Washington Post
    16 January 1985
    26 June 1986
    27 September 1987
    14 November 1987
    13 January 1988
    2 February 1988
    18 February 1988

Interviews

Clark, Jeff (U.S. House Select Committee on Hunger)
1986   Washington, D.C., September.
Dunne, Stanley (CARE/Ethiopia)
1986   Addis Ababa, 8 August.
Dwyer, Don (USAID/Ethiopia)
1986   Addis Ababa, 14 August.
Franklin, Tom (WFP/Ethiopia)
1986   Addis Ababa, August.
Gold, Richard (USAID, Food for Peace)
1987   Arlington, VA, 12 May.
Gordon, Cathy (USAID/Ethiopia)
1986   Addis Ababa, 13 August.
Goyder, Hugh (OXFAM/UK)
1986   Oxford, England, 22 July.
Heller, Roger (SCF)
1986   Addis Ababa, Ethiopia, 15 August.
Janardanan (CARE/Ethiopia)
1986   Assebetefari, Ethiopia, 21-22 August.
Kirch, Terry (CRS/US)
1986   New York, 18 June.
Narula, Raj (CARE/Ethiopia)
1986   Dire Dawa, Ethiopia, 16 August.

Ramp, Rudy (CARE)
1986   New York, 18 June.
Tekul, Ato (CRS/Ethiopia)
1986   Addis Ababa, 26 August.
Whitaker, Corrine (Bread for the World)
1987   Washington, D.C., 28 May.
Worrick, Thomas (USAID/Ethiopia)
1988   Addis Ababa, 19 July.

Index

Abate, Y., 29, 50
Abegaz, B., 52, 54
Aboucher, A., 52, 57
Adugna, S., 60
Africa Bureau (USAID), 95
Africa Confidential, 65
African Famine Relief and
  Recovery Act (AFRRA), 93,
  94, 96, 106, 107
Africa Report 66, 72, 128, 146
Agricultural Marketing Corporation
  (AMC)
  and NRDC, 32
  food trade, 50
  procurement targets, quotas, and
    levels, 49, 53, 54, 61, 84
  supplying military, 51
  warehouses, 149
Agyeman-Duah, B., 39, 40, 41
Alameya Agricultural College, 40
All Ethiopia Peasant Association,
  57
Amin, S., 34
Amnesty International, 35
Angola, 190
Appleby, A., 17, n. 1

Armed Forces Coordinating
  Committee, 28
Arsi, 49, 50, 54, 56, 57, 81, 115,
  139, 163
Atwood, D., 49
Australia, 65, 112, 118
Australian Development Assistance
  Bureau, 62, 85, 116
Austria, 112, 118
Ayele, N., 53

Bale, 49, 50, 54, 56, 81, 130, 139,
  163
Balsvik, R., 40
Banti, T., 30
Barnes, L., 147
Barre, S., 31
Basic Commodities Supply
  Corporation (BCSC), 61
Bates, R., 10
Bayeh, B., 64
Bazyler, M., 14
Bekele, D., 36
Beneficiaries and Beneficiary
  status, 82, 83, 117, 137-38,
  140, 151-58
  conflicts over criteria, 153

215

criteria, 156
Ethiopian controls, 153
infrastructures, 149-50
macropolitics of, 188-89
sector criteria, 156
status determinations, 153-54
Berliner Missionswerk, 87
Bezabih, A., 61
Biafra, 14
Bible Society of Ethiopia, 56
Bienen, H., 10
Bilateral Program, 122, 128-30
CARE assistance, 129-30
change in U.S. policy, 128
congressional deference, 100-101
distribution plan, 129-30
prohibition of aid to resettlement, 129
RRC performance, 130
transfer authorization, 129, 138 n. 5
Bloch, J., 72
Bolling, L., 121
Bondestam, L., 44, 58
Borton, N., 96, 122, 132, 135, 138 n. 1, 144, 162
Boserup, E., 7
Boyer, P., 73
Brandenburg, P., 145
Brauman, R., 114, 124
Bread for the World, 71, 98, 130
Brietzke, P., 177
British influence, 174, 176, 177
British Broadcasting Corporation, 73
Brooke Amendment, 41, 104-5, 106, 141, 182
Bulgaria, 112, 118
Bureau for Refugee Programs (USAID), 95
Bush, G., 128, 131

Bush, R., 43, 173

Canada 65, 91, 112, 117, 118, 148
CARE
aid to SCF, 120
and beneficiary status, 154-55, 156
and bilateral, 129-30
and commodity shortages, 165 n. 5
and cross-border program, 128, 137
and Djibouti, 165 n. 1
and House bill, 98
and villagization, 164
aspirations, plans, distributions, 121
distribution shortfalls, 162
expansion, 150, 155
flexibility, 157
food distributed, 133
food distribution centers, 158
food transport and costs, 146, 148
initial survey, 138 n. 4
rations, 157
staff, 136
start-up, 119
trucks, 147
warehouses, 149
Carter, J., 188, 190
Cartwright, J., 36
Castro, F., 190
Catholic Relief Services (CRS)
aid request, 135
and aid criteria, 156
and beneficiary status, 155
and cross-border program, 128
and development assistance, 107
and Food for the North, 102, 131, 137, 160
and House bill, 98

and resettlement, 137
aspirations, plans, distributions, 120-21
churches and religious institutions, 159-60, 165 n. 7
conflict with USAID, 134-5, 148
FY1983 program, 71
flexibility, 157
food arrivals, 146, 147
food distributed, 133
food needs assessment, 138 n. 4
food transport, 146
initial aid request, 67, 69
prefamine programs, 68
rations, 157
staff, 136
start-up, 118-19
trucks, 146-47
warehouses, 149
Cease-fire negotiations, 130
Chase-Dunn, C., 16, 173
Chat, 180
China, 112, 118
Central Intelligence Agency, 66, 67, 74
Christian Relief and Development Association (CRDA), 69, 136, 137, 138 n. 2, 147
Christian Science Monitor, 136, 165 n. 2, 185
Church Drought Action Africa/Joint Relief Partners (CDAA/JRP), 121, 133, 138 n. 2, 155, 146-47, 150, 155, 160
See also Catholic Relief Services
Clapham, C., 29, 30, 32, 38, 43, 47, 52, 57, 63, 82, 85, 127, 160, 163, 164, 177
Clark, J., 148
Clark, L., 55, 102, 127
Clarke, J., 86

Clay, J., 31, 51, 62, 63, 64, 71, 87, 90, 103, 138 n. 7, 155, 162, 164, 183
Coffee, 180, 181
Cohen, J., 32, 35, 53, 56, 115
Commission for Organizing the Party of the Working People of Ethiopia (COPWE)
and Party formation, 30, 58, 62
and Resettlement Authority, 63
formation of, 37
headquarters, 56
Second Congress, 83
Commodity Credit Corporation, 72, 108 n. 3
Congo, 40, 191 n. 4
Congress, U.S., 91-108, 127-32, 176, 184, 186, 187, 188
See also U.S. House, U.S. Senate
Congressional Record, 97
Conquest, R., 10, 11
Conte, R., 97
Coup attempts, 172, 179, 191 n. 3
Crocker, C., 131, 183
Cross-border operations, 124, 128, 137, 185
Cuba, 175
Cultural Survival, 103
Cuny, F., 68, 82, 137
Currency ties, 34, 180, 181
Cutler, P., 62
Czechoslovakia, 112, 118

Dalrymple, D., 10
Danforth, J., 72, 75
deCastro, J., 7
deCeullar, P., 69
Declaration of Socialism, 27, 28
Degefu, W., 43
Dejene, A., 24, 33, 54, 57

Dependency, 4, 33-34, 169, 170, 173-82, 190, 191 n. 1, 5
Deressa, J., 183
Desta, F., 64
Dines, M., 52, 125
Doulos, M., 57
Dunn, S., 149
Dwyer, D., 135

Early Warning and Planning Service, 62
Early Warning Service, 43, 62, 136
Eicher, C., 10
Emergency Planning and Preparedness Group, 165 n. 2
Erlich, H., 28, 31
Eritrea, 47, 49, 50, 51, 54, 56, 81, 82, 83, 91, 102, 114, 115, 117, 125, 127, 128, 130, 131, 132, 139, 152, 155, 157, 161, 162, 172, 177, 178, 190
Eritrean People's Liberation Front (EPLF), 30, 51, 84, 126, 127, 159
Eritrean Relief Association (ERA), 64, 126, 128, 136, 137, 161-2
Ethiopia, external relations, 34, 35, 43, 44 n. 1, 171, 172-73, 175-76, 177, 178-79, 179-80, 181, 182-83
See also U.S. policy, Soviet Union
Ethiopian Catholic Secretariat (EOC), 121, 131, 160
Ethiopian development
economic, 179-80
famine and relief, 169
foreign aid, 178-79
foreign intervention, 175-76
indicators of, 17 n. 2
national autonomy, 173-5
political agendas, 176-8

Ethiopian Domestic Distribution Corporation, 54, 84
Ethiopian Evangelical Church Makane Yesus (EECMY), 56, 121, 160
Ethiopian famine
and military activity, 81, 83
and AMC procurements, 84-85
cycle of, 44
factors, 3, 44
interpretations of, 4-5
mortality levels, 16, 55, 79, 80
regional distribution, 80
shelter populations, 1985, 152
See also Revolutionary food policy, Ethiopian food production and shortages
Ethiopian famine relief
and military activity, 74
effect of, 81-82
initial response, 68-70
normative factors, 169
role of media, 73
See also Food distribution, Primary distribution
Ethiopian food production and shortages
consumption requirements, 22
consumption shortfalls, 24
declining productivity, 22
food deficits, 21-22, 43, 48-49, 51-55
food needs assessments, 67, 72, 123-24, 134, 138 n. 4
persons affected by shortages, 80-81, 24-25, 140
production estimates, 23
production subsidies, 24
prospects for food security, 189
rationalization of production, 32
regional and sectoral production, 22-23

See also Revolutionary food policy, Ethiopian famine
Ethiopian Herald, 57
Ethiopian National Alliance to Advance Democracy, 190
Ethiopian Nationalities Institute, 62
Ethiopian Orthodox Church, 59, 131, 160
Ethiopian People's Democratic Alliance, 65, 66
Ethiopian People's Revolutionary Party (EPRP), 30
Ethiopian Red Cross Society, 64, 70, 119, 122, 138 n. 2, 155, 158-59, 161
Ethiopian revolution, 16, 26-39, 175
European Court of Auditors, 100
European Economic Community (EEC), 38, 65, 91, 100, 108, 117, 189, 190

Famine
  defined, 17 n 1
  external factors, 8-9
  internal factors, 9-11
  natural and normative factors, 43, 44
  types of, 7-8
  See also Ethiopian famine
Famine relief
  and rehabilitation, 15-16
  and sovereignty, 13-14
  cross-border operations, 14
  donor responsibilities, 11-12
  norms of, 6, 12-13
  outlooks on, 4
  See also Ethiopian famine relief
Farer, T., 34, 39, 61, 182, 190
Faught, W., 23, 49
Fida, H., 44 n. 1
Finland, 112, 118

Finney, L., 42
Firebrace, J., 126
Food distribution, 132-38, 158
  and militarism, 125
  and nationalism, 124, 125
  division of functions, 113
  dualism in, 111-13
  emergency phase, 82-83
  expansion of, 149-50
  foreign donations, 113-14
  military involvement, 162
  norms and standards, 132, 134, 137
  role of PVOs, 134, 137
  secondary level, 144-50
  stabilization, 140, 142-50
  tertiary level, 143-44
  See also food shipment, food transport, primary distribution
Food for Peace Bureau (USAID), 95, 148, 186
Food for Peace Plans, 122
Food for the North initiative (FFN), 101, 102, 121, 130-31, 137, 160, 165 n. 5, 185, 186
Food policy, *See* Revolution food policy
Food shipments
  arrival of U.S. food, 144-45
  diversion to Ethiopia, 143
  UN coordination, 144
Food transport
  airlifts, 144-45
  military involvement, 146
  ports of arrival, 145-46
  PVO strategies, 144-46
  responsibilities for, 147-49
  supply lines, 141
Foreign aid
  openness to, 11, 13
  viability of, 11-12, 17 n. 3
Foreign Assistance Act, 104, 107

Foreign Assistance Appropriations Act, 104-5, 107
Franklin, T., 144

Gamo Gofa, 49, 50, 54, 56, 81, 130, 139, 163
Geiger, T., 186
George, S., 9
German Democratic Republic, 112, 118, 178, 190
Gilkes, P. 37
Gill, P., 65, 69, 73, 107, 131, 144
Gojam, 49, 50, 54, 56, 81, 88, 139, 163
Gonder, 47, 49, 50, 54, 56, 68, 81, 86, 130, 133, 139, 152, 163
Gonder Public Health College, 40
Gonzalez Amendment, 42, 109 n. 9
Gordon, C., 101, 148, 157
Goyder, H., 59, 84, 108
Green, S., 13, 184
Griffin, K., 24, 32
Gurr, T., 14

Hackett, K., 102
Hadwiger, D., 95
Haile Mariam, Mengistu, 26, 30, 35-36, 36-38, 45 n. 3, 73, 131, 163, 170, 172, 175, 177, 179, 190
Hancock, G., 43, 59, 108 n. 2, 180
Hansen, A., 14
Hansen, R., 186
Hararghe, 49, 50, 51, 54, 56, 81, 115, 122, 130, 133, 138 n. 4, 139, 146, 152, 157, 161, 162, 163, 165 n. 3, 4, 7, 8, 180
Harbeson, J., 60
Harff, B., 14
Harris, M., 117
Harrison, P., 6
Hay, R., 24, 32

Heller, R., 150
Henze, P., 30, 35, 36, 37, 39, 57, 171, 176, 180
Hess, R., 34
Hickenlooper Amendment
  and PVO operations, 106
  and rehabilitation, 141
  and trucks, 148
  and U.S. response, 105-6
  authority of, 104
  displacement of, 182,
  extension of, 109 n. 9
  imposition of sanctions, 41-42
  waiver of in AFRRA, 106-7
Hoben, A., 184
Holcomb, B., 51, 63, 64, 87, 90, 182
Holland, S., 126
Holt, J., 61
Hopkins, R., 188
Horowitz, I., 6
Human rights abuses, 41, 73
Hungary, 112, 118
Hussein, A., 44

Ibnet, 126
Iceland, 112, 118
Ilubabor, 48, 49, 50, 54, 56, 81, 88, 139, 163
India, 112, 118
Insel, B., 12
Institution-building, 158-64
Interagency Group on Ethiopia and Sudan (IGETSU), 71, 95
Interagency Task Force on the African Famine, 62
International Committee of the Red Cross (ICRC), 69, 119, 121-2, 125, 128, 131, 138 n. 2, 161
International Development Association (IDA), 43

Index

IDA Act, 109 n. 9
International Disaster Institute (IDI), 61
International Labor Organization (ILO), 62, 189-90
International Security and Development Cooperation Act, 103
INTERACTION
  and H.R. 1096, 98
  and resettlement, 103
  objectives, 105-6
  role of, 95-96
INTERTECT, 135, 138 n. 4, 160
Iran, 112, 118
Isaksson, N., 115
Israel, 112, 118, 179
Italian Embassy, 63
Italy, 173, 174, 176

Jacobs, D., 14
Janardanan, 149, 161
Jansson, K., 4, 64, 89, 104, 114, 116, 122, 132, 136, 137, 138 n. 7, 144, 154, 163
Jeune Afrique, 155
Joint Relief Partners (JRP), 118-19, 120-11
  See also Church Drought Action Africa

Kaffa, 48, 49, 50, 54, 56, 81, 139, 163
Kagnew, 34, 40, 178
Kampuchea, 14, 144
Kaplan, I., 36, 41
Kaplan, R., 51, 673, 84, 117, 125, 126, 140, 153
Kasten, R., 96
Keating, R., 137
Keleman, P., 52
Keller, E., 37, 103, 181

Kennedy, E., 95, 96, 97
Kennedy, J., 189
Kent, R., 11
Kenya, 143
Keyes, A., 103
Kirch, T., 145
Kjekshus, H., 9
Korea, 40, 191 n. 4
Korn, D., 4, 39, 41, 43, 59, 61, 70, 75 n. 1, 86, 89, 101, 102, 111, 113, 128, 131, 144, 183
Korten, D., 172

Lasswell, H., 186
League of Nations, 34
League of Red Cross Societies (LICROSS), 119, 138 n. 2, 150, 161
Lefebvre, J., 191 n. 1
Lefort, R., 30, 44 n. 1, 47
Legum, C., 36
Leich, M. 191 n. 7
Leland, M., 97, 107
Lewis, A., 7
Lewis Amendment, 98
Libya, 97, 112, 118
Lindblom, C., 186
Lirenso, A., 31, 32, 54
Loescher, G., 15
Lyons, T., 191 n. 1
Luckman, R., 36
Lugar, R., 95
Lutheran World Federation (LWF), 121, 128, 160
Lutheran World Relief (LWR), 69, 128

Magistad, M., 87
Malhuret, C., 89
Manchester Guardian, 106
Marcus, H., 29, 34, 35, 40, 103, 176, 179, 181, 182

Mariam, A., 178
Marine Transit and Service Corporation, 146
Maritime Transit Authority, 143
Markakis, J., 53
Mazrui, A., 33
McCann, J., 165 n. 6
McClellan, C,. 88
McClosky, R., 107
McPherson, M., 97, 98, 102, 105, 107, 109 n. 6, 109 n. 7, 127, 131, 137
Medhanie, T., 42
Medecins Sans Frontiers, 136, 138 n. 7
Meillassoux, C., 9
MEISON, 29, 30, 44 n. 1
Mengisteab, K., 44
Menelik II, Emperor, 27, 34, 36, 173
Mercy Corps International, 128
Military activity and militarization, 31, 172
 and food deficit, 51
 and war economy, 35, 52
 controls, 177-78
 growth in, 36
 peasant march, 31
 recruitment, 52, 83-84
 Soviet aid, 36, 45 n. 3, 175, 177, 179
 U.S. aid, 35, 36
Ministry of Agriculture, 62, 108, 116, 163
Mmuya, T., 17 n. 2
Mudge, G., 11, 60
Mutual Defense and Assistance Agreement (MDAA), 40, 41

Narula, R., 138 n. 4, 164
Nasserism, 39

National Development through Cooperation Campaign (Zemecha), 28, 29
National Meteorological Service Agency, 62
National Military Service Proclamation, 52
National Revolutionary Development Campaign (NRDC), 32
National Security Council (NSC), 71, 109 n. 6, 184, 186
National Transport Corporation, 62
National Villagization Coordination Committees (NVCC), 163
Nelson, H., 36, 41
New York Times, 96, 101, 107, 146, 171, 190
Newsweek, 74, 96
New Zealand, 112, 118
Nichols, B., 15
Nigeria, 14
Niggli, P., 87, 88, 90, 153, 171
Norway, 112, 118
Nyerere, J., 14

Office of the National Council for Central Planning (ONCCP), 57
Office for Foreign Disaster Assistance (USAID), 62, 95, 123, 148
Office for Private Voluntary Cooperation (USAID), 95
Ogaden, 69, 114, 175
Oliver-Smith, A., 14
Operation Red Star, 51
Operation St. Bernard, 145
Operation Tesfa, 145
Organization for African Unity (OAU), 68

Index 223

Oromo Liberation Front (OLF), 30, 84, 87, 89, 115, 159, 162
Oromo Relief Society (ORS), 64
Ostefeld, D., 17 n. 2
Oxfam-U.S., 165 n. 6

Pakistan, 112, 118
Pankhurst, R., 39, 44, 180
Pascoe, W., 183
Pateman, R., 85, 125, 126, 128
Patinkin, M., 108 n. 2
Peace Corps, 41
Peasant Associations (PAs)
    and agricultural productivity, 53
    and aid criteria, 155
    and beneficiary status, 154
    and food distribution, 156, 158, 171
    and political power, 151
    and power building, 115
    and PVOs, 139
    and villagization, 163
    aid requirements, 153
    corruption of, 162
    party control over, 57
    politicization of, 85
    responsibilities of, 162
    taxes, 162
Pentagon, 184, 186
People's Democratic Republic of Ethiopia (PDRE), 170, 171, 183, 189, 190
People's Democratic Republic of Yemen (PDRY), 177
Perham, M., 40
Peterson, D., 39, 42
Pezzullo, L., 189
Phillips, J., 12
Poland, 112, 118
Porter, B., 175
Ports, 143, 144, 145, 146, 147

Pre-Disaster Planning Program, 62
Primary distribution, 150, 151-58
    and exchanges, 159
    administration and control, 157-58
    controls over, 152
    emergency phase, 165
    establishment of DCs, 154
    expansion of DCs, 154, 155
    institutions, 159
    procedures, 156-57
    processes, 151-58
    rationing and criteria, 154-58
    stability phase, 153
Private Voluntary Organizations
    and beneficiaries, 151-52, 156
    and cash grants, 123
    and Ethiopian development, 136-37, 171
    and DCs, 154
    and normative distributions, 134
    and religious institutions, 159-60
    and resettlement, 163
    and villagization, 163
    and voluntary institutions, 161
    accountability measures, 162
    aid criteria, 153
    aspirations, plans, distributions, 120-21
    competition and cooperation, 122
    delegation of authority, 184
    dispersion of DCs, 153
    distribution styles, 157
    domestic constituencies, 187
    Ethiopian controls, 185
    independence of, 123-24, 134
    institution building, 158
    modes of adjustment, 118-20
    party supervision of rehabilitation activity, 142
    reimbursements for transport,

148-49
relationships with RRC, 111, 139
roles and power of, 112, 135, 138
transition to stability, 141
See also CARE, CRS, SCF
Producer Cooperatives (PCs)
and agricultural productivity, 53
formation of, 44 n. 2
growth of, 33
increasing memberships of, 85
Program of the National Democratic Revolution (PNDR), 29, 44 n. 1
Provisional Military Administrative Council (PMAC), 28, 175, 176
Provisional Military Government of Socialist Ethiopia (PMGSE), 62, 63, 74, 113, 114, 116, 120, 127, 130, 133, 134, 135, 136, 137, 142, 143, 146, 147, 148, 152, 153, 159, 160, 161, 162, 163, 180, 190
Provisional Office of Mass Organization Affairs (POMOA), 30
Public Law 480 (PL-480), 118, 119, 121
and CRS, 68, 134
and foreign policy, 185
amendments to, 95
annual budgets, 66
appropriations, 92, 93-94
costs of distribution, 148
distribution of food, 132-33
dominant source of aid, 117
donations, 122-23
effect of Hickenlooper, 106
FY1983 program, 71
levels in, 98
PVO registration requirements, 122
proposals, 96-97
regulations, 135
reinstatement of, 71-72
USAID planning and targeting, 99-100, 122
See also U.S. Food Aid Policy, U.S. Policy, USAID

Rahman, M., 44 n. 2
Rahmato, D., 57
Reagan, R., 72, 186, 188
Reagan Doctrine, 12, 15, 102, 65-66, 92-176, 182, 186
Red Terror, 29, 176, 177
Rehabilitation, 141-2, 165 n. 6
Reimer, R., 179
Relief and Rehabilitation Commission (RRC), 134, 139, 140
and aid criteria, 153, 156
and beneficiary lists and screening, 151, 154
and bilateral program, 122, 129, 130
and Ethiopian Orthodox Church, 160
and foreign donors, 63, 114, 116
and institution building, 154
and Ethiopian military objectives, 60-61
and PVOs, 118, 120, 121, 122, 124, 134, 135-36
and resettlement, 89, 115, 126-27
and villagization, 127, 163
and WPE authority, 62-63, 126, 142
administrative infrastructure, 59, 115
approval of food distribution, 149

conflicts over operations, 58-59, 60-61, 83
constraints on, 59
criticism of, 136
decreased aid levels, 142
estimates of, 80-81, 152
failure of PMGSE support, 85
food distribution system, 79, 115-16, 124-27, 154
food needs assessments, 62, 67, 100, 124
functions of, 61
funding appeals, 85
in rebel regions, 125-26, 153
loss of control, 113-115
origins and structure, 60
policy role, 138
political mandate, 111, 113-17
programs and operations, 64, 111
relations with USAID, 132
resists retrenchment, 116, 142
restrictions on mandate, 142
restrictions on staffs, 136
shifting mandate, 143
sources of funds, 61-62
staff, 62
truck fleet and warehouses, 62, 147
Relief Society of Tigray (REST), 64, 126, 128, 130, 137, 161-62
Resettlement, 14, 79, 83, 158, 171
and bilateral program, 129
and colonization, 87-88
and dual food distribution, 117
and famine relief, 86
and food distribution, 113-14, 115
and MSF, 136, 138 n. 7
and political consolidation, 85
and PVOs, 136, 163
and RRC, 126-27
and State Farms, 90-91
and U.S. policy, 102-4, 137
and villagization, 91
death rates, 86-87, 90
explanations of, 89-91
moratorium on, 104
objectives of, 87-88
origins of, 89
prohibition of U.S. aid, 137
RRC's role, 89
resettlement conditions, 90-91
rhetoric of, 88-89
Soviet and Libyan support, 97
targets, 86, 87, 88
Warsaw Pact aid, 86
Restorationist movements, 34, 190
Revolutionary Ethiopian Women's Association (REWA), 57
Revolutionary Ethiopia Youth Association (REYA), 57
Revolutionary food policy
and the revolution, 27-33
collectivization, 32, 51, 52, 53
economic controls, 31-33
factors in, 26-27
state farms, 32, 90-91
theory of development, 28-9
See also food production and shortages, Ethiopian Famine
Rogge, J., 52
Roth, T., 183
Roukema, M., 97, 104
Rubenson, S., 33-34

Safe passage negotiations, 130-31
Samuels, J., 13
Sauldie, M., 29
Save the Children Federation (SCF)
and beneficiary status, 155
aid request, 135

aspirations, plans, distributions, 121
development goals, 162
expansion of, 150
food arrivals, 146, 147
food distributed, 133
food needs assessment, 138 n. 4
food transport, 146
rations, 157
staff, 136
start-up, 119, 138 n. 1
trucks, 147
warehouses, 149
Schellinski, K., 157
Schraeder, P., 15
Schwab, P., 28, 57, 177
Scoville, O., 14
Selassie, B., 39, 177, 183
Selassie, Emperor Haile, 7-8, 25, 27, 28, 30, 34, 36, 40, 56, 165 n. 7, 174, 176, 177, 178, 179
Settlement Authority, 63
Service Cooperatives (SCs), 33, 44 n. 2, 53
Shawcross, W., 14, 44 n. 1
Shehim, K., 30
Shengo, 171, 172
Shepherd, J., 60, 68, 80, 130, 131, 161
Shoa, 49, 50, 54, 56, 81, 86, 88, 121, 130, 139, 146, 152, 162, 163
Sidamo, 49, 50, 54, 56, 81, 86, 88, 121, 130, 139, 146, 152, 162, 163
SIM, International, 69, 108, 119, 160
Sivini, G., 86, 88, 89
Smith, G., 100, 128, 184
Snyder, C., 73
Solomon, R., 73

Somalia, 15, 31, 52, 97, 115, 157, 175, 177
Soviet Union
and dependency, 181-82
and deportation, 14
and Ethiopian media campaigns, 73
and Ethiopian radicalism, 37
and resettlement, 117
adoption of Mengistu, 66
aid responsibilities, 13
attraction of Ethiopia to, 33
Ethiopian alliance, 36, 38, 169, 185, 189, 190
food aid, 85, 189
foreign intervention, 175
influence of, 37, 174
military aid, 45 n. 3, 175, 177, 179
model of development, 38, 57, 176
nationalities policy, 178
support of revolution, 175, 176
trade restrictions, 180
treaty of friendship and cooperation, 174
Spencer, J., 34, 38, 40, 176, 179
Sudan, 14, 51, 52, 65, 87, 89, 97, 119, 127, 128, 161
Survival International, 63, 87, 88, 90, 91
Sweden, 112, 118
Swedish International Development Agency (SIDA), 35
Swenson, J., 95, 120
Switzerland, 112, 118
Szymanski, I., 191 n. 5

Tanzania, 14
Teferi, A., 32
Tekul, A., 135, 165 n. 7

Index 227

The Challenge of Drought (RRC), 60
Thomas, M., 160
Tidy, M., 33
Tigray, 47, 49, 50, 51, 54, 55, 56, 81, 82, 83, 86, 87, 88, 89, 91, 102, 114, 115, 117, 125, 127, 128, 130, 131, 132, 139, 152, 153, 161, 162, 172, 177, 190
Tigrayan People's Liberation Front (TPLF), 30, 51, 84, 87, 89-90, 126, 127, 153, 159
Torrey, W., 17 n. 1
TransAmerica, 145
Trucks, 146-47, 148
Turton, D., 81, 114

United Arab Emirates, 112, 118
United Kingdom, 100
UN Conference on Least Developed Countries, 59
UN Chronicle, 144
UN Development Program, 62, 144
UN Disaster Relief Organization, 69, 75 n. 3, 144, 188
UN Food and Agriculture Organization (FAO), 23, 64, 67, 69, 74, 127, 189
UN General Assembly, 186
UN Institute for Training and Research (UNITAR), 11, 15, 143
UN Office for Emergency Operations in Africa/Ethiopia (UNOEOA/E), 67, 69, 100, 111, 112, 124, 144, 165 n. 2
UN Research Institute for Social Development (UNRISD), 7, 17 n. 1
UN World Food Programme (WFP), 43, 64, 69, 73, 74, 108, 111, 112, 144, 147, 188
UN WFP Trucking Operation in Ethiopia (UNWTOE), 147, 148
U.S. Agency for International Development (USAID)
and bilateral program, 129-30
and commodity give-aways, 165 n. 5
and development assistance, 107
and ideology, 186
and institutions, 159
and PVOs, 117-18, 121, 134-35, 138 n. 3
and rations, 157
aid functions, 122
annual estimates of requirements (AERs), 122
approval of aid requests, 100, 123
assessment team, 72
budgetary power, 122
bureaus of, 95
capacity and strategy, 117
congressional testimony, 95, 97, 98, 102, 127
effect of Hickenlooper Amendment, 105
Ethiopian operations, 1979-83, 100
Ethiopian influence over, 185
expansion of distributions, 124
food needs assessments, 67, 124
locus of decision making, 184
opposition to US Air Force transport, 141
planning and control, 99
policy changes, 141
regulatory direction, 185, 188
relations with RRC, 132
relative autonomy of, 182, 184-85

roles of, 101, 135
trucks, 148
transport costs reimbursements, 148
U.S. Department of Agriculture, 10, 74
U.S. Department of Commerce, 183
U.S. Department of Defense, 146
U.S. Department of State, 66, 71, 100, 102, 129, 184, 186, 190
U.S. food aid policy
  and Ethiopian population redistribution, 132
  and Ethiopian programs, 127-32
  and institution building, 158-64
  and villagization, 104, 163
  accountability concerns, 74
  beneficiary status, 152
  commitment levels, 1983, 74
  competition in Africa, 66-67
  declaration of emergency, 71
  democratic constraints, 185-87
  development norms, 182, 188-89
  diplomatic role, 169
  early responses, 70-75
  efficiency and lag time, 100
  food allocations, 98-99
  Food for Peace policy, 188
  funding levels, 92-94, 98-99
  ideological factors, 70, 185-6
  influence of PVOs, 187
  logistical arrangements, 75, 99-101
  macropolitics of, 185-88
  New Directions policy, 188
  objectives of, 133-34, 158, 159, 189
  prohibition on developmental aid, 107-8, 183, 189
  restrictions on, 83, 99
  role of media, 96
  shifts in assessment, 127

  See also USAID, PL-480
U.S. General Accounting Office (GAO), 42, 48, 67, 71, 100, 105, 128, 138 n. 3, 143
U.S. House of Representatives, 41, 42, 67, 71, 72, 73, 74, 80, 92-99, 101-7, 108 n. 5, 109 n. 6, 109 n. 7, 125, 126, 130, 131, 135, 138 n. 3, 143, 145, 148, 164, 187
  See also Congress
U.S. Policy on Ethiopia
  development diplomacy, 39-40, 175
  famine period, 83-84
  objectives, 99-104
  prefamine interests, 65
  prerevolution, 40, 175, 176, 177, 178-79, 181-82
  presidential determination, 91, 103
  structural characteristics, 91-92
U.S. Senate, 41, 71, 73, 87, 94-99, 101-7, 109 n. 6, 109 n. 7, 127, 128, 130-32, 187, 191 n. 6
  See also Congress

Vandevelde, K., 109 n. 9
Vestal, T., 40
Villagization, 153, 158, 163-64, 171
  and Ethiopian authorities, 163
  and famine and relief, 115
  and food distribution, 113-14
  and Peasant Associations, 115, 163
  and PVOs, 136, 137
  and PCs, 85
  and religious institutions, 164
  and social services, 115, 164
  and stabilization of relief, 15
  peasants involved, 104

RRC authority, 127
Walczak, J., 188
Wall Street Journal, 66
Walters, V., 131
Warsaw Pact, 113
Washington Post, 66, 71, 171, 190
Weiss, T., 97
Welega, 49, 50, 54, 56, 81, 87, 88, 89, 139, 163
Whitaker, C., 103
Wiarda, H., 173
Willets, D., 180
Wolde, G., 131
Wolde Giorgis, D., 44, 55, 58, 59, 60, 62, 63, 73, 80, 85 88, 114, 122, 125, 126, 129, 146, 154, 175
Wolde Mariam, M., 75 n. 1
Wollo, 47, 49, 50, 54, 56, 68, 81, 117, 130, 133, 139, 146, 152, 161, 163
Wolpe, H., 72, 73, 97, 98, 105
Wood, A., 17 n. 2, 80
Worker's Party of Ethiopia (WPE), 62, 139, 142, 153, 154, 159, 163, 164, 165 n. 1, 177
  and political power, 151
  authority over famine relief, 63
  celebration of, 59
  control over relief, 64, 79, 113, 142
  creation of, 57
  inauguration of, 84
  radicalism of, 83
  regional First Secretaries, 126
  resettlement program, 86-91
  supervision of RRC, 114
World Affairs Report, 59
World Bank, 17 n. 2, 32, 33, 109 n. 9, 189, 190
World Vision Relief Organization (WVRO)
  aid request, 135
  and Ethiopian government, 137
  and Food for the North, 131, 137, 165 n. 5
  aspirations, plans, and distributions, 121
  churches and religious institutions, 159-60
  expansion, 150
  food arrivals and transport, 146, 147
  murder of staff, 162
  prefamine programs, 68
  staff, 136
  start-up, 119
  trucks, 147
  warehouses, 149
Worrick, T., 49
Wubneh, M., 50

Yugoslavia, 112, 118

Zartman, I., 31
Zewde, B., 44
Zimbabwe, 112, 118